Chandi Wyant's route on the Via Francigena

● Milan

○ Fidenza
○ Costa Mezzana
Medesano ○
○ Fornovo di Taro
Cisa Pass ○ ○ Cassio
○ Pontremoli
○ Aulla
Cinque Terre ○
○ Lucca
● Bologna

● Florence
Altopascio ○ ○ San Miniato
○ Gambassi Terme
San Gimignano ○ ○ Colle Val d'Elsa
○ Siena
○ Buonconvento
Montalcino ○ ○ San Quirico d'Orcia
Radicofani ○ ○ Acquapendente
Bolsena ○ ○ Montefiascone
Viterbo ○
Vetralla ○ ○
Sutri ○
● Rome

RETURN *to* GLOW

A Pilgrimage
of Transformation
in Italy

Chandi Wyant

To my Grandmother, Florence Ena Isherwood.
Let us go then you and I,
When the evening is laid out against the sky.

And to the doctors and nurses
of San Giovanni di Dio in Florence
who saved my life.
E quindi uscimmo a riveder le stelle.

Courage means to tell the story
of who you are with your whole heart.
~ Brené Brown

Contents

ONE

Lost

I'm limping on both feet—if that's possible—in scorched wheat fields somewhere south of Siena.

I'm a woman alone and I'm lost.

The sun's heat pummels the earth, and my limbs are like basil leaves, crushed by the stone pestle of the sun. Dusty tracks are scratched across the brittle fields. Sharp rocks push into the soles of my shoes, and I chide myself for bringing trail runners instead of day hikers with thicker soles. My spine is slimy against the pad of my pack and my teeth clench at the pain in my feet.

A farmhouse comes into view, suggesting a greener, shadier route to come. When I reach the farm, the trail disappears. I shift my weight from one foot to the other, trying to relieve their ache, wondering which way to turn.

The sound of a motor causes me to look toward a field where a man on a tractor waves me over. As I walk closer, he calls out, *"Devi tornare indietro!"* (You have to go back.)

I call to him, *"Ma quanto indietro?"* (But how far back?)

"The signs are incorrect! Go back!" I hear his shouts in Italian as he plunges the tractor into chunks of earth and rumbles away.

I return slowly on the dusty tracks to the brittle fields. Finding a handkerchief-sized patch of shade, I take off my pack and sit on it. My head drops toward my feet. Silence reigns, as if in the piercing heat even the crickets and birds have been struck mute.

I've been walking alone for twenty days, crossing the Apennines, climbing the hills of Tuscany, and skirting the edges of busy highways, and I've not been lost until now.

Lost. That's why I undertook a pilgrimage in my favorite place in the world. In the past year, my foundation had been swept away by both a divorce, the pain of which surprised me, and a sudden traumatic illness. These ordeals left my physical and emotional health in such a terrible state of disrepair that I feared I would never get my glow back.

I lift my head from my hands. The silent, brittle fields offer me no solution.

I must not fail. If I fail at this, I will fail to get my glow back.

I've made myself a promise with this pilgrimage. *Un voto*, a vow.

Slowly, I stand, heave my pack on, and begin retracing my steps. My legs feel as if they cannot manage the weight of my body. Sweat threatens to drip into my eyes, and I stop to squint at furrows in the field—mini trails made by mice. Then I see a tractor track on a hill above me. I aim myself toward it. A tractor track will surely lead to a farmhouse at some point. Deciding on a direction brings relief, but I make slow progress. "Please," I murmur to the sun, "you don't have to keep pounding me."

I hunker under my hat, my eyes cast downward, my shoulders cringing. Just put one foot in front of the other and you'll arrive somewhere, I tell myself.

You'll arrive somewhere.

Arrive. From the Latin *ad rīpa*, to the shore.

Am I getting there now, to a new shore?

TWO

Pericolo di Morte

The decision to walk over four hundred kilometers (more than 250 miles) alone from northern Italy to Rome did not begin with the divorce. It began with the emergency surgery, which happened during a vacation in Italy just before I filed for divorce back in Colorado.

I was in my early forties and had been separated for a year when I went to Italy (a country I'd been returning to frequently for over twenty years), hoping to get rejuvenated and come back fortified, less in grief, more shored up, and ready to face the divorce process.

Two days into my trip, I was at my friend Sydney's apartment in the historic center of Florence when I was struck by nausea, vomiting, pain in my abdomen, and fever. It was Sunday morning and the doctor who made the house visit said I had a virus. By Monday night I was in the emergency room at the hospital of San Giovanni di Dio.

"You're awake," the anesthesiologist says. I try to follow her Italian through my anesthetic haze.

"It was." She uses a word that stays with me: *bruttissima*. Horrendously, disgustingly nasty.

Whatever it was, it was *bruttissima*, and that's all I know. Days pass before I grasp how close I'd come to dying in that hospital seven thousand miles from home.

I'm wheeled into a large room that contains five other beds with five other urgent care patients. I can neither move nor eat.

When I see my oddly distended and bloated stomach, I think of the naked woman in Giotto's *Last Judgement* who cowers under the clutches of a hairy blue creature. She's a medieval product, before painters studied anatomy, and her distended pouch of a stomach is where her *mons pubis* should be.

If whatever happened didn't kill me, surely the pain I'm in will. My reflex to deal with the pain is to pull my hair. That's all I do for days when I'm not asleep—yank at my hair. My fingers have a will of their own, scouring my skull, seeking more hair to pull, like an invertebrate scouring the bottom of the sea in search of algae to consume.

When Sydney visits, I don't know if I've been there two hours or two days. I sense she's telling me what happened, but I can't comprehend her words.

"Half an hour more and you would have died," the surgeon tells me on the one occasion he comes to my bedside a few days later. "It was really acute. One of the worst I've seen. Why did you wait so long?"

I try to sort through his Italian words. Half an hour?

My mind is like a lane in a bowling alley, his words hurtling through it, knocking over the remaining few pins. I gasp as the last smidgen of stability is knocked away.

"Peritonite acuta," he says, providing me with a two-word diagnosis.

My brain moves the second word to the front. *Acute peritonitis.* But the words aren't familiar, even in English. Or perhaps my brain is too strung out from pain and drugs.

When Riccardo the nurse struggles to find a vein in my arm to change my IV, I ask, *"Cos'è peritonite acuta?"*

"Arg! Your veins are so small!" he says, taking another stab. My breath jumps in my throat and I avert my eyes, focusing on Lolle, one of my roommates. Every night when she starts her hollering, two nurses march in like a SWAT team and tie her arms to the bed.

"Acute peritonitis. Fatal if neglected." Riccardo snaps the words, and I think of a martial artist snapping a board with the side of his hand. "Ruptured appendix. Walls of the abdomen inflamed. Deadly bacteria. Sepsis."

Days turn into weeks. Round green bruises grow on my thin arms, my feet swell, and a blinding pain develops daily in my head. Sometimes someone gives me a damp cloth that I hold to my forehead for hours in a daze as loud family members visit other patients in the room. At night, the bedpan is left too long by busy nurses and I sleep with it pressing into the flesh of my bottom.

Then I realize I'm having trouble breathing.

"You're just nervous," the doctor tells me.

I repeat myself for two more days.

A pulmonologist comes and sticks a gigantic needle in my back. "You're coming with me," he says.

To Heaven? I almost voice my thought.

The only clear thought I have is of my grandmother saying, "The train is leaving. Don't be late!" when she was in the process of dying.

Pneumonia has developed, perhaps because of the sepsis in my lungs. It is a brutal setback, filled with more pain.

Four weeks after the surgery, I fly home. United Airlines refuses to change my return date in spite of the doctor's letter to them stating I'd been in *pericolo di morte*—danger of dying. I change planes in Chicago and the wheelchair awaits. I almost cry with gratitude as the assistant wheels me through customs, onto the train between terminals, and to the gate.

On the jet bridge in Denver, my carry-on at my feet and my back feeling the hot Colorado air through the thin wall, I watch the other passengers pass by until no one remains except the flight crew. Trembling like one of those skinny hairless dogs, my eyes plead with the vacant jet bridge for the requested wheelchair to appear.

The flight crew begins to pass me.

"Can you help me?" My words whisper from white lips to a female flight attendant.

She pauses and looks at me perplexed.

I point limply to the carry-on at my feet. "I can't lift it."

She picks it up and slows her pace to match mine. I want to lean on her, this stranger I don't know.

It's a portent, I think, of how much I'll have to lean on others who have no commitment to me. I'm far from family, and my divorce awaits.

THREE

The Orange Room

My house in Colorado is in a cohousing community, so at least I know my neighbors—important when all my family live in other states.

Cohousing is a concept brought to the United States from Denmark. The idea is to foster community, so homes are placed on pedestrian walkways and cars are left in parking lots a distance from the houses. Interaction is created by walking past other people's front porches along the pedway to reach one's home. When I return there from hospital, five of my neighbors bring me dinners for five nights.

The meals I receive are a godsend, but after five days, I'm still not very capable on my own. Asking for help and relying on community members are uncomfortable for me. The women friends I have in the community all have husbands and kids, and while they may have an alternative lifestyle, they appear just as busy as their counterparts in suburbia. And because there is a lot of turnover in the community, there are many members I don't know well.

A severe pain develops in the surgical site. I have no idea who to call. My doctors are in Italy. I have no medical insurance and no primary care doctor in Colorado. I gingerly make my way downstairs, my hand pressed over my abdomen. In the fridge I find carrots and onions that someone brought over and I find lentils in the cupboard. I could make soup.

I hold onto the counter and tell myself to breathe as pain tightens in my abdomen. Then I rinse a carrot and begin to cut it. After a few minutes, my legs are buckling and I abandon the soup making.

Back on my bed, I call a few community members. I reach Sita, who comes over with an amethyst bio mat and a Byron Katie book.

The heat of late August fills my upstairs bedroom, making my cotton sundress adhere to my frail body. Curled on my side on the bio mat, I have a view of Sita's summer-tanned legs and bare feet.

"Really, the bio mat is gonna be great for this," Sita says as she adjusts the swamp cooler in the window. Air smelling of damp straw whooshes toward me. Sita squats next to my face. "Chandi, have you heard of Byron Katie?"

I lift my head to peer at the cover of the book she holds. *Loving What Is* the gold letters say.

"The pain you're in. Suffering is optional. She'll show you how." Sita sets the book down, and I put my head on it. "Just, you know, when you're better. . ."

I groan and press my hand to my abdomen, my cheek on the smooth book cover, my eyes closing tightly.

Footsteps sound on the stairs and someone calls my name. It's Jill from the north pedway.

"Chandi!" She rushes in and I open my eyes to look up.

"Thanks," I say weakly.

"She's in pain. She doesn't want to be taken anywhere," Sita says as Jill kneels next to me.

"Here," I say, taking a breath. "The surgeon in Italy told me if I got a pain here, it could be a hernia in the surgical site."

"Do you need to go to the ER?" Jill asks with worry in her voice.

I clutch my hand around hers. "I just can't face another ER trip. The flashbacks. It will traumatize me."

"Oh, baby girl, we need to get the trauma out of your body," Sita says, tucking herself next to Jill and putting a hand on my stomach.

"I don't have insurance, and I'm afraid of the cost," I grunt.

"What about ibuprofen?" Jill asks.

"Yes, okay," I say weakly in agreement.

They stay a while, Sita dabbing lavender oil on the bottom of my feet and Jill sitting me up to drink water and take ibuprofen.

Sita goes on retreats all the time and sits at the feet of a guru. I consider her wise. Jill is an atmospheric scientist who exudes gentleness.

"This bursting of my insides in Italy. . . do you think I had some kind of festering wound, you know, from the marriage, that caused my insides to blow up?" I ask them.

"I'm sure it's symbolic," Sita says quickly. "Yes, that fits." She nods firmly.

Jill intervenes. "I'm not so sure. I think random things happen."

Then Sita stands up. "I've gotta get Micah his dinner now. He started school this week, and I have to get him going on his homework."

"Me too, Chandi," Jill says. "I have to make Alice's dinner. I'll see about getting you a doctor appointment if you're not better tomorrow, okay?"

Halfway down the stairs, they turn and tell me to call if I get worse.

I lift a hand in a weak wave. "Yes, I'll be fine."

I lie on my back on the bio mat, looking at the ceiling. I try on both of their theories about my burst appendix, but I can't tell which makes me feel better. I focus on the deep blue color of the ceiling. I'd called it "Tibetan Blue" as I was painting it. The color had reminded me of the particular blue I'd seen on a Tibetan temple when I'd first visited Nepal way back when I was twenty-one. Way back when I'd had my glow. Long before I was married.

Images of how the house had looked when Darrell and I had bought it flit through my mind: dirty white walls, cheap linoleum floor, and layers of grime under the washer and dryer, which were in a closet in the kitchen; a stinking pee-stained carpet in the two little bedrooms upstairs. There had been no front porch or back deck. But I had a down payment, a precious down payment that meant at thirty-three, I would no longer have to deal with the horrors of bidding wars for rental places in Santa Cruz and Silicon Valley.

Not being able to afford to buy in those home turf locations, Darrell and I had moved to Colorado over housing prices alone. But it was going to be worth it. I had my little pot-of-gold-down-payment, and I had a plan for the rundown house.

I planned to take $10,000 out of the down payment and put it toward new floors, a porch, a deck, fresh paint, and landscaping. It never occurred to me to ask Darrell to share the cost of any of it. It didn't matter. I was excited to buy our first house. I was eager to have fun picking out paint colors together and planting a garden together. Working on the house would surely create the sense of team that I had been so disappointed not to feel during the wedding.

The pain in my abdomen presses forward like the hurricane I watched once, coming across the sea toward me as I stood on the rooftop of a condo in Playa del Carmen.

The room is now dark, and I roll to my side, wondering if the warm amethyst mat is working any magic.

Should I go to the ER?

I see myself in a wheelchair, heading down a hall—a white fluorescent sanitized hall of searing pain where the figures in scrubs are blurry, where voices cannot be heard over the silent scream from the hot, blinding eruption in my body. I am more afraid of the flashbacks that the ER will bring than of lying here in the dark, alone with this pain.

I nix the idea of calling my mother. She'd already been with me in the Italian hospital. During my hospital stay, she'd arrived in England for a preplanned and sad event: to clear out the family home in Devon and sell it. It was the home she'd grown up in until the war began and she moved to the US. She loved that house in Devon and the land around it more than anything else in the world. But instead of going down to Devon when she arrived in England, she got a flight to Florence to be with me. Her time to clear out the house had been cut in half, and she'd only just taken the long flight back to California.

No, don't call her, I tell myself. She'll have jet lag and might already be in bed.

I roll to my other side and watch the bottoms of the sheer white curtains fluttering and lifting. I remember that after hanging them, I had been so pleased that when the moon passed by those windows at night, I could see its spirit-white face from my bed, through the sheer curtains.

I think about my enthusiasm for fixing up the house.

"Let's take a class on Pergo flooring at Home Depot! It will be fun! I bought a tree for the yard! Let's plant it together!" I would say to my new husband, but it was like throwing my enthusiasm against a wall and watching it splat and then slide off.

"Which project should we do today? Should we get the floors done first or paint first? What do you think?" I asked one Saturday morning, noticing that my enthusiasm was forced.

"Do we have to do any of it?" he replied, inserting himself onto a small patch of available couch and opening a book.

I felt set at great distance, as if I had been picked up by a giant unseen hand and placed on an iceberg in the North Atlantic. I looked at the mattress on the living room floor where we slept because the bedrooms weren't useable and at the boxes piled shoulder height across the rest of the room. "Yes, I think we do need to get going on it," I said weakly.

But I dropped it. A few days later, I offered to take out the carpets reeking of urine on my own and do all the painting myself if he'd do the Pergo floors. He conceded and did them, but he never covered the gap between the floor and the baseboard with quarter round.

In the meantime, I found my enthusiasm again. I was going to create my orange walls. I'd wanted orange walls for a very long time, since my first India trip twelve years earlier. On the threshold of adulthood and awed by the world, I'd been stunned and startled by India. I'd been caught immediately in her tidal pulls, challenged and beckoned, drawn in and spit out, pummeled and caressed.

Reverence and celebration were marked by the color orange: the garlands of marigolds, the sadhu's robes, the *tilak* on the forehead of the holy people. And then in Varanasi, from a boat on the Ganges, I was enveloped by the devotion to Agni, the fire god who burns away darkness and brings the light. Under the sky studded by orange embers, on the river anointed by orange petals, I thought, faith here is not like in my culture, which to me was white and weightless, like baby's breath. Here faith was orange. It was gutsy and deep like a birthing canal. It was something that connected you to the womb of the earth and then birthed you out, wearing a garland of marigolds, celebrating.

To paint a room orange was to remind myself of a time when my spirit had rejoiced.

I knew pure orange would be too heavy for the room. A color wash was the thing to do. I spent four days working on those walls, learning to rub the color wash with a cloth in that sfumato way I had seen on walls at estates in Tuscany. When I was done, the furniture arranged and the candles lit, the room positively glowed.

Yet throughout the ten-year marriage, every time I looked at the gap between the floor and the walls around the edge of that room—the gap that filled so easily with debris—it was like a scar, reminding me of the disappointment I'd felt in those first months of the marriage.

I had thought that if I put all of my money, and all of my enthusiasm, and all of my energy into creating this house for us—into making it an attractive sanctuary in which to build our marriage—I couldn't go wrong; the marriage couldn't go wrong.

I pull my knees toward my chest on the hot mat. My fingers go to the place between my hip and stomach where the scar is. Strange, I think. Strange, that glowing orange room of my spirit. There's a scar around it. Is it the scar of my marriage, of my bad choices? Is it tightening in on me?

I remind myself that I have my head on a book called *Loving What Is*.

Can I love what is?

Can I love the pain?

Can I love having no money and no primary person?

Can I love the fear of healing alone?

FOUR

A Minefield

In the morning, Jill takes me to a doctor who orders a CAT scan. I get on a payment plan to cover it, and Sita calls my worried mother with an update.

In the waiting room, Jill tells me about her ovarian operation.

I've been there, her story tells me, and I squeeze her hand. For a moment I stop feeling conflicted about having taken her from her daily duties.

The doctor who reads the scan has little to say. "It seems something ruptured in there. Do you have a history of ovarian cysts?"

"No, I've never had any."

"Hmm."

"It must somehow be related to the surgery. I had to take the flight home sooner than the doctors in Italy advised. Maybe something—"

"Most likely a cyst. It's gone now. Take these painkillers though."

The painkillers knock me out so thoroughly that I don't leave my bed for two days.

When I become aware that I need to eat, I stress about who to call. Sita and Jill have done enough, I reason. I call six other community members before I reach someone. She says she'll send her boyfriend over. He never appears.

I crawl to the bathroom, and I eat nuts instead of cooked meals. It's easier than dialing a half dozen numbers again. And then the aloneness hits. I understood it clearly during those weeks in the hospital, this aloneness. The word lonely is not strong enough for it. It's an excruciating aloneness that scrapes like a razor.

This will pass. This will pass. I say these words over and over, attempting to trust and surrender like I did when I was wheeled into the operating room in Italy. But fear and excruciating aloneness barrel toward me.

I don't think I'm going to die. No, the pain is not as bad as what I endured in the hospital in Italy. And I survived that. What makes me now gather my reserves into my small fists and push through on my own is the discomfort of calling busy people multiple times in one day because I need help. It seems that only a relationship partner or a family member would truly work in this situation. I feel like I've been sucked into a muddy, stormy river that is racing out of control, swallowing everything in its path.

All I can do is curl on the bed repeating in my mind *This will pass, this will pass, this will pass* like a catatonic mental patient.

A week later I file for divorce. I push myself to reach out to someone to go with me, to drive me in fact.

A community member says she's not comfortable going. "Darrell was a fellow community member for a long time. I'm still friends with him. It would be weird."

I call Baxter, who lives in town and is neutral.

"Sweet Jesus, you are skin and bones," he says when he sees me.

"You look good too, Bax," I say, trying to make light of it. I'm determined to make light of the whole day, of the whole darn process of filing for divorce.

"You didn't consider putting this off until you're better?" Baxter asks as he drives up Canyon Boulevard.

"You know, we planned to face the nitty-gritty of it when I got back from Italy. We've been putting it off long enough."

"It's hard, man. It's harder than ya think it's gonna be."

"Yeah. Okay, Bax. Thanks for being here."

"You ready?" he asks as he pulls up at the courthouse.

"Yes. Let's get it over with."

That's all I say to myself as I walk from one counter window to another in the courthouse. *Just get it over with.* I'm tired of my emotions. I don't want to have any today. *Just get it over with.*

The wild geese begin to land in the pasture beyond my house, and the meat doesn't return soon enough to my bones to ward off the cold of snow in October. I'm not working. I'd gone to grad school during the two years of my separation from Darrell to pursue my passion for

Florentine Renaissance history, and I'd started teaching as an adjunct instructor at local colleges before the burst appendix trip. But I'd returned from the hospital too ill to take on the fall classes.

There is hardly anything in my bank account, so I try to do the divorce on my own, hiring a lawyer for only a few hours' consultation. But I find I'm ill-equipped to do it on my own. The paperwork surprises me. It keeps coming, like the May snowstorms in Crested Butte that drop ten inches and snuff out the spring.

One day, as I try to complete the paperwork, my mind becomes too numb to accomplish anything. I read and reread the small sentences on the form, but my mind won't budge. I picture someone next to me, someone who feels healthy and strong and can make short work of the forms. I call a neighbor I've not asked anything of. She works in high tech and is more mainstream than most of the community members. She comes by and takes a look at it. Then she looks at me and says, "You've got to pull yourself together."

"I'll try that," I reply, mustering bravery in my voice, although I thought I had been trying that.

I feel ashamed—ashamed for finding the paperwork hard; ashamed for finding my life hard.

Everything has so quickly unraveled.

One day a friend shows me her new iPhone. No one else I know has an iPhone yet. In fact, I only have a landline. She also tells me about Facebook.

"I've been under such a rock," I say.

"Look," she says, bringing Facebook up on her phone, "I'm friends with your ex."

"He's not my ex yet," I remind her.

She magnifies the page and hands me the phone. I orient myself and read a comment from a girl who appears to be from the nursing program he is in. "It's so fascinating that you lived in Italy! How wonderful. Tell me about it!"

"Oh." I feel an inward wince as I hand the phone back.

Her eyes flash. "He never would have lived there if you hadn't been in his life!"

I try to shrug it off. And yet, divorce is like crossing a minefield. You never know when something is going to blow up right in front of you and make you hit the deck, cowering.

In this moment, it seems that any valiant effort I'd made during the marriage to provide us with a colorful, creative warm life has left me in an empty gray room shivering without a blanket.

What is it about divorce that makes me so fragile?

I will not look at his Facebook page. This is a good resolution, I think, and surely it will all be over by Christmas. With a grimace, I remember that the troops in August of 1914 were told this as they headed to war.

I borrow money from my parents to meet with the lawyer again.

"You deserve maintenance in your situation," he says.

"He doesn't have a job right now," I reply.

"When he gets one then. Has he usually had a steady job?"

"Well, it's complicated."

When I met Darrell, he was working on becoming a stockbroker at Shearson Lehman, but it wasn't for him. Within a few months he had switched to the call center at Charles Schwab. He regaled me with ideas for businesses he was going to start. I hadn't thought much about owning a business. Growing up, my concept of job possibilities had begun and ended with being a teacher.

In our early days of dating, Darrell had told me he was going to start a car wash. I was surprised when he said earnings could be a hundred thousand in the first year. That was way more than I'd get as a teacher, although surely not as fulfilling. But I was intrigued. My long-term boyfriend before Darrell had been a hippie. I'd heard he was now collecting seaweed on the beach for a living. Darrell, on the other hand, seemed to have business savvy.

I paid little attention when the car wash talk disappeared. As use of the internet began to be more prevalent, Darrell decided he would start a web development business. He paid a printing shop to print up thousands of postcards to advertise his services.

I had thought people just threw mail solicitations in the trash, but he told me that direct mail gives the lowest cost per lead and that four percent respond. Thousands of postcards were sent out, but no work was generated except for two websites he did for friends, and then his interest in it flatlined. I was wary about the next business idea he brought to our kitchen table.

"But what job does he have now?" The lawyer's question prompts me back to the present.

"Uh, he decided to become a nurse. He's graduated but doesn't have a job yet."

"But there's a huge nurse deficit here in Colorado. He should be finding one right away. Is he trying to wait until the divorce is over?"

"I don't know. But I don't think we can plan on maintenance," I reply.

In November, when the land turns its face downward and the shine disappears from the sky, aloneness hovers like a permanent ghost-guest in my cold house. My body doesn't feel strong enough to resume many of my activities. Although I'm going to a divorce support group every Sunday, I have not resumed my dance classes. This is a problem.

"Dance is very important for removing grief from your body," my sister tells me over the phone. She had once been a dancer in a modern dance company in New York.

"I know. Not only that, it's a key way I get in touch with joy."

"Maybe you can go and lie on the floor, and just absorb."

"True. Yes, I could do that."

I decide to say an affirmation for the rest of the day. *I will be able to dance again by December. I will be able to dance again by December.*

FIVE

From a Distance

On the darkest night of the year, December 21, I huddle with Kari on Boulder's Pearl Street Mall. It's my first night out since the hospitalization and my return from Italy in August.

"There are some 'specimens' for you!" Kari gives me a conspiratorial nudge as we come upon three college boys, their pants hanging off their butts and their caps propped sideways.

I lean into her, away from the wind. "How about this?" I say, grinning. "In my personal ad, I'll say, 'Please ignore body ruined by sepsis!'"

"Catchy, but a personal ad? We're not supposed to date."

Kari and I met in the divorce support group. The facilitator had encouraged us to get out and have fun—but not to date yet.

We stand in the freezing air at the end of the pedestrian mall, arms linked, waiting for the light to change. A bitter wind blows the hood off my white Victoria's Secret coat. The coat usually makes me feel sexy and young, but tonight it isn't working its magic. I feel nervous and weak.

"Can we just move to Mexico?" I say, holding my hood in place as another bitter blast sweeps down the nearly empty block.

"Yeah, where's the beach?" Kari's words come through her cinnamon-colored hair, which is blowing across her face.

We pass closed shops and edge toward a restaurant emitting a lively beat. "Hey! Salsa!" I call out over the wind. "The next best thing to being in Mexico!"

We hesitate at the door. Kari's eyes question me.

A Latino man in a black leather coat is at the open door. "Two dollars."

I shrug a yes at Kari. She nods, we pay, and we enter. A band plays in one corner where tables and chairs have been pushed to the side. Although the atmosphere is friendly, I know both of us are afraid that our efforts to get out and have fun will fail, and if we fail, our feelings of grief and loneliness will be magnified.

I dance with a guy from El Salvador whose head reaches my chest. Kari dances with a pale lanky guy who doesn't move his hips. The cheer and liveliness of the music makes me smile, but after two dances, I drop to a bar stool and ask for water.

Kari joins me.

"Kari, I'm sorry. My body's exhausted."

"It's okay. We can go."

We huddle into each other as we make our way down the dark street, our teeth chattering.

I settle into the car seat, clutching my coat around me tightly. "I miss my glow," I say as Kari revs the engine. "I have to get it back."

"Is that like getting your groove back?"

"Yeah. You know when I last felt it?" I notice my voice rises with anticipation. "I was in Playa del Carmen when Italy won the World Cup, and I was on a rooftop bar with a friend, drinking Mojitos. We looked down to the street where the Italians were waving their blue shirts and chanting *Viva Italia!* I was caught up in the excitement; I took my top off!"

"Wow! That's so different from. . . "

"From how I am now? I know." I lean forward to warm my cold hands at the heater vents. "That was more than two years ago. I haven't felt that way since."

"I know what you mean."

"I thought I was going to get my glow back when I went to Italy this past summer."

"But you landed in the hospital instead."

"Yeah. Definitely didn't get my glow back." There's a shiver in my chest, but it's not from the cold, it's from recognition. "It's more than that, Kari." I turn toward her, feeling a sparkle inside me like the beginning fizz of a firework. "My glow is when I loved the world and it loved me back."

"Oh." Kari shoots me a questioning look. "What do you mean exactly?"

"Like. . ." I pause trying to remember how it felt. "There were times when my sense of purpose was clear and my heart was like a balloon on a string. Like I was holding the string, and my heart was out in front of me, higher than me, seeing all the cool things that were ahead and urging me to come along. And I'd be all in, you know, not hesitant, not looking behind me."

"Wow, I don't think I've ever felt that. It's worth getting back—for sure." Kari pauses, her forehead scrunching up. "Why do we even have a grief process if we know we were unhappy in the marriage?"

"Because there's still the death of the dream."

"Yeah." Kari sighs. "I gotta let go of the fantasy of him, of us."

"Letting go doesn't happen overnight," I say, turning my gaze to the dark farmland stretching cookie-sheet-flat from Baseline Road. I had met Darrell right after I turned thirty, and we separated soon after I turned forty. My relationship with him defined the whole decade of my thirties, and I could see now that the loss of something that had defined me for ten years had more impact than the loss of the actual man.

Turning to Kari I say, "You know, marriage is such a fundamental way women have defined themselves for hundreds of years. Even if I decide I don't want to get married again, still, without this definition, right now I feel unmoored."

"Afloat in an aimless boat!" Kari laughs.

I'm heartened by her laugh, and I manage a chuckle. "My boat's gone missing!"

"You know what I did?" Kari looks at me conspiringly. "I got a boob job because he wanted me to!"

"Oh, Kari!"

"I know. Right?"

"You know, if I had allowed myself to really pay attention to my soul, I would have known that he wasn't right. But I plowed forward, with my head leading me recklessly."

"Your soul? I wasn't thinking about my soul either!"

"Well, I did think about it once," I say quietly. "There was this time after the engagement and before the wedding. It was morning; I'm always more emotional in the morning. I had this mini breakdown. I was crying and saying to him, 'I want to know that you love my soul!'"

"Oh!"

"I think he saw it as one of those perplexing female meltdowns that a man has to bear."

"Don't be hard on yourself. I think plenty of people get married without feeling a soul connection."

There's a compassion in Kari's green eyes that I want to press to my chest like a hot water bottle.

"My ex is fighting so hard not to help me and Amber," Kari says. "She's only eight. It's heartbreaking."

"Sorry. That sucks."

"Yeah." Kari sighs. "Divorcing with a nice chunk of cash coming in each month has got to soften the blow a bit. You know, if we could take a trip to Mexico or afford massages—"

"It would make it easier."

Kari's frown deepens as she drums the steering wheel. "Damn holes we've gotta crawl out of."

"We'll get there." I force my voice to be cheery, but I fear our holes are deep. And while remembering my glow has cheered me up, I'm looking at it from such a distance that it seems it happened to someone else, not me.

SIX

The Message

The next day, I throw up in the bathtub. With my hands gripping the edge of the tub and my head hanging dangerously near the vomit, I remember Kari's words: *Damn holes we've gotta crawl out of.*

I wash the vomit down the drain, rinse my mouth, and slump on the bathmat against the side of the tub, too weak to get up. I have never heard of throwing up from exhaustion, but I instinctively know this is what's caused it.

I think about the interview with a movie star I'd read in a magazine the day before in which she said you have to be nurtured emotionally and spiritually for a relationship to work. Reading it, I felt the hole inside of me, and I started to obsess. This looping CD that won't stop playing had cropped up at the time of the wedding and afflicted me throughout the marriage. I want so much to turn it off.

I don't know how to negotiate all this: my out of commission body, my heart without its glow. I've gone back to the island of razor-scraping aloneness.

When I was in the hospital, my two local friends in Florence had done everything they could, and yet, it didn't take away the aloneness, which scraped more ferociously at my insides when I talked to Darrell on the phone. I had just spent a year trying to separate from him, but while I was in the hospital and in a half-dead state, all I wanted was for him to be my man—be the man I always wanted him to be.

My feebly weak mind, strung out from pain, grasped at what it could, and it couldn't understand that Darrell was gone. That he was not my man. That he'd never really been.

When he called me in the hospital, he dutifully asked how I was, and I'd give him snippets with what energy I could muster. I told him that the nurses chided me for having a headache again, and he had murmured that it sounded hard. I told him how the nurses and doctors argued at the foot of my bed, and he had replied that Italians are loud. During one call, I told him that the surgeon had finally visited me and informed me that I'd had half an hour left to live when I arrived at the hospital. My fingers had tightened on the small cell phone as my words choked out.

I'd hung on to the compassion I could find in his voice, but his voice was small and far away, and my wilderness was vast. A part of me wanted him there, holding my hand in the hospital, but I was supposed to be moving on from him, and when he made no mention of coming, I knew we were really over.

The calls always ended with me sobbing and my five roommates pausing their moaning or their conversations and turning to me with questioning eyes.

"*Mio marito.*" (My husband.) I'd manage the two words, gasping at the physical pain and at the razor-scraping aloneness.

"*Ah, sì,*" they would say, nodding knowingly.

The bathtub is cold against my back. I should get up and make some ginger tea, I think, but I remain on the bathmat. Tentatively, I probe the scar on my belly. The skin has dot marks along each side of the scar where the staples were. When I first saw my stomach in the hospital, once I ceased the demented hair tugging and started to focus, it was unrecognizable—distended weirdly with large staples marching up one side of it, like a body part created by Victor Frankenstein.

An acupuncturist friend had told me that in an emergency appendectomy like mine, the doctors would have scooped out my organs and put them on a tray. "That's why you have so much trauma in your body," he'd said.

I wasn't sure if that could be accurate, but the image appalled me.

The surgeon had instructed me to deeply massage around the scar to break up scar tissue. But doing that made me nervous, so I hadn't done it.

Ineptly, I poke around the sides of it but my brain fails to force my fingers to dig in. It would feel like digging through my emotional life.

Is there a message in this mess? I have to admit, for many years, long before I was married, whenever I thought about what the universe might want to tell me, I secretly hoped it would give me a blindingly strong sign that I should move to Italy, something I couldn't ignore, like Constantine seeing that flaming cross in the sky.

My head reels with nausea again. *Breathe*, I tell myself, and I close my eyes. A patch of bright blue sky opens in my mind right then on that dark December day, and across that patch of blue, like an airplane pulling a banner, I see the message: *Walk across Italy.*

Yes, I think, *yes*. It will be a pilgrimage of sorts, a chance to get my glow back. It will be an offering, what the Italians call *un voto*. My body may be too weak to dance, but one thing I can still do is walk. I will walk across Italy, from sea to shining sea.

Maybe I'll start at the Tuscan coast, heading east through Tuscany and on to Le Marche, across Italy's waist, to the Adriatic. I stop slumping, my spine straightening against the tub, the Mary Oliver poem in my head, the one about the journey where she conjures the image of a woman striding into the world after a hardship, determined to salvage her life. It will be like that, I tell myself.

SEVEN

Is It Logical?

By spring the divorce goes through, but I feel little relief because the condo hasn't sold. The condo—the albatross around my neck. Darrell was gung ho about investing in real estate, and with a financial gift I'd received, we'd bought the condo, but it had been a money sucker. One set of renters had created a bad flood that was costly to fix. The most recent renters had let their dog and cat pee on the carpet. And the condo had not gone up in value. It was now empty. Renters could not be found, but the mortgage had to be paid. Even though it was a buyer's market, it was time to unload it. But Darrell didn't want to use a realtor and resisted listing it at market value. His voice on the answering machine saying things about the condo created an anxiety that latched on to my chest, making me feel jittery.

Then one day when I open the curtains as soon as I get out of bed, as is my ritual, I see Darrell coming out of the neighbor's house. I adore the way the sun shines every morning in Colorado. And even on days when shame or depression are my dominant emotions, if I pull the curtains and let the sunlight pour in, something lifts inside me and turns toward brightness, toward possibility. But this morning, I see Darrell coming out of the neighbor's house. Turns out he's dating her.

"Of all the women in Boulder, he picks your *neighbor*? *Jeez . . .us!*" Kari almost shouts when I tell her about it over the phone.

One night soon after, I return to the community, park in the dark, and begin walking toward my house. I realize that the person walking just in front of me is Darrell. He doesn't live here. He's going to Jane's house. I hesitate, wanting to hide. It should be embarrassing for him, not me, but I feel embarrassed.

He turns onto the pedway, where there is better lighting. He's carrying something that looks like roses. My body stiffens and my feet halt. I cringe into the shadows, immobilized. Holding my breath, I wait a minute and then edge into the pedway. Only when I'm assured that he's turned into Jane's house can I allow myself to scamper on.

The next morning I realize to my dismay that my usual delight in pulling open the curtains has vanished. The window by my bed looks directly toward Jane's front door, as does my kitchen window. Instead of joy at the morning light, I feel panic. I try to calm myself. I try to think of what Byron Katie would do. But I don't manage to open the curtains.

A few weeks later I'm in my front yard weeding. The blossoming results of all the bulbs I planted are springing around me: white snowdrops, yellow daffodils, and purple hyacinth. It's therapeutic to pull weeds and clear the debris from around the tender shoots.

But then Darrell and Jane saunter past, holding hands, no more than five feet from where I squat.

Everything in my body speeds up except my hands, which remain frozen in fists around clumps of weeds. My bones seem to shake, and even my teeth feel as if they are rattling. Limbs have come unmoored. I feel myself scattered like flotsam in the garden. I scramble to the house, lunging for the doorknob, as if fleeing a giant wave.

I tell myself to sit down. I'm knocked off course and things have become blurry, like the time I accidentally jibed on the sailboat, and the boom hit me in the head.

My palms press into my thighs, and I command myself to take deep breaths.

I reach for the phone and call Kari.

"That's probably a panic attack," she says.

"I don't know what to do."

"What about prayer?"

Prayer? I don't even know how to start, or who to pray to.

No one ever talked about God in my family. We were *intellectuals*. My mother carried on the progressive educational ideas of her

British parents. It was her mission to raise us without a TV and in the outdoors as much as possible.

My mother was so creative with children's games that we didn't notice the lack of TV. And we had books. Floor to ceiling shelves proudly presented hundreds of hardback books from England. During our early years, my siblings and I were so immersed in the classic British storybooks that when we stepped outside of our hilltop home, we expected to see the high walls and climbing roses of Mary's secret garden or Lake Windermere and the crew of swallows and Amazons, instead of the Santa Cruz hills with acres of apple orchards edged by towering redwood trees.

We worked every weekend morning, raking chicken droppings from the floor of the coop and wheelbarrowing them carefully down a steep dirt road to the compost pile, where we shoveled them into a fecund mix of decaying vegetables, horse manure, and earth. We mucked out the horses' stalls, pruned fruit trees, and watered vegetables. My parents' vegetable garden was almost an acre big.

My dad's corn took me hours to water *thoroughly*, as I was told, slowly moving the hose to each basin down one long row and back up another long row. I would sit in the dirt next to the stalks with the hose on low and carefully shore up the mud basin with my hands as the soft blond corn silk waved above me.

Doing it thoroughly seemed to take half a day. I felt beholden to a family credo that everything must be done properly.

We ate meals from the garden, and we discussed presidential primaries and the Queen's Silver Jubilee, but we never discussed God. It was something other people did, not us.

"Why?" I asked my mother by the time I got to college.

"Well, because dogma demands authority, rather than intelligent thought," she replied as she cut curls of lemon rind.

"Bertrand Russell," my father said, momentarily lifting his eyes from the giant book he was reading on Winston Churchill.

"Back in Devon, Bertie and your grandfather—"

"Yes," I said impatiently, "they had issues with organized religion. I get that. But what about individual experiences of something. . . well, otherworldly?"

"Well, talk to your grandmother about that."

Talk to your grandmother. Now, shaking from an anxiety attack, I think of those words. I need to pray to someone I can imagine. And I can imagine my grandmother, the only spiritual person in my life throughout my childhood and teen years. She was my only grandmother and she was British, although by the time I came along, she was living just around the Monterey Bay from us, in Carmel.

I know what I need to get started: the breathwork CD that Gregg gave me. Gregg, a life coach, led workshops Darrell and I had taken. It seemed that Gregg knew me better, psychologically, than almost anyone, so I'd sought his help while drowning in the troubled divorce waters. He'd told me to listen to the CD daily. This I had not done.

We don't do those things. We're intellectuals.

The breathwork CD leads me to a place where I am able to visualize my grandmother. At first, she and I are sitting under an apple tree. And then, as I'm guided further into the process, an image comes of her and me on a swing in the sky. It's got a wide wooden seat, big enough for the two of us. Long ropes descend from gold-dipped clouds. We are swinging in a baby-blue sky where wafting rose-colored forms seem to indicate angels. And then Jesus joins us. He's standing in bare feet behind us on the swing, his hands holding the ropes.

Later, my mind thinks *of course it was Jesus*, I was only falling on an image from my culture. But I like the image of the three of us on the swing. It cheers me. It gives me a sense that I'm not alone. And isn't that why humans created religion? So they wouldn't feel alone, so they'd feel that a great benevolent power is with them in their time of need?

In the following months, when the divorce stress hammers me flat, I do my best to turn my mind to the visions from the breathwork CD, and when my mind is calm, it sneaks back to again ponder the banner with its message, *Walk across Italy.*

I wonder which town on the Tuscan coast to depart from. I think of the nude beach near San Vincenzo where I used to go with Sydney and Antonio to escape the ferocious Florentine heat. There I swam naked in a peacock-colored sea and felt whole and complete in mind, body, and spirit. This idea of walking across Italy is a revolving beam of light that I push aside when it swings through my mind. But it keeps coming back. I want to check in with Gregg about it, but I can't afford a session with him, so I build a list in my head of why not to walk across Italy: no money to get there or to pay for accommodation for a walk that would take at least a month; have already not worked for a semester due to illness and am subsisting on next to nothing; more responsible to get a full-time job as soon as my health can handle it; no designated route between the two coasts.

After a few months of taking my list seriously, I know there's something wrong with it—wrong in fact with my whole approach to my life.

Gregg agrees to my idea of a trade. I'll do office work for him in return for the session.

Sinking into his couch, I'm happy to again be in his compassionate teddy bear presence. I tentatively tell him my idea of walking across Italy and then quickly counter it with, "It's irresponsible."

"Why?" he asks, looking at me intently.

"Because I have no money. I need to get a job."

"Chandi," he says evenly, "what about trusting your heart? This idea is coming from your heart, not your head, and your head is getting in the way. Your head has always gotten in the way of following your passions."

I shift uncomfortably. It's true, and it's come up before, but I make another stab at hanging on to the way I was trained. "Things have to be logical, reasonable, for me to be okay doing them."

"Whoever said that following one's passion is logical?" He crosses his ankle over his knee and lets his words sink in.

I think of the book I'm reading titled *The Passion Test*. The authors suggest that people who play it safe aren't as energetic, passionate, and excited about their lives as those who dance on the edge and go for their dreams. I realize I *have* danced on the edge. I did it when I traveled. I was doing it when I last had my glow, in Playa del Carmen.

I sigh. "I don't know, Gregg, I'm so exhausted."

"It takes a lot of energy to *not* be you."

That one strikes home.

EIGHT

Desiderata

In spite of Gregg's encouragement to get out of my head and into my heart, I dither for another month. My head remains dominant, arguing that a job and health care should be my focus. Yet I want to believe Gregg has it right, that there's another way to approach living my life.

I develop the idea of a fundraising campaign. Trying to overcome my trepidation, I type a blog post presenting my idea of a long-distance walk across Italy, peppering it with phrases: Have you ever had to start your life over? Did you know how to figure it out? With your help, I can take this step in rebuilding my life.

I add a PayPal link and suggest that if one hundred people donate $10.00 each, I'll have enough for my plane fare. But I don't push the publish button. I wander to the porch, pick up my cat, and look out absently at the garden. A butterfly lifts from the tall stalks of iris that I'd planted. Its orange wings flicker in and out of the purple petals.

The caterpillar turned into a butterfly just when she thought she was dying.

The thought alights in my mind, and I hug my cat against my heart. With an inward smile, I go back to the computer and press the publish button.

My walk should be forty days, I tell myself. There's a jumble of spiritual traditions in my head. I'm not sure which ones say that forty days is a period of testing and trial, ending with restoration and renewal, but I'm pretty sure a lot of them do.

To complete the walk before July when the temperatures will be blazing, I decide I have to depart by the end of May—in three weeks.

The donations come in from friends, from family, from members of the divorce support group and the Italian speakers group. My parents say that they find the campaign embarrassing, but they go ahead and donate. My siblings donate, and an acquaintance from the divorce support group lends me an iPod to take. Most importantly, my housemate, who I have taken in to help me cover household costs, commits to taking care of my cat while I'm gone.

The donations encourage me to believe in myself. After all, if these donors believe in me and my proposed walk, then my idea might have value. Many times, I choke up while reading the comments people write on my blog and the heart-warming and unexpected cards that arrive in the mail. Some come from people I barely know.

One woman who stumbled onto my blog tells me that my adventure reminds her of the woman she used to be, the woman hiding inside of her, and the potential in us all. And I realize I am reminding myself of the woman I used to be. I'm going off on this solo trek to find that person again.

I thought I was alone, but I'm not. There are many people cheering me on. I practically skip across the parking lot as I head to the Italian speakers meet-up.

Ah, but then there are the naysayers.

"You're crazy." "I'm afraid for you." "You've come undone." "You're risking your life." The naysayers fling doubts in my path.

Pascal, a friend living in Italy, writes to me, "There's absolutely no safety on the roads; there's no safety in sleeping outdoors. And you need a good solid regime of exercise and building yourself up. Come to Italy when you're stronger, and then do something you like to do here, but not a walking tour of any kind."

His comment alarms me. It encourages the part of me that's fearful, the part of me that isn't sure a net will appear if I leap. But I remind myself of my travels on my own twenty years ago, when I'd learned to trust the universe, when I had embraced leaps of faith, when my glow was a frequent visitor.

I'd been in love with Italy since my first trip there at age nineteen, when a girlfriend, Dana, and I had set out with backpacks, youth hostel cards, and Eurail passes for an extended jaunt around Europe.

We'd taken a night train from Switzerland and arrived in Florence in the morning. Groggy and stiff from sitting in a second-class train compartment all night, we wandered toward the Arno River. As I stood on the Ponte Santa Trinità, gazing at the faded yellow backsides of the shops on the Ponte Vecchio and hearing the melodious Italian language around me, I began to experience what my grandmother had so poetically described.

She had testified to me about the beauty and the art of Florence, a city she'd visited more than fifty years earlier. She was named for the city, as she often reminded me, because her mother (also British) had been mesmerized by Florence's striking beauty.

I get a message from a man on the Slow Travel forum. He's an experienced long-distance hiker.

"There are some key elements to being a successful solo hiker: introspection to make all that time on the trail of value to you; resilience in being able to overcome the hardships; and a sense of adventure to make it all worthwhile. It appears that you have all three."

I close my eyes and think of orange-winged butterflies.

That evening, as I drive home from the Italian speakers meet-up, I realize that the naysayers and the supporters are mirroring my struggle between the head and the heart.

But even if I get my heart up front and center, leading me like the warrior queen Boadicea, what am I going to do about my route? Am I just going to turn my back to the Tuscan coast and start walking in an easterly direction? How can I create a list of possible places to stay if I have no idea where I'll be at the end of each day?

For a minute, I become my own naysayer. This idea is radically unrealistic. Am I going to walk on highways? Through farmers' fields? How will I maintain a sense of direction?

I rush home and anxiously Google towns that might be on my route, seeking B&Bs or farm stays in the vicinity. Averaging the cost of accommodations, I multiply it by forty nights. Over three thousand dollars. My heart sinks.

In desperation, I go to the Slow Travel forum for Italy, a forum I'd been a part of for years. I post this note: Hi everyone, I am going to be walking across Italy for the month of June. I'm thinking I want to go from Cecina on the Tuscan coast to Fano on the coast of Le Marche. The crazy thing is, I have no idea if there are trails. I leave in less than two weeks.

My post elicits comments such as, "First you inspired me, then you frightened me," and, "I have done a couple thousand miles of solo hiking and have also done enough mountain climbing to destroy a fair amount of brain cells. The biggest lesson I could impart is that there are many things in life that you can do spontaneously. Long-distance hiking is not one of those things."

I read their comments a few times, letting the reality sink in. This is harebrained. There is no route to follow, and I have no idea how to read a compass. Figuring this out with only two weeks left is ridiculous. But I'm determined now. A stubbornness kicks in. I write to Italian friends asking advice, and I again examine my map of Tuscany, tracing possible routes, hoping for something to click into place.

I go to bed full of nervous energy, refusing to admit to myself that my plans are foolhardy. I want my Constantine cross in the sky. I want to believe in the walk across Italy message. It has to work.

The next day on the Slow Travel forum I read this: "Hello Chandi. Consider walking the Via Francigena, a pilgrimage route to Rome. If you do it, you will belong to a special select group of people who have walked the route. Let me know if you have questions. Julia."

I write her back immediately, my fingers flying on the keyboard, my heart soaring with hope.

I look up the pilgrimage. *Yes*, my heart says. *Yes. A pilgrimage.* Hadn't I called it that in my mind?

With only two weeks left, my preparation becomes frenzied. I find a few websites about the route, mostly in Italian, which often provide conflicting information. I download a list of religious institutions that will accommodate pilgrims, sometimes for free, sometimes for a small fee. And I learn how to obtain a pilgrim passport—a booklet that a pilgrim presents at each destination to be stamped and then presented at Saint Peter's in Rome, the spiritual ending point of the pilgrimage.

Julia, who walked it the previous year with her husband, tells me, "The route has only recently been revived by the Italian Ministry of Culture and signposts are erratic. Plan to get lost."

On the fledgling Yahoo group for the Via Francigena, I learn about two guidebooks to the route, one in Italian, titled *Guide to the Via Francigena, 900 Kilometers on Foot on the Pilgrimage Roads to Rome*, and one in English, published independently by an American couple who had walked the route. I inquire about purchasing it, but the couple is out of the country and can't sell it to me.

Then I bump into a website created by Alberto, an Italian in Milan. Apparently, the Italian Ministry of Culture had hired him to walk the route and write up directions. I e-mail Alberto, and he confirms that his directions are recent. All I have to do is download and print them. Thank goodness.

I'm computer savvy, but I don't have any of the latest gadgets like iPods and iPhones. However, Alberto proudly tells me he's just posted the "way-markers" for GPS on his website. I have never used a GPS—not driving or hiking. I don't know what way-markers are or how I would get them onto a GPS if I owned one. But it gets me wondering. Do I need a GPS?

When I inquire at the REI store, I'm told that Garmin—whoever that is—doesn't publish GPS maps for Italy. I e-mail this information to Alberto. No, he insists, Garmin has published them. He's sure of it. So I call Garmin's customer service, and no, Garmin hasn't published them. Just as well. I do not have money for a GPS and I have a penchant for low-tech travel.

If Freya Stark traveled by herself in the 1930s in the wild parts of Iran where no Westerner had ever ventured, then I can do a solo pilgrimage in Italy without a GPS.

As I rush through REI, poking at the hanging sleeping bags, looking for the lightest weight one possible, I decide not to take a tent. Instead, I'll do what's necessary to get to lodging for the night, even if it means taking a bus to the next town instead of walking.

I have a hard time deciding on shoes. Years ago, I'd finally seen a podiatrist about the blisters I always got when hiking. After taking one look at my heels, he informed me that my bone stuck out more than most people's, and unless I cut out the insides of my boots in the heel area, I'd always get blisters. Subsequently, I'd found that with day hikers, I can usually be blister free, but with the above-the-ankle boots, blisters are inevitable.

But should I go with shoes that are lighter than day hikers? My Keen sandals are going to be my backup. I know that with a light backpack and a trail that isn't crazy difficult, I can feel supported enough by Keens. But on days when I walk in my Keens, will the day hikers with their heavy soles be too bulky strapped to the outside of my small pack? I settle on Salomon Trail Runners and spray them twice over with waterproofing spray.

As I prepare to depart, I remember the poem "Desiderata" on my grandmother's bedroom wall. A line from it—"no doubt the universe is unfolding as it should"—was the main piece of spiritual wisdom I carried with me as a teen in my nonspiritual family. I had said it to myself back then whenever I struggled to sort through the confusing things that happen in a teenage world.

I remember my grandmother saying, "Desiderata means desired things."

Will I find my *desired things* on the pilgrimage?

NINE

Coraggio!

From Denver, I wing my way to Chicago. The man next to me asks why I'm heading to Italy. I tell him about my pilgrimage.

"Where do you meet the group?" he asks.

"There's no group."

"No group? You mean you're doing it *totally alone?*"

"Yes."

"That's brave!"

At the counter for my gate in the Chicago airport, an elderly couple approaches. They try to ask for information in stumbling English and cannot make themselves understood. I recognize their accent as Italian, so I chime in and begin translating. The man exclaims, "Thank God, an Italian!"

With my strong American accent, I don't know how he can think I'm Italian, but I'm pleased. The American Airlines employee breathes a sigh of relief. "Thank goodness you can speak that language."

Charlemagne said, "To have another language is to possess a second soul." Learning Italian is the greatest gift I have given myself. Each time I arrive in Italy and hear and respond to the *bella lingua* around me, a secret, dormant place in me springs to life like a Bernini fountain in Piazza Navona, turned on again after having been shut down for some time.

The woman in the seat next to me, like the man on the prior flight, asks why I'm going to Italy. When I tell her, she also says, "You're meeting a group, right?"

"No group."

"No group? You're brave!"

After hearing this word a second time, I have to ask myself what I make of it.

Perhaps I'd not attached the word *brave* to my pilgrimage because of what happened in the first twenty-four hours during my first time traveling alone.

At age nineteen, as I set out on a budget backpacking European adventure with my friend Dana, I had no plans to travel solo. I didn't know any other female who had traveled alone, so it wasn't a concept. In 1984, if you didn't have a friend who had done it or hadn't read a book about it, you had no examples—unlike the online world today, where travel blogs are awash with examples of female solo travel.

Three months into our trip, we were in the Greek city of Thessaloniki, staying at a place called the Farm School, when we realized we could take a night bus to Istanbul.

Istanbul. No one we knew had been there. In fact, our parents had told us in no uncertain terms *not* to go to Turkey. Traveling to Turkey at that time was not on the backpacking circuit, and certainly not on the radar of most nineteen-year-old girls.

Our night bus ride would enter the country that was depicted in the movie *Midnight Express*, which had come out five years before and had scared the pants off Americans who watched it. Moreover, the Iranian Hostage Crisis had ended only three years earlier—an event that had caused panic and fear about the lands between the Bosphorus and the Persian Gulf.

At the Turkish border, we obediently exited the bus while the Turkish guards pulled all the luggage out of the bus's belly. The dark faces of the Greek and Turkish men were lit by the glows of their cigarettes. The few women present had their heads covered. We were the only foreigners. I had never been so removed from my culture or so conscious of male dominance. Nor had I been close to someone who brandished a machine gun.

Two Turkish guards shouldering machine guns had walked up to Dana and me, stopping a foot in front of us. Planting their legs slightly apart, they moved their dark eyes from our heads to our toes and back to our faces. With a smirk and a laugh, they turned back to poke at the assortment of baggage on the ground.

Dana tucked her arm through mine and whispered, "My God, we're far from home!"

I was slightly daunted, and yet I tingled with anticipation as I stood on the edge of what felt like a very different world.

Oddly, Dana and I chose this very foreign city in which to split up. She'd committed to a job back in California and planned to head to Paris on her own to get her flight home. I was in no way ready to end my adventures. I decided to take a night bus back to Greece and then venture into Yugoslavia. Dana stood in Divanyolu Street next to a Turkish man with one foot who had befriended us, waving as my bus pulled away.

The bus I'd boarded was supposed to take me to the large bus station where I could get a night bus back to Greece. But after sitting on the bus for over thirty minutes, my confidence waned. The surroundings looked more and more like outskirts and less and less like a place where one would find a major bus station. I began to try to communicate with people on the bus, but no one spoke English.

The bus driver pulled over when the passengers began to chatter about my predicament. It was clear to me that no one knew what to do because no one understood where I wanted to go. Then a man in business attire who spoke English climbed on the bus. With relief, I explained to him where I wanted to go.

"I'll take you there," he said.

We got out at the next stop and boarded a minibus. He expressed excitement about meeting someone from California and gave me his business card. When we arrived at the big bus station, he led me to the ticket booth, ensured I wasn't cheated, and loaded me onto the correct bus.

After this, I bullet pointed some guidelines for myself and my travels:

- Rid my head of the voices of the media that tell me that the world out there is scary.
- Carry with me a belief that people are good, and want to do good for others.
- Embrace the world and it will embrace me back.

On the Turkish side of the border, the same sullen army men with machine guns made the same demand that luggage be pulled from the bus's hold and searched, and once again, the Greek and Turkish men shot me piercing looks.

On the Greek side, the luggage was searched yet another time. Finally, the bus pulled into Thessaloniki at about two in the morning. Only a taxi ride lay between me and the friendly Farm School.

I didn't relish the idea of getting into a taxi with any of the male drivers who swarmed around me. They seemed too eager and too full of testosterone, but I went with one who insisted he knew the location of the American Farm School. The place he took me didn't look right, and when I challenged him, he became angry. Being in a forest alone was preferable to being in a taxi with an angry Greek man at two in the morning, so I got out.

After he pulled away, I found myself standing next to a locked gate and a fence. Beyond it, I could see woods and possibly a farm. I thought it might be the back of the Farm School. Perhaps he'd brought me to the back gate instead of the front.

I threw my pack over the fence and climbed it. As I dropped to the other side, a barking dog came racing toward me—a German shepherd. I braced myself and considered putting my pack between it and my body. Then I told myself to relax and be friendly.

I called softly to it, *"Entáxei,"* a Greek word I was pretty sure meant *all right/okay*. I must have picked it up at some point in the past month in Greece without knowing I'd done so.

Happily, the dog became my guide and protector, staying with me as I stumbled through the woods and ditches. I trudged, bleary-eyed, past dark shapes of barns and wondered about crawling into a stall to spend the night.

Over an hour later, I came upon a road and then a hut with a night watchman sitting at a gate. I asked for directions to the Farm School, but he didn't understand my English. He was short and swarthy, and he had a pleasant face. I must have looked desperate because he invited me to sit down and made me coffee. Once seated, I couldn't get up. I didn't notice when the German shepherd left. Perhaps it believed I'd been delivered to safety.

Because I couldn't communicate with the watchman, I simply pulled my sleeping bag out and put it on the floor of his hut. Too tired to do anything else, I had to trust him—and summon a more complete trust than ever before. I went to sleep, and he left the hut.

Did he usually leave the hut at three-thirty in the morning, or was he giving me privacy? I'll never know.

When the sun rose, the watchman returned bearing thick, luscious Greek yogurt. I almost burst into tears when he handed it to me. Once revived, I was able to recall that a brochure written in Greek about the Farm School was somewhere in my pack. Reading it, the watchman gave me a reassuring look, took me to a bus, and told the bus driver where to drop me. I finally made it safely to the Farm School, which wasn't at all near where the taxi driver had dropped me.

Thus, my first twenty-four hours of solo travel were replete with the discomforts of being utterly lost *and* with comforts provided by strangers. After that, I had no qualms about solo travel. I had learned that the best experiences await on the other side of fear.

But now, on the plane to Rome, I dissect the comments about bravery that have been made by total strangers on hearing that I am traveling alone. Even if I don't hesitate to arrive in an unknown country on my own, I still fear plenty of things.

I fear being in a damn hole.

I fear the judgments from the outsiders about my marriage.

I fear that I'll never stop obsessing.

I fear I won't regain my glow.

So what do I *want*?

I want to believe in the *walk across Italy* message.

I want to believe I can be tuned in enough to listen.

Wrestling into awkward positions in the confines of the economy seat, I think of the line by Rumi, "The door is round and open, don't go back to sleep." Am I seeking a religious connection?

I don't know, but I get it that people turn to religion after crisis and trauma. I have a cousin who became religious after her ten-year-old daughter died of cancer. Like me, my cousins were raised in a household in which family members were either relatively nonreligious or adamantly nonreligious.

Eyebrows were raised and shock was registered by the adamant ones when my cousin got herself baptized and began sprinkling her e-mails with the word *God*. But I quietly understood. I understood how the need to believe in something arises when too much trauma is in one's veins, when too much of one's foundation is yanked away.

When teaching Western civilization, I cover the historical Jesus, making a distinction between the historical and the faith-based Jesus. As an academic, I can only understand the historical one. Yet, when a priest came to my bedside in the hospital and asked if I was Catholic, I felt regret when I shook my head no. As he moved away, I wanted to call out, "Wait! Tell me about God!"

Arriving at my Rome hotel at noon, I check in and immediately take a shower once in my room. But it is a quick shower because I don't want to miss the lunch hour.

I step into the narrow pedestrian *via*, stop, exhale, and feel a lightness in my heart for the first time in months.

Two Roman women move languorously in front of me, confident in their high heels on the uneven cobblestones. A long-haired man sits behind a small table displaying jewelry. The silver catches glints of sun angling into the wisp of a street.

The earthy-red hues of the walls are mottled and chipped. I imagine that I'm moving the way the Roman women do over the ancient cobblestones. And it feels as if my heart is leading instead of my head. The narrow street gives way to a small piazza where tiny cars—Cinquecentos and Smart cars—are scattered in disarray in the rare open space. Two men in business suits, both on cell phones, pass me, their rich voices rolling through melodious words like the sound liquid dark chocolate would make when poured into a cappuccino cup.

I pause to make sense of the jumble of narrow streets in the Campo dei Fiori zone, a part of Rome I know relatively well. Not like the back of my hand the way I know Florence, but still, I've been to Rome more times than I can count. And yet, there are hundreds of corners of the city I've never seen and an opulence of museums and churches I have still not entered.

Oh, Rome is burnished with treasures! How I've loved this city ever since my first visit when I was a wide-eyed nineteen-year-old with no nice clothes and no makeup in my pack, only jeans, T-shirts, a pair of hiking boots, and a budget of ten dollars a day. I had been blissfully unaware of the Italian protocol, making of myself a *brutta figura* instead of a *bella figura*. To "make a bella figura," I would have needed at least to wear handsome shoes. I later learned hiking boots in a city make a *brutta figura*.

I arrive at a simple trattoria and settle into a chair at an outdoor table. A charming boyish waiter takes my order and immediately compliments my Italian.

After twenty hours of travel and economy class airplane food, I eat that first plate of artichoke pasta like a person possessed. My waiter admires my spotlessly clean plate and asks what I'm doing in Italy. As if on cue, his response to my plan is, *"Coraggiosa!"* which means *brave*.

Crossing the Ponte Sisto, I make my way to the Church of Santa Maria in Trastevere. Said to be the first church in Rome dedicated to Mary, it was built in the third century AD, and its richly carved Ionic capitals are supposedly from an old Roman temple of Isis. Perhaps it is the lingering goddess energy that makes the church so appealing to me.

Late afternoon light stretches through the small arched windows in the apse. My eyes linger on the stunning twelfth-century gold mosaic that fills the half-dome. Mary and Jesus are on a throne in heaven. Large halos encircle their heads, and their golden robes shimmer brightly. This is nicer than Jesus hanging mournfully on a cross. He's relaxed, with one arm around his mother and an open book in the other hand.

I slide into a pew and ponder my intentions for the pilgrimage. I write in my small notebook:

- I will know how to trust my heart and trust the universe.
- I will regain strength in my body and empowerment of my spirit.
- I will experience surrender.

In the silence of the church, I feel I can hear its heartbeat, pulsing with centuries of prayer. My eyes go back to the mosaic in the apse, and I'm reminded of the vision I had, months ago, of my grandmother and Jesus on the swing.

A message comes to me. *We've been here all along. You only have to turn your heart to us.*

TEN

The Kukui Nut

The cobbled street is shaded while the ancient red-brick wall at the back of the Pantheon glistens in the sun. My heart gives a leap of joy as I approach. The Pantheon is one of the oldest intact structures in the world, and it is my favorite one to marvel at, apart from Brunelleschi's dome in Florence.

I think of my students in Colorado and how much I'd enjoyed sharing the magnificence of this building with them. Built in 27 BC by Marcus Agrippa (deputy to the first Emperor Augustus), it was destroyed and rebuilt twice, the last time by the Emperor Hadrian. Its concrete dome, made without steel reinforcing rods, is a testament to Roman architectural ingenuity, and it has now been with us almost nineteen centuries. I want to reach out and touch the worn red bricks and the fragmented marble columns. Who made those bricks with the date of 130 AD stamped on them? Slaves or skilled workers from a guild?

Below the street is a patch of grass at the base of the Pantheon. There, chunks of marble, grey and broken, lie scattered. I round the corner to the piazza that slopes toward the stately rows of columns flanking the front of the temple.

There it is.

Could there be any better representation of what the Greeks and the Romans gave the world? It is a perfect blend of the two cultures, the Hellenistic columns at the front of the temple giving way to a Roman creation, the dome—that crazy genius of a dome with its open-to-the-sky oculus at its top. This is the dome that gave up its secrets centuries later to Brunelleschi, the great architect of the Florentine Renaissance, allowing him to understand how to create the dome of Florence's cathedral.

Ah, my heart stirs as if in recognition. The Pantheon is the womb of the city, its round shape rendering it feminine. It was built and conceived by men, but by men who worshipped goddesses as well as gods.

There's an angelic quality to the light that slides into this cylindrical space through the oculus. As I stand at its base, I'm sure that it's a conduit from the human to the divine. In this light, there are centuries of voices: voices of Romans and barbarians, voices of ancient pagans and early Christians, voices of wars and survival, voices of song and religiosity. The voices curl around me, erasing age and time.

Outside I pause, looking to one of the pillars where a couple is locked in embrace. The girl's back is against the pillar, and the guy has set his long legs on the outsides of her thighs, his feet in designer leather shoes hemming her feet in. They begin to kiss.

Simultaneously, I want to look and pretend I'm not looking. With a pang of regret, I remember walking through the twisting Florentine streets on hot summer nights with Darrell. I had longed for him to feel impassioned by the sparkle of the Neptune fountain, by the honey-colored light on the Arno, by the sounds of a Simon & Garfunkel tune sung by the American busker ringing around the walls of the Uffizi Gallery. I had wanted him to pause in the perfection of the piazza and kiss me the way I saw Italian guys kissing their girlfriends in the streets, oblivious to passersby. I envied the way they seized the moment, the way they prioritized passion. I had tried to create that feeling between us on those summer night walks through those wonderful Florentine spaces, but he never responded.

Turning from the Pantheon, I consult my map and head to the Vodafone store to get a SIM card. Waiting in line in the cell phone store gets me obsessing. I don't want to, but my mind has a will of its own. The cell phone incident happened soon after Darrell and I arrived for a year of living in Florence. I was meeting with Father Casparian of Saint James American Church in Florence to arrange a wedding for clients.

"What's your cell phone number?" he had asked me.

"Um, I don't have one." I immediately felt idiotic and unprofessional.

"Why? You need one for this line of work!"

I averted my eyes as I replied, "My husband is worried about the expense."

"You need one for this job," Father Casparian said with finality. And at the wedding dinner, he told Darrell this. Only then did I get a cell phone without a battle.

Release, release, release, I tell myself sternly as I square my shoulders and walk up to the Vodafone counter.

I hand the guy ten Turkish lire instead of ten euro. When I'd grabbed my leftover currency that was stashed with my passport, I hadn't noticed the Turkish lire note tucked in with the euro.

With currency exchange, I'm hopeless. I can spend months in a foreign country and still not be able to convert their currency to dollars in my head. The only time I was able to convert in my head was in the eighties in Italy when the dollar was strong against the lire and all I had to do was take off the zeros and divide in half. Ten thousand lire was five dollars. Fifty thousand lire was twenty-five dollars. And the euro has stayed mercifully close enough to the dollar that my head can stay above water. But with any other currency, I've become cross-eyed and tangle-brained.

Friends I've traveled with have had an astonishing ability to become immediately familiar with the local currency. Within a day of being in Sri Lanka with my friend Robyn, I asked her, "What's this in dollars?"

She drew on some kind of inner calculator and replied, "Oh, that's about twenty-two dollars." She looked at my scrunched brows and pursed lips as my mind made cartwheels of decimal points and division signs and said, "Just multiply 3200 by .0069."

"Huh? In my *head?*"

"Well, I'm not really doing *that* in my head. The idea is to simplify it to a fraction of a ten-based number, then multiply that by the bottom number of the fraction—"

"Whoa! Hold your rickshaws!"

My ineptitude with math has always been at its most obvious when I travel. I bumble along, getting myself ripped off due to lack of focus on cash exchanges and numbers.

By evening I'm in a booth in the narrow back room of Cul de Sac, a small, affordable wine bar. Eyeing the wine bottles in the cabinet next to my table, I admire the Tuscan superstars: Le Pergole Torte Montervertine, Solaia Antinori, Sammarco, Castello dei Rampolla, Biondi Santi Brunello. I read their names, letting my mind roll over the words.

The cheese list is pure indulgent delight: from Burrata Pugliese to Camembert Piemontese to Pecorino in many forms and to Gorgonzola, either *dolce* or *piccante*. Scanning the wine list, I note the dessert wines: Pedro Ximenez for €3 a glass, Moscato Passito for €4.50. Even at my income level, I could enjoy wine here frequently.

The Gorgonzola speaks to me with such sensuality, I want to take it to bed. If I don't have an Italian lover, at least I have this cheese plate.

In this moment, I cannot fathom why I'd live anywhere but Rome.

Leaving Cul de Sac, I step into the Roman night. The street seduces me with its ivy-draped wall and the sexy sounds of Italian voices that float toward me from outdoor tables. I can't help thinking about the sensuality that only Rome can give when one walks home at night on the arm of a lover.

When Darrell and I lived in Florence, we came down to Rome after Christmas, swapping apartments with the author, Alan Epstein, of *As the Romans Do*. I remember us walking along the Lungotevere and how I turned to him saying with delight, "We're in Rome!"

We ate dinner at Luna Piena in the Testaccio district, joining the conviviality of the Romans in the crowded, festive trattoria. It was one of the rare times I felt happy with him during our eighteen months in Italy.

What am I nostalgic for? Not for him or for us, but rather, for that kernel at the core of me, like a seed that wanted to grow and flourish in the marriage. I picture it like a kukui nut, the ones from Hawaii that are polished and strung on satin ribbons.

Shiny mahogany, full of promise.

ELEVEN

Monks

Fidenza, a town north of Parma in the region of Emilia Romagna, is the place where I'll start the pilgrimage. This is a decision I made in haste before I departed, calculating that it would take approximately forty days to walk from there to Rome.

Before the five-hour train ride from Rome, I walk to the *forno* in Campo dei Fiori. This bakery doesn't look like much on the outside, but their pizza *bianca* has created a cult following. I'm going to do as the Romans do and eat a slice for breakfast. At their neighboring annex, I buy a panino for the train ride and then walk over to the statue of Giordano Bruno, to sit under it and eat my soft, chewy, olive-oiled warm and toasty breakfast.

It's not really fair that I'm eating the best pizza bianca in Rome and there's Giordano Bruno, hanging over me looking awfully hungry. The poor guy was burned at the stake for his ideas by the Catholic inquisition. Poor Jesus—to have an institution founded in his name behave with repression and violence contradicting what he stood for. How far the Catholic Church had strayed at that point from what the early Christians were about. How far we humans stray from our core. How separated we become from our true essence.

On the Eurostar train, I pull out the papers I'd printed about the history of the Via Francigena. I cover pilgrimages in the Middle Ages when I teach Western civilization, and while I know that a pilgrimage to Rome—or to Santiago de Compostela or to Jerusalem—symbolized the greatest goal for a Christian in the Middle Ages, I'd never heard of the Via Francigena until a few weeks ago.

Apparently, in about the ninth century, it became mandatory

for all archbishops to journey to Rome and receive from the pope a *pallium*, a wool garment distinguished by a cross. Sigeric was one such archbishop who made the long walk to Rome after he became the Archbishop of Canterbury in 990 AD. On the return journey, he wrote detailed notes in his diary about the route.

Sigeric's diary was somehow rediscovered in the 1980s by Italian researchers, which resulted in the revival of the Via Francigena, and the official route became the one dictated by Sigeric in his diary. My information says that there are a few thousand pilgrims a year on the Via Francigena—a minuscule number compared to the popular Camino in Spain that receives over a hundred thousand a year.

Roughly translated, the name Via Francigena means "the way of the Franks" and comes from the fact that the route enters Italy from France via the Alpine passes. From Canterbury to Rome, it is about 2,083 km—around 1,290 miles. This takes about four months to walk. The part in Italy is about 944 km, or 587 miles. It starts at the Gran San Bernardo Pass, which connects the French Canton of Valais in Switzerland with the region of Valle d'Aosta in northwest Italy. I had liked the idea of walking over the pass, but since it typically opens in June, there was no guarantee that I would have found it open in the last days of May, and starting that far north wouldn't allow me to get to Rome in forty days.

In Sigeric's time, Christians made religious journeys to seek a cure, to expiate a sin, or to deepen faith. Why is there a revival in modern times? I suppose it's dissatisfaction with modernity. Augustine endorsed spiritual travel as a retreat from worldly concerns, and I'm pretty sure that's one of the main reasons people do it today.

I stop reading and unwrap my panino of zucchini flower blossoms, arugula, tomatoes, and mozzarella. The only condiment? Olive oil, of course. The focaccia bread is moist and salty with a perfect crust, the greens are abundant, the tomatoes taste like they've just been picked, and the mozzarella—something that invariably disappoints me in any other country—is the real deal.

I could have eaten two of those. Wiping away the crumbs, I turn to look outside, where green pastures, like a movie on fast-forward, race across my window. What will the countryside look like on the first days of my walk? I've hardly spent any time in the region of Emilia-Romagna. How detailed are Alberto's directions? Will I really find my way just reading those, with no maps?

How different this was going to be from the Italy I know. I run through the things I love most about Italy: riding a bike around Florence; eating at a homey trattoria; relishing the *dolce far niente* (the sweetness of doing nothing) on the Italian islands.

I will not be in Florence on this pilgrimage. I might not have enough money to indulge in a trattoria. And not only will I not be on islands, but with the physical demands on my weak body, I doubt I will experience a sense of dolce far niente. How will my body handle the physical challenge? Is it smart to be doing it alone when I've felt overly alone for the past year?

The train slows, and the outskirts of a city clutter my view.

I close my eyes and remember how Florence had captured my heart on that first trip when I was nineteen. At the end of those six months of travel, I found myself taking a marathon train ride from southern Portugal, just to get back to Florence one more time.

It was before Portugal, Spain, France, and Italy undertook projects for high-speed trains, and the old trains I rode at the end of August dragged themselves for two nights and a day across Portugal and Spain, over earth baking like a potato in an oven. My well-worn khaki pants were sticky on the vinyl seat of the second-class compartment, and my sandals were held together with duct tape. I ate oranges and nuts from my backpack and watched the wildfires lighting up the hillsides at night.

Prior to the European Union and the Schengen Agreement, the border crossings were laborious, with checkpoints on each side. Additionally, Spain's railway gauge was a different size than the French one, so we all had to exit the train at the Spanish border and hike across to the French side.

The heat and grime of the journey urged me to stop in Nice, where I got a cheap *pension* and took a bath. I watched the water turn brown as it sluiced off of me. After one more long day of train travel and another long border crossing, I finally arrived in Florence.

I called my parents from the Florence post office, telling them I had to stay and learn the language.

"You have college money you've not used. Just be sure the school is connected to an American one so your credits will transfer," they advised.

I spoke no Italian, but I got a phone book and managed to look up language schools for foreigners. Then I went knocking on their doors, asking if they were affiliated with any schools in the US. Four months later, I was enrolled in a program and went to live in Florence for six months and learn Italian.

I was able to get back to Italy in my late twenties by leading groups of American teens on summer abroad trips. When I was twenty-nine I spent the year in Lugano, Switzerland, as an intern for my first master's degree. Nothing about living in Lugano excited me more than knowing Italy was right across the border and that I could train down to Florence for the weekend. I was sure that when I finished the degree, I'd move to Italy, once and for all. But instead, while writing my thesis at home in California, I met Darrell.

As the Eurostar speeds north to the start of my pilgrimage, I pull out Alberto's directions. I would have liked to have maps, but with only ten days to get organized, finding a good map of each section of the route had been too challenging. His directions include trails through woods and fields, as well as small and large roads, in an attempt to follow the route Sigeric took.

From Fidenza, he suggests walking to Fornovo di Taro, a distance of thirty-four kilometers, or twenty-seven miles. Twenty-seven miles? I don't think so!

But there's a place called Costamezzana at the eleven-kilometer mark. Seven miles. Much more reasonable.

I had e-mailed the monks at the Convento di San Francesco in Fidenza to book a room before departing from the US. From the station, I take a taxi through town to the outskirts. There, we pass a park and then turn down a tree-lined drive that ends at the Church of San Francesco. I note the church's simple but tall façade with a round window above the large main door. The convent, a two-story red-brick building, is attached to the left side of the church. Both the church and monastery are quite new for Italy, having been built in 1878.

A smiling slender monk about my age and wearing a Capuchin robe comes to the door and leads me down a hallway. We enter a large room where five monks sit on benches against the walls, a long table in front of them. Four of the monks are Italian; one is Chinese.

As a lone female in hiking clothes, I feel out of place entering their dining room. The most elderly monk peers at me and asks who I am. The monk close to my age says that I am an American pilgrim. The rest of them give me a simple *buona sera* and continue with their meal.

On a table in the middle of the room are various pots and bowls of food, a pitcher of white wine, a loaf of bread, and a half wheel of cheese.

"We're not formal here. Just help yourself," the monk says, indicating a bench on the other side of the room.

Sensing that the monks eat more meagerly than I do, I'm unsure how much food to put on my plate. I take plain spaghetti with olive oil and parmigiano as well as some of the green salad. One of the monks tells me the lettuce comes from their garden. Through the windows, I see a large yard with tidy rows of vegetables.

The monks eat with silent concentration. I watch them and ponder why this particular male bastion feels unusual. Because these men are concerned with holiness? It feels in odd juxtaposition to my other travel experiences when I'd found myself in distinctly male strongholds.

On my first trip, after the saga of being lost for twenty-four hours from Istanbul to Thessaloniki, I had, a few days later, taken a night bus to Skopje in what was still Yugoslavia. I found accommodation with female students at the university. The young women were wonderful, and they were eager to ask me about my country and my travels. The male students were something else. I was approached by one who said very matter-of-factly, "I want to sleep with you tonight," indicating it was his turn.

When I questioned him, he explained that since I was a woman traveling alone, I had to be a whore. In a moment of feistiness (and having no clue about his culture), I told him he was ridiculous. That night, another male student pushed his way into the dorm room with the same idea, saying it was his turn.

I managed to physically push him back out of the room. He could have overpowered me, but I could only assume that when I set him straight that no turns were being taken, he allowed me to push him out of the room.

The more I traveled, the more I was a constant intruder into male trenches. They were everywhere. Where were the women's bastions?

Five years after my first trip to Europe, I was in Turkey again, this time with my boyfriend Ted.

Attempting to take a night bus from the Black Sea town of Trabzon to Lake Van near the eastern edge of the country, we ended up in a dusty outpost near the Iranian border called Agri. The bus unceremoniously dropped us there in the morning, despite our understanding that it went all the way to Lake Van. Learning that there was no transport to Lake Van until the next day, we checked into the local rat's-nest hotel. There were no women to be seen outside, so I hid in the room while Ted got food.

The boredom of hiding in that unsavory room all day got the better of me, and I ventured out with Ted by day's end. I wore the Turkish balloon pants I'd bought in Istanbul, and I had a scarf over my head across half my face. Ted, eager to interact with the locals, kicked a soccer ball in the dusty road with children.

I decided that this womanless town might not be so bad, and I took a kick of the soccer ball, which must have demonstrated I was a wanton hussy. Two guys snuck up behind me. A hand shot between my legs and grabbed. I whirled around ready to strike. The palm of my hand, fingers pulled back, aimed for the nostrils, as I'd learned in self-defense training. But I hesitated and retracted my arm, realizing in an instant that I had no rights in that country. So I yelled at the men instead, and they sauntered off, laughing.

Ted, who had missed the encounter, trotted over after hearing me yell. My heart raced and I gasped for breath as I pointed furiously at the departing men and told him what had happened.

"Um, Chandi, there's nothing I can do," he said in a flat voice.

"I was about to slam into his nose, but—"

"You were right not to hit him," Ted replied in an even tone. "Can you even imagine the judgment of a Turkish court?"

These monks in Fidenza are a different species. I watch as they clear their plates in the same contemplative way that they ate.

They appear uninterested in my femaleness. In fact, they appear not to notice it. There might be times when I'd like to be noticed, but I don't think the pilgrimage will be one of those times. Traveling as a woman alone requires being on guard frequently, which in turn requires stamina. Here I am, the only woman in a building full of unknown men, and I don't have to be on guard. How blissful.

TWELVE

The Yellow Saint

In the hour of sunlight left in the day, I walk to the center of Fidenza to see the cathedral, called San Donnino. Construction of the cathedral began in the early twelfth century. In front of it stands one of the world's first road signs, a statue of Saint Peter holding a scroll that says "This way to Rome." It's a reminder that Fidenza was an important stop for pilgrims on the Via Francigena.

I find my way to the cathedral by following my instincts. I'm surprised to find a loud band playing smack dab in front of it. The band not only blocks the entrance, it blocks my ability to inspect the statue of Saint Peter with its road sign.

A pedestrian street takes me to the heart of the town. I pass a shop displaying leather handbags. A red one triggers a memory of when Darrell and I had first moved to Florence.

We had spent months preparing, storing belongings in the attic, and clearing the house for renters. But the final stages of the move were still frantic, and I arrived in Florence without a purse. Soon after, I needed to visit the event manager at the Grand Hotel Villa Cora about a wedding I was organizing, and a ratty daypack would make a brutta figura.

I had looked in the outdoor market, and I was surprised that most of the purses cost the equivalent of $70 and up. The next day, Darrell and I passed a small leather shop near Piazza Santa Croce, and I popped in. There was a nice looking red purse, large enough to hold documents, for only $30. Relieved to find one in the nick of time—my appointment at Villa Cora was in an hour—I bought it.

Outside in the street, Darrell berated me for not bargaining in the shop, angrily telling me we wouldn't make it in Florence if I was so reckless with spending.

I'd slunk away, feeling as low as a homeless wet cat, to find the bus to Villa Cora. I wondered if later, when he was calm, he would apologize. He didn't. And once again, I didn't tackle it. The same type of thing had happened only a month earlier, and I'd responded the same way: deflated, sinking to an airless place, the bottom of a well.

While preparing for the move in Boulder, I'd networked and pursued leads online for two months, trying to secure an apartment in Florence. Darrell had insisted I find one for under a thousand euro a month. But each one I found was deemed horrible by a friend in Florence who was viewing them for us. Then he viewed one I'd found in Settignano, a village in the hills above Florence, and said it was cute, but it was a thousand euro a month. I told Darrell that it might be our best bet.

I was startled by the fury in his voice as he said he couldn't believe I'd considered it at a thousand euro. He shouted that I'd been wrong to let the landlord think we were interested. I'd never seen him so mad, and I started crying. To my horror, he charged out of the house, and I felt my joy about our move to Italy sliding from my heart, leaving me limp and sobbing on the couch.

I hadn't raised it later. I didn't know where to begin. All I knew how to do was to plow ahead with our move to my favorite place in the world.

I'm so ashamed to be obsessing, I want to take a surgeon's tool and extract the marriage from my brain. Wincing, I almost bump into a pram. It's pushed by a couple who walk arm in arm, he nuzzles her ear and she laughs.

"*Scusate,*" I say, my face flushed. My acute aloneness puffs from my chest, filling the street like a spinnaker.

I am alone, and I am the girl who came with her husband to live in the most romantic place in the world but couldn't make it work.

I force my obsessing from my mind and check e-mail at a *punto internet*. When I'm done, it's dark outside. How do I locate the road back to the monastery?

A young congenial looking guy passes as I stand in the doorway. I ask him for directions to the monastery and he responds, *"Ma è lontano!"* (But it's far!)

It's probably not far compared to my walk to Rome, I think.

"Are you a pilgrim?" he asks.

"Yes!" I smile, suddenly liking this new label.

"How about I drive you back to the monastery?"

I check my intuition and get a feeling that as a pilgrim, I'm respected and appear nun-like.

During the five-minute drive, we chat about my pilgrimage, and I thank him effusively as he pulls up to the monastery. The word *angelo custode* comes to me in Italian. He's my first guardian angel.

That night, I dream of a saint dressed in yellow with a pilgrim's staff. As I stand at a crossing of two trails, he touches my shoulders, turning me south, and says, "From now on."

The feeling of the dream remains as the morning pours white like milk into the narrow room. I reach for my journal and quickly jot down some notes: *Symbolism of the color yellow? Of direction south? Crossing of two trails, obvious.*

I sit up, set the journal aside, and pull my knees toward my chest. The deep bronze sound of bells from the church encircles the monastery and moves over the gardens and toward the wooded hills. I remain in bed, my arms around my legs, feeling the lifting and lowering of the bells in my core, as if they could recalibrate the rhythms of my heart, of my breath.

In this space the answers come. Yellow, *awakening*. South, *glow*.

I quickly slide off the bed. Rome, here I come.

THIRTEEN

Our Common Human Nature

"It's somewhere over there," the monk says.

Our backs are to the church, where I intercepted him when he left mass. He waves his arm, indicating that I will turn right out of the driveway. Alberto's directions are no use because they lead from the town center, not from the monastery, which is at the edge of town.

"So I walk down that road, and then. . . ?" I ask hesitantly.

"We are not very informed about these things," he replies casually.

"Oh!" I remain standing there without more words for a moment, mouth agape.

The monks don't know how to get to the Via Francigena? Don't monasteries and pilgrimages go together, like mozzarella and tomatoes?

"I'm sure I'll find the way," I say, attempting to reassure myself as much as him.

Turning out of the driveway into a quiet tree-lined road, I think of my solo travels over twenty years ago, when I'd always found my way.

I try to hold this thought like a shield against any anxiety that I'm sure must be hovering nearby, ready to pounce from behind a garbage can. The road comes to a T, and I don't know which way to turn. Pulling Alberto's directions from my pocket, I try to figure things out. It seems I have to find a long field with a church at the end.

Checking my instincts, I choose the street to my left. The few people I encounter can't tell me where the Via Francigena is. I tell myself to see it as an adventure, as a treasure hunt, like the one my father created for me and my siblings and friends at Easter, which would take us tearing across the apple orchards and into the redwood forest, following his clever clues.

I encounter a Polish man walking a dog who, thankfully, has heard of the Via Francigena.

"My son is the priest of the Pieve di Cabriolo," he tells me proudly, "and the Via Francigena is not far from there."

The Pieve di Cabriolo is the church mentioned by Alberto at the end of the field. I walk with him for a few blocks and we come to a large field.

"My son's church is there." He indicates a knoll at the end of a flat expanse of barley. The wet shoots of barley shed water on my shoes as we cross the field. With his thick Polish accent, I have trouble understanding the man's Italian. Reaching the *pieve*, he stops. "I'll turn back now. Just cross that road and you'll find a Via Francigena sign," he says with a kind smile.

"Mille Grazie! Buona giornata!" I call to him as I head to the road's edge. See, my heart says to my mind, that was another little angelo custode!

Across the road, I find a Via Francigena marker and enter a silent wooded area. I have a moment of trepidation, and then in my mind I hear the words *Non aver paura!* Don't be afraid.

These were the words the Italian ambulance drivers had said to me. They had carried me down the steep stairs from Sydney's apartment when my appendix was bursting, repeating, *"Non aver paura!"* as we descended the six steep flights.

Stepping over a stream and clambering up a bank, I see a gravel road wind up the hill in front of me. I pause to read the directions: Straight along the rock road. Turn right and climb toward the ridge. I lift my eyes and examine the land. Look at that, it matches! I feel as if I've made a discovery of Darwinian proportions.

I take a reassured breath and begin pushing my way up the road. A guy on a mountain bike passes me. My pace slows. I'm slogging up the hill. Why is it a slog? It's a simple hill, not a fourteener in Colorado.

I remember Kari's words, "Tell me you're going to train for this."

"I can't really, I don't have time," I had replied.

Why had I not had time? Why had I rushed so much? I'm a crazy lady with a butterfly net running after my glow.

On the ridge, I congratulate myself. I've gone about three miles and I have about five hundred more to go.

I peek into a barn, admiring the round bales of hay stacked inside. On the other side of the road, roses bloom in front of a farmhouse and a dog barks behind a wire fence.

At the seventh kilometer, I come to the Church of Siccomonte. Here, Alberto's directions say to leave the road and go into the fields next to the church. I descend, walking over stubs of cut hay.

The hunger in my belly is like an empty fish net. I hadn't eaten breakfast except for energy nuggets from Colorado because the monks had all been in mass, and I wasn't sure it was appropriate to scrounge in their kitchen. Italian breakfasts are skimpy. The standard is a cappuccino and a *cornetto*, which is similar to a croissant but with a more cake-like texture. They don't provide the sort of sustenance a pilgrim needs, so I'd packed protein nuggets and protein powder.

Will I arrive by the lunch hour? There must be a trattoria in Costamezzana. Don't all self-respecting Italian villages have one? I cross a gully, hike a few kilometers on mostly car-less roads, and arrive at the bottom of the hill that leads to Costamezzana. It is very steep. My body aches and I'm tempted to hitchhike. Instead, I sit down, pull out the list of accommodations, and call the town priest.

A woman answers and introduces herself as Luisa, the sister of Don Rino, the priest. She says they don't put up pilgrims but the hostel does. "Come by the church when you get to the village, and I'll call Signora Gorzanelli, who is in charge of the hostel."

I slowly persevere up the hill. Entering Costamezzana, I note a church, a restaurant, and a tiny grocery store with its grate pulled down. I ring the bell at the house next to the church.

Luisa, who has white hair and black slippers, answers the door. "You're here!" she says enthusiastically.

She hasn't been able to reach Signora Gorzanelli, and the hostel is locked for the day.

"Leave your pack with me." She opens the door and points to the entryway. "The trattoria is open. Get lunch, then come back to the church."

I think about my budget and how I should be eating bread and cheese by the roadside. But I quickly rule that out because I'm exhausted, famished, and chilled. Inside the restaurant, I'm warmly greeted. Only two other tables are occupied. Classical music creates a pleasant background, and the two male waiters move languidly.

I speak with one of them about their offerings and choose a plate of mixed *salumi*, crepes, and a green salad, as well as a quarter liter of wine.

A gigantic plate of prosciutto, salami, *sopressata*, and *pancetta piacentina* arrives. My first thought is, I won't eat all this! Then I promptly do.

I chat with the waiter about the sopressata, and he carries over a book titled *La Suina Commedia* (The Swine Comedy). It's got photos of pigs and farmers and information about the artisanal way of working with pork in the province of Parma.

After hearing why I'm undertaking the pilgrimage, he brings me a magazine I didn't know existed about the Via Francigena. In it, I read an interview with Don Mario Lusek, Director of the National Office for the Pastoral of Free Time, Tourism, and Sport. One of Lusek's comments about pilgrimages stands out. "There is nothing more secular and more Christian than considering life as a journey, a search, a pilgrimage toward the discovery of the source of our common human nature. We believers call it God. No one, in the name of God, is a stranger to me."

The source of our common human nature. I repeat this in my mind as I consume piping hot crepes with their casing of béchamel sauce. When I go to pay for my meal—having no idea what it would cost because there has been no menu—the waiter says, "Nothing!" with a smile. When I protest, he responds, "It's the first day of your pilgrimage. I insist!"

"You Italians are the best. It's why I come back again and again," I say.

It's more than that, I think, as I walk the short distance to the church. It's why I travel alone. Solo, these moments with strangers— moments when we experience the source of our common human nature—are more apt to appear. Perhaps, too, these travel moments give me joy because I go into them with little expectation, and thus, disappointments are few.

FOURTEEN

A Foreign Field

Outside, under the gray sky, I walk to the church and gently push the door open. Inside, on a pew, sits Don Rino, Luisa, and a woman from the village. I slide into a pew behind them. Don Rino seems to be holding a service, even though he's sitting with the two women and not standing at the altar. Suddenly consumed with exhaustion, I tip my head into my hands and close my eyes, my elbows propped on my knees, hoping it will appear that I'm fervently praying.

Once in a while when I look up, I see Don Rino's white head drop forward in the unmistakable way a head does when someone falls asleep sitting up. Whenever this happens, Luisa elbows him and his head jerks.

Then Don Rino rises and goes to the organ. He plays and sings. His clear voice fills the little church and I think of my mother, who used to sing to us kids for hours in the car when we drove to the Sierras in the summer. My eyes fill with tears as I think of how she had adjusted her important England trip to be with me in the hospital. She was supposed to be in England packing up the house that had been my grandmother's and saying good-bye to it. Instead, she was helping me survive so she wouldn't have to say good-bye to me too.

Selling the Devonshire house called Golden Meadow that my grandmother had bought in 1936 weighed heavily on my mother. She'd lived there as a child during World War II, when they had to put black paper on the windows and abstain from using electricity, when they had to scrounge the countryside for things to eat, when the American soldiers practiced D-Day landings on the beach below the house.

It was where I spent occasional summers as a child. It was there that my grandma and I recited Rupert Brooke's "The Soldier" while on the high green hill above the hedgerows. I was sure he spoke of that precise corner of land when he wrote,

That there's some corner of a foreign field
That is for ever England.

Selling the house meant clearing the attic of generations of family memorabilia, finding homes among our relatives for the antique furniture, and sorting my great aunt's musty hardback books. We'd planned that I would go to England to help my mother after my trip to Italy.

But then I landed in the hospital. My father was on the flight to London with my mother to be part of packing up Golden Meadow and saying good-bye to it. But he'd not flown with her to Florence to be with me in the hospital. He'd remained in London, waiting for my mother's return.

I'd been in the hospital twelve days at that point, and I was on the edge of the bed in anticipation. My Italian friend Rosella was at the Florence airport picking up my mother. Over and over, I mentally calculated how long it takes to go through the Florence airport and how long it takes to drive from there to the hospital. I wanted to know how many minutes it would be until my mother walked into the room.

I knew I looked awful. When I finally saw myself, I was horrified: hollow cheeks, sunken eyes, ashen skin, wrinkles standing out tenfold, and a wisp of a body with a bizarre, distended stomach hanging from it.

My mom walked in, sat on the bed next to me, and held me. I put my head on her shoulder and cried.

Rosella found out that the main place to stay near San Giovanni di Dio was a nunnery. She went to check it out, and the nun told her the only room available was up a flight of stairs. Rosella recounted to me how the nun pointed to the stairs and said, "A seventy-eight-year-old? How is she going to do it?"

"That nun doesn't know my mom," I replied. "My mom is strong."

Every morning in the July heat, my strong mother walked from the nunnery to the hospital, passing the gypsies sitting by the entrance. She arrived each morning by nine o'clock and stayed all day until after I'd eaten dinner. Then, with an hour left of daylight, she walked to the Tavola Calda, a simple restaurant that Rosella had showed her. There she sat by herself, ordered to the best of her ability without speaking or understanding Italian, ate dinner alone, and then walked up the hill to the convent, ringing the bell to get in just before the nuns went to bed.

My mother had hastily booked her flight for four days in Florence, but she stayed with me for the last nine days until I was passed to a nunnery. The airline wouldn't let her move her return date, so she had to forfeit that ticket and book another. I felt terrible that I wasn't up for arguing with the airline.

"We didn't realize how sick you were when we booked me for four days. It was all such a scramble," she had explained.

I had the novel *Rebecca* by Daphne du Maurier with me. I had read it last when I was about twelve years old. It was a perfect book to share with my mom because it takes place in England and describes the English countryside she loves. We sat on the narrow hospital terrace that was strewn with cigarette butts. I wore a support band Velcroed around my stomach on top of a nightgown. Across from the terrace, the merciless July heat pressed into the yellow hill like a rolling pin.

I had to interrupt my mother's reading often, forcing myself to rise and make the journey to the bathroom.

"The bathroom again?" she would ask, and I would nod with determination.

It was a journey I dreaded. It was too far to the toilet with no seat. I had to pass through the room of crowded beds, go down the hall, and pass the men in undershirts to get there. While they were keeping me alive, the antibiotics had killed everything good along with the bad. Not only did I have diarrhea, but a yeast infection had taken hold with the ferocity of a rabid dog. The nurses wanted to give me more drugs. I asked for vinegar.

"*Non si fa!*" (It's not done!) the nurse cried out.

I wrote the word for vinegar in Italian, and my mom went into the blazing streets.

How could someone be that sick without a mother or a spouse to hold their hand? I wonder this as Don Rino's voice circles the church like a lonely bird. I am crying, but I try to quell my tears as he comes back to the pew.

The village woman takes her leave, and Don Rino and Luisa turn to talk to me. I imagine it's my visible exhaustion that prompts them to say, "Are you sure this won't be too difficult for you?"

"My spirit is stronger than my physical body." I don't know where this sentence comes from.

I see recognition in their twinkling blue eyes. "Yes, that's right," they say.

"What do your parents think of you taking such a long trip?" Luisa asks.

"They're used to it."

Luisa proposes that we go to the house, where she will call Signora Gorzanelli again. I talk to Don Rino outside while Luisa makes the call.

"No," she says, shaking her head as she comes out. "She still isn't answering."

Don Rino suggests I go back to the restaurant, which doubles as the village bar. "Wait there. Her house is directly across the street. The bar proprietor can get her for you when she gets home."

As I collect my pack from Luisa, she and Don Rino bless me. I'm pleased by their blessing but embarrassed that I don't know how to cross myself.

I wait for two hours for Signora Gorzanelli. My long-sleeve layer and my rain jacket don't ward off the chilliness. I hug myself, too tired to write in my journal. When Signora Gorzanelli arrives, she keeps repeating, *"Per stasera?"* (For tonight?)

As a pilgrim without transportation, I'm not sure where else I'd go at six in the evening.

The hostel is in a two-story palazzo with stone steps leading straight from the road to the tall wooden door. Along a corridor are a handful of rooms, each with about four beds. There's one bathroom, which has a shower but no hot water. I'm too tired to shower anyway, and I don't feel sweaty on this cool day.

The signora gives me one of the rooms to myself. I pull my sleeping bag from the bottom of my pack, and quickly climb into it. Ah, to be warm and feel all of my limbs relax.

Before I fall asleep, I realize that ever since the burst appendix,

I have struggled to find something *good* about it. It took everything out of me physically and made it considerably harder to bear the challenges of the divorce. But one positive thing occurs to me. My mother had been there for me, in a particular way—a way that had perhaps changed something in me. It wasn't my father, or my not-yet-divorced husband who came to Florence when I was half dead in the hospital. It was my mother.

When I was five, without verbalizing it even to myself, I decided that I would be the one who didn't need help.

We lived in London that year, and my mother took my sister to a psychoanalyst because she was considered "overly shy." This unpronounceable word, *psychoanalyst*, I understood to be a special doctor, one my mother went to when she was anxious.

And two years later, I saw my mother anxious again. It was on the flagstone patio outside my Uncle Reggie's farmhouse. My brother was throwing a tantrum, and as my mother made an attempt to stop it, my Aunt Mari clucked her tongue and Uncle Reggie shook his head, and the unsaid message I picked up was that my parents should be ashamed.

My child's mind decided a second time that I would be the child who didn't need help.

When the divorce and the anxiety attacks compounded my struggles to recover from the burst appendix, and when the razor-scraping aloneness cut deeper than ever, I did not raise the idea with my parents that maybe I should come home for a while. When my father told me later that it hadn't occurred to him to suggest it, I understood how well I'd perfected my role. I was the one who no one saw as needing help, even if I was drowning.

If my mother had not already had the flight to England, she would have made a motion about coming over the phone, and I would have told her I was managing. It would have been a lie—one I would have made out of my habit of fighting my own battles.

And yet, circumstances were otherwise, and I got something I'd never experienced with her or with anyone else—the feeling of someone *being there* one hundred percent. I stopped being the stoic child and simply sat in the Pepto-Bismol nightgown and listened to my mother read *Rebecca* to me. She was fully there, keeping me alive, with every line of *Rebecca* that she read.

FIFTEEN

To Awaken Quite Alone

When I awaken in the dark room, I don't know where I am. I fish for my phone from under my pillow. It's five a.m. Sitting up, I adjust my eyes to darkness and see a row of beds, each with a thin green spread and a flat pillow. Brown shutters on the tall windows block the light.

I think of a Freya Stark quote: "To awaken quite alone in a strange town is one of the most pleasant sensations in the world. You are surrounded by adventure." [i]

I first heard about Freya Stark when I was twenty-one, living in London. The best respite from the miserable East End bed-sit where I lived was visiting Aunt Mari, who was married to my Great Uncle Reggie. She and I would sit on her bed and drink cassis. She would have a plush boa around her neck and call me "dear girl."

I was planning my first trip to India when she gave me a few Freya Stark books. "Dear girl! You haven't heard of her? You must read her!"

And so I stayed long over the cassis, reading chapters of *The Valleys of the Assassins* and of *The Southern Gates of Arabia*. I was immediately smitten by Freya. She was bold, outlandish, and totally unperturbed at being a Western female in the most foreign places possible.

"She started learning Arabic at age thirty," my aunt informed me. "She said that when she looked at maps, she was filled with a certain madness."

My spine tingled as I heard these words.

Despite malaria, dengue fever, and dysentery, Freya traveled through harsh terrain for long hours on donkeys and camels. She outwitted French captors in Lebanon, and in Baghdad during a pro-Nazi coup, she was taken prisoner in the British embassy.

My aunt had waved her glass of cassis dramatically as she talked. "My dear girl, she traveled to remote regions of Iran where no Westerner had gone! And she traveled without a man. Do you know how radical that was?"

There in my aunt's London apartment, I felt a thread pulled through the tapestry of history. I felt it pull directly from the core of Freya's determination and loop through the core of my own with a tug and a knot. Her maverick movements in the world were much greater than mine. I was not in the Victorian era and I was not traveling to a place no Western woman had gone. Still, the determination that thrust us forward was the same.

I was lucky to come of age at a time when it was relatively acceptable for a woman to leap into the world and embrace any number of new experiences. But even in my generation, we have to face double the challenge—perhaps ten times the challenge—of a man doing the same thing. It's as if we're taking part in our own act of revisionist history when we travel alone.

Freya's bravery is a particular kind, different from male bravery. Hers is a bravery without backing.

Consider the encouragement men have received from Western literature. From the *Odyssey* to the *Divine Comedy*, and from *Don Quixote* to *Huckleberry Finn*, the male quest is so upheld that it has long been an integral element of the Western psyche. And because it's so integral, it is not a radical act for a man to travel solo or be adventurous because he has the backing.

We are sitting on the spines of piles and piles of books wherein the characters who have grand adventures and who are portrayed as the brave ones are male characters. In turn, this gives real life men an entitlement to take these journeys. They don't have to agonize about their desire to be adventurous. They don't have to deal with horrified reactions to their proposed journey.

Sure, there's a young man here or there who clashes with his father because he wants to take a year to backpack around the world instead of going to law school. But overall, the red carpet is rolled out for men to do their quests. Since the inception of patriarchy, women have had zero encouragement from society—and often, active discouragement—and almost no representations in literature for such adventures. And yet, there are women who have managed to believe in themselves and their right to explore and they set out and make it happen.

Every time I teach a history class, I'm confronted with how brutally women's achievements have been left out. I'm confronted by how incredibly hard it was for women to achieve anything because they were denied education, jobs, and freedom. Doors were shut in their faces. They were sometimes deemed insane and locked up. And when they did manage to make achievements despite all that, they were left out of the history books.

When I tell my college students about the suffrage movement, very few have heard of it. Sometimes a few of them have heard of Elizabeth Cady Stanton and Susan B. Anthony. No one has yet been able to say who Alice Paul was when I initiate the topic. And at every college where I've taught, my male colleagues either do not cover this topic or touch on it only briefly. Yet, it was the longest and greatest social movement in the history of the United States.

We've built Western civilization on the backs of the Greeks, who are infamous misogynists. When Homer wrote the *Odyssey*, the idea was codified: Men make adventurous quests and women tend the hearth. And the women wait. They spend their lives waiting, wondering when it will be their turn. But some, like Freya, say "screw it," throw down the distaff, and leave on their own quest.

There was Gertrude Bell too, another British explorer enamored of Arabia. Twenty-five years older than Freya, Gertrude first went to the Near East in 1899 and spent the next ten years there. She learned Arabic and Persian and gained keen insights into Arab culture. She was much more discerning of the differences between tribes than were her male British counterparts, and she traversed and charted wide swaths of the Arabian lands.

Gertrude was the first woman ever hired by the British military as an intelligence officer. T. E. Lawrence—better known as Lawrence of Arabia—would not have been able to carry out his campaigns without the intelligence provided by Gertrude Bell.

Her knowledge of Arabic and of Arab history gained her the respect of powerful sheikhs. She mapped the route for the British advance on Baghdad in 1916 and fought with the troops. She attended the Paris Peace Conference at the end of World War I, where she met Prince Faisal of Mecca. She created the border of Iraq and Kuwait and advised Churchill to instate Prince Faisal as Iraq's ruler. Churchill relied on Gertrude more than T. E. Lawrence. Her achievements in an extremely male world were remarkable.

In the history classes I teach, I sometimes ask for a show of hands on who has heard of Lawrence of Arabia. Then I ask who has heard of Gertrude Bell. Many hands rise for the first; none for the second. So it does occur to me, every so often, that we women still have to prove ourselves ten times over and ten times harder to get some credit. And even if we possess bravery without backing, we tend to be crossed out of the history books.

Patriarchy is often uncomfortable for me. Yet I love the world. I'm stunned by the improbable floating green and blue planet that we've been given and which, as humans, we have not proven we deserve. I love the medley of the mountains and the mountain people, the congregation of the islands and the island people, and the moon seen from so many different shorelines and crested crags. Along the way, I often bump into the patriarchy, and it stings me, as if I have against my skin the poisoned dress that Medea sent to her rival, Glauce.

I'm willing to struggle out of that dress each time it is thrown over me in order to visit these lands and fold their magic into my heart.

SIXTEEN

Breakfast for a Pilgrim

Extracting myself from my sleeping bag, I open the shutters, expecting to see morning sun. Instead, rain, like a startling naked baptism of a baby.

Pulling on pants and a shirt, I pick up the magazine that the waiter at the restaurant had given me, and in the pale light I read, "The main journey of the pilgrim is from head to heart."

I read the sentence a second time and then set my hand against the cold window.

That's what Gregg had said: "Get out of your head and into your heart."

Creeping out of the hostel with a rain cover over my pack and a waterproof shell over my hiking pants, I step into the tenebrous six-in-the-morning street. Nothing moves except the rain. There are no cars; there are no people. Grates are down and shutters are closed.

Crossing the street under a steady rain to the same bar/restaurant—the only one in town—I read the sign on the grate: *Chiuso Lunedì.* (Closed Monday.)

I had imagined getting hot milk for my oatmeal package. I'm going to obsess about breakfast now, I just know it.

I'm a big eater. Italians call me a *buona forchetta* (a good eater). A typical breakfast at home has me eating hearty oatmeal made from steel cut oats with almonds and dried cranberries, along with a wedge of whole grain toast covered in almond butter.

Reluctantly, I pull out the emergency energy nuggets. If no breakfast happens often, I will need to make the energy nuggets last. Shops in these small towns will not likely have backpacker food items that provide a dose of protein in a few bites.

The cold water from my CamelBak is unappealing. Now I'm going to obsess about tea too.

With a deep breath, I say, *"Coraggio!"* and start down the hill, following the way-marker.

A left off the road takes me to a steep, narrow path through woods that are green-black and dripping with water. On my left is a ravine with a stream, while on my right, beech and pine trees tangle in a wet, heavy canopy up a hillside, blocking the sky.

It's almost like walking at night.

What if a boar charges me?

My shell pants are nonbreathable, and they generate an alarming heat as I hike up the hill. You could grow tomatoes in these pants.

Turning onto a tractor track next to a vineyard, I experience another clothing challenge. As I walk through the wet grass on the track, my socks feel suspiciously wet, and I discover that my trail runners (twice waterproofed) are letting in water. Then the clay-like mud on the track begins to cake to them, making it seem like I'm wearing uneven platform shoes. I stop every few feet and knock off the huge cakes of mud with my trekking poles.

The track along the vineyard is silent and misty, and I tell myself I'll come to a hamlet with a bar where I'll have breakfast. But the countryside yields no sign of people. I pass a barn and walk over straw that smells of cows, reminding me of my Uncle Reggie's farm in Herfordshire.

I pause and look at the Old World brick barn that has molded itself over the damp, green land. I imagine that its floor is warped, like the floor of Uncle Reggie's barn, which sagged and sloped this way and that. The brick walls of Uncle Reggie's barn held mounds of hay. To my child's eyes, it was a castle of hay. We went to England every two or three summers during my childhood, and upon arriving at Uncle Reggie's farm, my siblings and I made straight for the barn. There I became one with the Dylan Thomas poem "Fern Hill" that my grandmother had coaxed me to memorize.

I stop walking, and with my wet feet in the tall grass, I lean on my poles, wondering if I can conjure up some of the lines.

And as I was green and carefree, famous among the barns
About the happy yard and singing as the farm was home…

I smile. What was the one about the house high hay? Those are the lines I called out to my sister after I climbed to the top of the bales.

> My wishes raced through the house high hay
> And nothing I cared, at my sky blue trades. . .[ii]

What a brilliant poem. It's one of those rare and wondrous achievements that humans are capable of at times. Like Michelangelo's David. It surpasses all that came before it. Moreover, look what my grandmother gave me. Here I am alone on a pilgrimage in the rain, but by reciting the poems she taught me, I feel her with me. My heart is light as I think about my wishes racing through house high hay.

A paved road brings relief after the mud. It leads to a hamlet of homes, but there is still no one in sight. Through the mist, I admire a tall green house with stately rows of windows. Coming closer to the houses, I imagine seeing people sitting outside on a sunny day. I'd chat with them, and they'd invite me in. Today, the shutters are closed.

To humor myself, I say, "Anyone want to give a pilgrim some breakfast?"

I know what my grandmother would have said if she'd been with me. She would have quoted "The Listeners."

> 'Is there anybody there?' he said.
> But no one descended to the Traveler;
> No head from the leaf-fringed sill
> Leaned over and looked into his grey eyes,
> Where he stood perplexed and still.[iii]

It's a comfortable landscape, bucolic and restful. I realize that the English landscape comforted my grandmother the way the Italian one comforts me. And thinking of my grandmother comforts me. Ever since she was there on the Dark Night of the Lungs in the hospital, I can reach her more easily.

The Dark Night of the Lungs happened about a week into my hospital stay. The pain in my head scalded and seared continuously, and then it doubled, screaming out of my back, under my ribs.

It was a Japanese POW camp pain. Beaten with a bamboo stick pain.

There were shouts and moans like shrapnel from shapes I could hardly make out in the five other beds. The buzzer screeched, a cry for help—all night. The nurses became irritable. I willed myself not to add to it. I would bear the pain. But on the Dark Night of the Lungs, I succumbed and buzzed for a nurse.

It was Caterina who came. The Polish nurse, the one I was awed by. She'd had a shouting match at the foot of my bed with a male Italian doctor. Boy could she hold her own, and in a language that wasn't hers.

"You've spent too much time in bed. You have to walk," she told me definitively.

She was sure of herself, and yet, I could not walk on my own. But if it would ease the pain, I would try. I didn't think to ask for painkillers.

Caterina got me to the hallway and left me at a ballet bar that ran the length of the wall. I clung to it and strove to put one foot in front of the other.

I didn't know how to move the jumble of bones that I couldn't recognize as my body. I'd become a half-dead phantom in Dante's purgatory, doomed to inch along the ballet bar, looking for my *real* body.

During this stupefying shuffle, I was aware of nurses, their important and nimble movements like squirrels in the hall. None stopped to ask if I was okay. Any minute, I was going to lose my grip on the bar, and the skeleton of me would surely break. Perhaps I'd become invisible. Perhaps I was passing to the next world.

A wheelchair—a life raft masquerading as a wheelchair. The bones folded into it. There was a glimmer of strength in my hands. I urged the chair to roll to my room.

I looked at the bed and heard Caterina's words. If the bed caused the pain, I would stay in the chair. The pain that had been beyond what I could handle was now beyond that. I didn't know someone could have such pain and remain alive.

I pulled a tray on wheels toward me. My head fell to it.

Then I heard a voice. "Ask for painkillers. Don't let the pain get the better of you." It was my grandmother.

My stupor lifted just enough for my finger to press the buzzer.

A male nurse came, and I croaked out the words, *"Non ne posso più. Non posso sopportare più questo dolore."* (I can't do it. I can't stand the pain any longer.)

The painkillers he gave me kicked in by early morning, and I managed to get myself onto the bed. *Please let me sleep for days.* That was all I asked of the world.

An hour later, the nurses clattered into the room calling out, *"Buon giorno."* They called it like a warning, as if what they really wanted to say was, "You'd better be awake and ready to get out of bed!"

As it turned out, that extra pain was from pneumonia. Caterina was wrong.

I follow the narrow paved road around the contours of a hill. The gorgeous landscape to my left—undulating hills and valleys smooth and gentle—is perhaps the prettiest I've seen outside of Tuscany. It is a picture of tranquility: the textures of each field with their shades of green and yellow; the farmhouses on the ridges and in the valleys, with their streams of mist lingering nearby.

The route has me turn onto another tractor track, one that descends into the landscape I'd been admiring. How pleasant this track would be in the sun on a dry day!

With every step, my shoes become impossibly caked; I scrape them constantly and make no progress. I try to do a silly shaking of my feet with each step. Oh well, I think as I plunge on, wobbling ridiculously on three inches of uneven mud. I'll just go down the hill like a donkey in platform shoes.

A farmhouse comes into view at the bottom of the hill, and I stop to scrape my shoes under a light rain. A dog's nearing bark causes me to straighten. For the first time today, I see someone, a man following the dog.

"Buon giorno!" I call out, glad that I am no longer walking like a donkey in platform shoes.

He responds in kind and then, in a perplexed tone, calls, *"Ma, piove!"* (But it's raining!)

Yes, I give an Italian *What to do?* shrug, and he invites me in.

I take off my muddy shoes at the doorstep and follow him upstairs. His wife fixes me coffee with hot milk served in a bowl. I sit at their kitchen table. My feet are clammy in their wet socks, and suddenly my body is spent—*fuso* I'd call it in Italian. But my heart is poking me gleefully. Look at this! You're in a kitchen of angels! Told you you'd be taken care of!

"Would you like bread and jam?" she asks.

"Oh, thank you!"

My grizzly bear hunger gives me self-control issues, and I tell myself to slow down and eat with some decorum.

In my first two days, finding my way has not been a problem. The lack of breakfast has.

Two teenaged children walk into the kitchen, blinking their startled, sleepy eyes at the wet American sitting at their breakfast table. When they learn I'm from California, the father tells me he's traveled there.

"There's a town in California named after me: Modesto!" he states with a big grin.

"I've never met an Italian with that name," I say.

"Italians use this name if they don't want to use a saint's name," his wife explains.

The son asks me pointedly, "What do you think of the death penalty?"

I chuckle. I'm often faced with this question in Italy.

The death penalty question leads to questions about health care and we share a stimulating conversation.

"My eyes were opened when I was in California," Modesto says. "There are *grossi problemi* in the US." He turns to his family. "It isn't all glamorous like what's portrayed on American soap operas." Then he wags his finger, admonishing his kids, who have raised their eyebrows in surprise.

I share my experience as an adjunct college instructor with no health care. "I can't afford to go to the doctor."

"*È assurdo! È tragico!*" (Absurd! Tragic!) exclaims Modesto.

As Modesto's wife makes me a prosciutto panino, we all agree that health care should be *un diritto umano* (a human right).

The son brings in a chunk of parmigiano and Modesto holds up a thigh of prosciutto as they proudly show me the two most famous products of their region. I take pictures of Modesto and his son holding their prized products, and everyone follows me outside, where I put on my wet shoes and tuck the panino into my pack. Modesto instructs me not to continue following the Via Francigena, which would have me walking along more impossibly muddy tractor tracks. Instead, he tells me to take the road to Medesano.

He points to a straight road along the valley. "A few kilometers up, there'll be a right turn to Medesano. You can't miss it."

"*Ciao! Ciao!*" I turn back at the start of their drive and call and wave again, so reluctant to leave their kitchen, their warmth. How long has it been since I was with a family in a kitchen?

It takes me almost two hours to get to Medesano. Although the road is quiet and flat, I find it hard, and I wonder if I'm carrying too much weight. In Medesano, the pilgrim accommodation is a Sunday school building next to the church. The priest shows me to a room on the second floor that includes an attached bathroom. He gives me keys to the building and answers my pressing question: Where can I eat?

Although I have the panino from Modesto's wife, I crave a hot meal for lunch. I'll eat the panino for dinner.

Following the priest's suggestion, I go down the street to a hotel that has a three-course lunch, including wine, for €12 (about $17).

The waitress brings me a risotto *con radicchio* the color of blackberry mouse with a pungent aroma of Taleggio cheese. The slightly bitter radicchio—that wonderful candy-striped vegetable— is rendered smoky-flavored once cooked and goes gleefully with the buttery, gooey, decadent Taleggio. Now this is comfort food!

This trattoria meal is *un grande piacere.* (A great pleasure.) It doesn't matter if I'm alone. No one is looking at me askance for indulging in it. I realize it's nicer to be in Italy without Darrell. Without *the culture of deprivation.* I had even given it a name.

During my first years with him, I thought he was simply frugal in a way that matched my own upbringing. My grandmother's stories of living through two world wars in England were so vivid that, as a child, I thought "the war" was still on. When she scraped half the peanut butter off my bread, I thought she was sending it to unfortunate children that somehow were in the god-awful trenches in Belgium with Rupert Brooke.

I'm able to be frugal, but I'm also willing to spend money to enjoy life. That willingness to enjoy gets brought out in me more when I'm in Italy. The Italians are so good at it.

One of my most cherished pleasures is a long, lively trattoria meal in Florence. For me, to be able to live in Florence and eat at a trattoria is to reach the pinnacle of existence. When Darrell and I lived there, I periodically mentioned how I would love to partake in this favorite activity.

"I refuse to spend the money," was Darrell's unchanging answer.

I understood that money wasn't pouring in, but what was the point of living there if we couldn't sometimes take in the pleasures the city offered? Here I was, surrounded by Italians who were so good at enjoying life, and yet my husband seemed to push the culture of deprivation into overdrive.

When we walked through Florence at night and came upon a triangle of a piazza bursting with revelry—outside tables full of diners, white candles dripping, ruby wine splashing into tumbler glasses—I wanted so much to be one of those shiny, happy trattoria diners. I'd have to turn away and cast my eyes down. If I pushed against it, it created tension so I usually let the culture of deprivation win.

"Signora? Altro?"

The waitress's words bring me back to the present in the empty restaurant. *"No, grazie, era perfetto!"* (It was perfect.)

Walking through the town, I decide I'm going to have lots of happy trattoria meals in my future. I'll double them, making up for lost time.

I start to hum the Oscar Mayer Weiner jingle, inserting "happy trattoria."

Oh I'd love to be a Happy Trattor EE A
That is what I'd truly like to be!

SEVENTEEN

Releasing

At midnight, I'm still awake. It's June second—the Festa della Repubblica Italiana. The day celebrates Italy's birth as a republic, and below my window is a bar where the locals are blasting music and shouting. I pull the mattress off the single bed and drag it into the inner hallway to distance myself from the noise. As I settle down, I realize I have a headache. I get up and sort through my belongings to find my stash of ibuprofen. Finally, sleep comes by one in the morning. When I awaken again, I'm in a fog and it takes me an inordinately long time to prepare my pack.

I eat a yogurt and begin walking at the late hour of nine o'clock, feeling a wee bit out of sorts. But I tell myself that a bad night now should not lower my spirits. No night could be as bad as the Dark Night of the Lungs eleven months ago.

The first part of the walk, as far as a town called Felgara, is pretty, which cheers my spirits. The route takes me along tractor tracks—this time dry—and I wonder how they could have dried overnight. The land is shiny green, and each chunky stone farmhouse sports a huge barn holding round hay bales. Red poppies peep up from under rows of grapevines.

After about an hour, I arrive at a particularly bucolic farm. The path leads up a verdant slope into the owner's gardens. On my right is a vegetable garden, and on my left, short rows of grapevines stud the terraces. A little farther up the slope, a circle of pine trees creates a shady glen. A short wiry man sinks a shovel into the loamy soil, and I admire the rich quality of the earth as I greet him.

Continuing, the path takes me to the central courtyard between the house and the other farm buildings. Pots of bright flowers crowd the gravel area in front of the house, and a large white sheet hanging from a second story window contrasts against the worn sand-colored façade of what is clearly a very old house. It's so tranquil I want to move in.

Exiting down the driveway, I spot the signs for the Via Francigena, and as I head up the crest of a hill, I have an intuition to look back. I see my first fellow pilgrim. When he reaches me, we walk together and chat. He's young and Swiss, and says he has walked from his front door in the French part of Switzerland. His blond hair curls from under a sun hat and his long, sturdy legs brim with lean muscle. He seems capable of walking to China without flagging, and I have to pick up my pace to walk with him.

We pass a house where a woman calls to us from her porch, asking if we want water. Even though I have water with me, I take the opportunity to chat. She has a round middle-aged face, bright eyes, and an enthusiastic voice. My companion and I take off our packs and as she tops off my water bottle, she asks, *"Siete fidanzati?"* (Are you a couple?)

I laugh. The Swiss pilgrim must be at least fifteen years younger than me. "We aren't fidanzati yet!" I joke.

She glances at him, comments on his youth, and then looks at me and says, *"Anche Lei."* (You too.)

This makes me laugh again. During the last year I'd felt so old and washed up, it strikes me as hilarious that she calls me young.

We leave the farmlands and enter residential streets, heading down to the town of Felgara. In its center, I look with interest at the *gelaterie* and wonder about getting a drink or a gelato to give myself a boost. Yet I want to keep up with the Swiss guy.

How nice to walk with someone! But in my attempt to keep up with him, I cease reading my printout with directions. We follow a sign stuck on a pole placed at a crossroads. Coming to a dead end, we turn around and retrace our steps to the sign on the pole. A group of African immigrants have gathered there, and we speak with them in Italian. They laughingly show us how the sign on the pole swivels around. I take out Alberto's directions and read them carefully as my companion continues to chat with the Africans.

We find our way under a highway and onto a vast flat riverbed almost devoid of a river. I try to ignore my need to pee as we walk at a fast clip along the sandy trail. My energy flags, and I finally tell my companion I have to stop, pee, and rest.

He continues on.

I feel limp as he tromps off down the dusty riverbed, the comfort of a strong man slipping away so quickly.

He had arms like Piero the Policeman.

Piero was placed on guard at my hospital room door because of the convict. This was after the nice doctor, who discovered my pneumonia, moved me to another ward.

I was pushed into the new room in a wheelchair. This one had only three beds instead of six. I hoped upon hope this room would be quieter. A short, plump Sicilian woman and a lanky Romanian woman were my roommates.

"She's a gypsy," Rosella had said under her breath to my mother, indicating the Romanian. "Watch your purse."

The bathroom was quite a distance down the hall, farther than it had been on the first ward. This room, like the other one, had a long, narrow terrace littered with cigarette butts. From the terrace, my mother and I could make out the edges of the nunnery where she stayed, a fifteenth-century villa on a hill surrounded by cypress trees.

My mother asked if I really had to wear the sheet I was wrapped in or if she could buy me a nightgown. My new Sicilian roommate piped up that she wanted to give me one of hers. Amid my assertions that it was too nice, the Sicilian woman insisted and presented me with a large flannel nightgown the color of Pepto-Bismol.

After a few days, the Sicilian woman was sent home, and I wondered who would be my new roommate. My mother hoped the other bed would remain empty, but that night, after my mother had departed for the nunnery, a heavyset woman in a wheelchair was rolled in. Her face was puffy and her eyes careened once around the room, as if a siren had gone off, and then they became stony. She did not acknowledge either me or the Romanian.

Two police officers appeared at the door. The sleeves of their blue cotton shirts were rolled up, and their heads were shaved.

They sat in chairs just outside the doorway. The nurses gave them each two chairs so they could put up their legs for the duration of an uncomfortable night.

"My goodness," my mother said when she arrived the following morning. "You've got two police officers camped outside your door!"

"Yes. The new woman is a convict."

"Heavens! I hope she doesn't have a knife under her pillow!"

A doctor came in and began to speak loudly in Italian to the Romanian woman. It was no use. The Romanian woman understood not a word. But I'd noticed that she could handle a bit of English, so I began translating for the doctor as my mother pressed her purse to her side and looked with consternation from the so-called gypsy on one side of me to the convict on the other.

When the convict announced she needed to go to the bathroom, the two police officers rose to their feet and followed her. "That's hilarious!" my mother exclaimed. "As if it would take two of those mighty men to bring her to her knees!"

"Mom! Don't make me laugh!" I tried to press my hands to my lungs as my laughter sent shooting pains through my ribs.

The next day, a new set of police officers arrived at my door. One of them was the most ravishing man I'd ever seen. Instead of a shaved head, he had dark hair curling just above his shoulders, and blue-green eyes like a Poseidon.

I stared at his arms. They were Roman-statue beautiful, and the sexy way the sleeves were turned up. . .

"Oh, my God, Mom, his arms!"

"Well, *you're* feeling better!" my mother retorted.

After squatting next to a cluster of small dusty trees, I gulp some water and assess the surroundings. The shallow river makes a series of paths through the flat plain. There's no shade and no comforting farmhouses in sight. I notice broken glass and rusty tins with pried off lids strewn between scrubby bushes. If unsavory characters are along the route, they'll be here. And I'm without the strong Swiss man at my side.

I lift on my pack and give myself a silent pep talk. Okay, you don't like the landscape. You don't feel safe. What will you do? Panic?

That won't help. Don't give fear any power. Get a protective image going! I imagine being surrounded by a thicket of white roses. The thorns keep out intruders while the white petals represent purity and light around me.

When it leads away from the shallow river, the trail becomes even more unappealing. I'm confronted with an abandoned factory behind a wire fence. Tall, tired buildings with broken windows and blotches of rust appear to have once contained apartments—clearly depressing ones—that perhaps once housed workers. It's a scene right out of Dickens's *Bleak House*.

The route leads along a rocky, dusty road that follows the fence for the long length of the factory. I pick up my pace, demanding my feet perform in spite of a throbbing pain in them that alarms me. Rocks seem to pierce through the bottoms of my shoes and my mind tumbles this way and that, first saying that I wouldn't have noticed the ugly buildings if I were walking with the Swiss guy and then chiding me for already forgetting the rose image.

I pass the factory and turn onto a paved road that leads to a bridge. Seeing people and cars, I breathe a sigh of relief. The long, straight bridge rises high over the riverbed, and as I walk along it, I note that the railing is no more than three feet high. It wouldn't pass muster in the US, I think, as I look down at the branches of water that move slowly between raw scrapes of riverbed.

If I fall over the silly railing, how deep will the water be?

I feel faint, and as I near the end of the long bridge, an old man on a bicycle rides by and calls out, *"Forza! Dai!"* (Have strength! Come on!)

I realize I'm stumbling.

Reaching the bridge's end, I lift my head just enough to see the sign for the Via Francigena. It takes me up a steep cobbled road into the center of Fornovo di Taro and deposits me at the main church. But a church is not what I want. I want food.

I have visions of meeting up with the Swiss guy and sitting outside a pizzeria eating a very large and luscious pizza from a wood-burning oven.

I see no eateries near the church. In fact, I see no people except one woman, standing in front of a shop that's got a grate pulled half way down. She responds to my exhausted question, "No, nothing is open. Today's a holiday."

As she begins to tell me where to eat, my heart sinks. It's back to the end of the bridge where I'd just been.

"There's a place that hosts pilgrims and feeds them," she says.

It sounds like the best bet for food. Still, my legs tremble.

When I get back there, I don't see the pilgrim house, so I ask someone who tells me that the place has been closed for three years.

Okay, I tell myself, forget the visions of a succulent pizza *al forno* with oozing mozzarella. Just get yourself to a bar and order a panino.

Up the street, I stumble into the first bar I come to and sink into a hard plastic chair.

The basic panino with prosciutto and a bottle of iced tea comes to €6 (about $8.60). The price seems steep for something so simple in an undistinguished bar in a small town. Perhaps I'm not being fair. Perhaps I'm overly obsessed about delicious trattoria meals because of the culture of deprivation.

I pull my phone out and call the *agriturismo* (farm stay) I had booked.

"*Dove sei?*" a voice calls into the phone.

"I'm in a bar in Fornovo," I tell her. "How many more kilometers to your place?"

"Just a few. I'll come get you? Which bar are you in?"

She speaks rapidly. I hesitate for a moment, feeling that I should walk all the way, but my feet are alarmingly painful. Soon enough, the proprietor of the bar is taking my phone and telling the woman where I am.

The farm is in the countryside, right next to the road where I'll continue the next day. I'm given an "apartment" in her home with a bedroom, bathroom, and kitchen/dining room painted mint green. It's homey and comforting, and I elevate my aching feet for a few hours before I am finally brave enough to stand on them to scrub my small supply of clothes in the sink.

Without a car, I can't get anywhere for dinner, but luckily, the proprietor provides dinner for an extra cost. She charges €40 for the night and €10 more for the dinner.

I must admit, €40 ($57) is beyond my budget for a night's lodging, but I rationalize that it's worth it. After all, the previous night cost nothing and the youth hostel the night before only cost €10. And I had donated €10 to the monks on the first night. I make calculations in my diary; I figure that my lodging has averaged €15 a night, so potentially, after forty days, the accommodation cost will come to €600 ($866). I don't have that much—not for lodging and food combined, never mind only for lodging.

A voice in my head taunts me. *Give up! Throw in the towel! You're not going to make it on this pilgrimage, not physically or financially! And you're not going to make it once you're back home either! Remember the article you read— that women divorcing in their forties fare much worse than their ex-husbands?*

I close my notebook, lean into the pillow, and shut my eyes. I tell myself to turn my thoughts around. But you *are* making it. You *did* get through the year. You took in a housemate, and you didn't go shopping except for necessities. Your friends and family donated money for you to come here. Look at the ways in which the universe is generous. It's all about what you believe.

Later that evening, I write, *My word for the day is "release."*
Release the bad night's sleep.
Release the desire to keep up with the Swiss pilgrim.
Release the expectation that the route will always be pretty.
Release your visions for lunch.

Having fixed expectations may block a miracle. If I release expectations daily, it will open me to the unexpected, to possibilities unconsidered, to seeing, as William Blake put it, heaven in a wildflower.

EIGHTEEN

Wild Beasts

This isn't the first time I've walked partway across a European country. A few years before the Berlin Wall came down, when I was twenty, I joined a group attempting a peace walk from California to Moscow. When my program in Florence ended, the group was in Germany, walking across the last stretches of free Europe, hoping they'd be allowed to walk across Eastern Europe and into the Soviet Union. I took a night train to Nuremberg and met them in the morning as they held a vigil outside the Palace of Justice, where the famous trials of German military leaders had been conducted by the Allies. The peace walkers stood in a circle holding hands outside the palace, their banners and flags draped around their shoulders. A few German police officers hovered nearby, arms folded across their chests, expressions neutral. I slipped into the circle, and into something larger than myself, youthful idealism bouncing in my heart.

Inside the palace, we toured Courtroom 600, where the trials had taken place. Chills went through me as I imagined the room forty years earlier when Rudolf Höss, the commandant at Auschwitz, admitted that under his order, two million Jews had been put to death by gassing and half a million by other means. Here, in this courtroom, the Allies showed films of the death camps they'd liberated, and the world learned the true horrors of the concentration camps.

Alan, a young man who'd been walking with the group since it had passed through his home state, introduced himself with a southern accent.

"What do you know about the Nuremberg trials?" I asked.

He told me that the trials set a precedent in international law.

The main defense of the German military officers was that they were just following orders and, therefore, were not guilty. The trials had determined that individuals couldn't get off the hook for war crimes by asserting they were simply following orders.

Standing in that courtroom, I had one of those moments. It had happened once before, a year earlier when I'd seen Rome for the first time. My love for history made me larger. It was as if I was connected to all the centuries of humankind, and with the hopes, fears, joys, and struggles of those who had come before me.

With the peace walk memories in mind, I leave the farm stay and walk along the white line between the paved road and the green fields. Stopping where the road crosses a brook, I look across the pastures where the low angle of the early light is sending long tree shadows toward where hay bales bask. I reflect on the youthful me who had participated on the peace walk in Germany. The memories make me wistful. What exactly do I miss? I still have an inquiring mind and still love to discuss history, so I haven't lost that. Yet I'd felt so unburdened then. In fact, my main concerns were about Reagan's policies in Central America and the nuclear arms race, not personal ones. What the heck has happened to make me feel so burdened, so focused on survival?

My question stretches long in front of me, like the shadows of the trees, and I continue on the road. A small chapel to my left causes me to stop. The rough wooden door is locked with an iron bolt, and the once-white walls are stained with blotches of gray. Tall rose stems reach up next to the old door, the pink petals almost touching the simple fresco above it. The fresco, done only in gray and white, depicts a man holding a child—undoubtedly Jesus—in one arm. Is the man a monk? He holds a long-stemmed flower toward which the baby Jesus reaches. I feel my heart open and receive a blessing, as if the chapel represents my hopes for renewal.

Walking on up the road, I come upon an elderly man tending a little patch of garden between the road and brook.

He asks, *"Sei sola?"* (Are you alone?)

With a sense of happiness, I respond, *"Si!"*

"Ma Lei non ha paura?" (But you're not afraid?)

"No, di che cosa?" (No, of what?)

He laughs. *"Vero, non c'è pericolo qui."* (True, there's no danger around here.)

At the turnoff for Bardone, I note that I've been walking an hour. This is where I'll begin to climb the Apennines. The directions indicate that it will be one of the hardest days between Fidenza and Rome due to the elevation gain of about 1,040 meters (more than 3,400 feet). The day's destination is the town of Cassio, twenty kilometers (just over twelve miles), which is enough to make me apprehensive.

On the previous day, I'd only walked 10.5 kilometers after which I was wiped out.

How am I going to walk twenty kilometers today if I was wiped out yesterday after only ten? I huff up the narrow road winding steeply to Bardone and tell myself that there's no point in being anxious. Just take it one step at a time.

Stopping to pee, I take off my pack and walk through the deep green grass and red poppies. There is a single line of grapevines curving down the sloping hill. I sit and look between two twisting vines to an emerald-colored hill sloping toward a row of verdant trees. Above my head, nubile bunches of grapes hang, and at my feet, the poppies contrast crimson against green like a Van Gogh painting.

Under the warm sun, I absorb the abundance of the land, then reluctantly shoulder my pack and continue. Not a soul in sight.

It's almost nine when I enter Bardone, a hamlet that seems to be built entirely of gray stone. The first thing I come upon is a stone marker depicting a pilgrim. The figure wears a hooded cape and carries a staff. At the bottom are the words *Romam Peregrinantibus.* I guess it has stood in that spot since the Middle Ages. *Peregrinantibus* is not classical Latin and is indicative of the grammatical changes that occurred in Latin during the Middle Ages, which is when pilgrims began to walk the Via Francigena. The word relates to the verb *peregrinato* (to travel/wander/roam) and also relates to the noun *peregrinationis* (pilgrimage). *Romam* denotes motion towards Rome. The phrase could mean, "For those who are making a pilgrimage to Rome."

This route, called the Via Claudia, connected the Parma area to Tuscany and to the Tyrrhenian Sea in the Middle Ages, and hospices (hostels) offering hospitality to pilgrims sprang up along it.

The hamlet of Bardone established its first hospice in 1004.

There may be history to discover in Bardone, but I don't see any place to buy food for lunch. Not knowing when I'll find food and facing a strenuous day, I feel a need to push on.

An hour of climbing up a quiet road leads me to the village of Terenzo. As I enter this fairy-like stone hamlet, my head is sweaty under my hat and my shoulders and feet ache. I stop at the village fountain. Its shaded stone wall hosts an array of herbs and flowers, and I sit with my back against the wall, enjoying the pungent scent as I rest my feet.

Surely there will be a grocery shop in this village. But after shouldering my pack and walking a few paces with no sign of a store, I leave the village behind before I realize it.

The Via Francigena veers off the road and onto a single-track trail heading steeply up through some woods. I stop and eat a few energy nuggets. I tell myself that I've got to figure out this food thing. The woman at the farm stay wasn't up when I left, and I hadn't thought yesterday to ask if she could make me a panino for today's walk. I thought I would come upon a grocery store today, but I now realize that there will be days when I cannot expect to encounter a fresh panino en route.

The woods give way to a bald hilltop. Gone are the charming villages and idyllic green pastures with red poppies. I look down and see all the way to Parma and Fidenza. Even though I'm sure I'm the slowest pilgrim ever, it looks like I've come a long way from this vantage point.

The trail continues upward, and I come upon a man resting at the side of the trail. He looks about sixty and wears an odd green wool hat, like the Trachten hat Bavarians wear. His backpack isn't made of the typical modern material. Instead, it's the olive-colored canvas style my parents used in the 1950s. But his doesn't even have a waist strap. His belly protrudes. Is he a pilgrim?

I nod to him as I pass.

He greets me in German in a raspy voice. *"Guten Tag."*

I adjust from Italian to German. "Oh, um, *guten Tag!*" I don't know if he's a pilgrim or if we have a common language, and I continue on, worried that if I break my feeble rhythm, I will not make it up the mountain.

Marching through the rest of the woods, I come out on the Statale 62, which I'm pretty sure leads to Cassio, my destination for the day. But the directions have me turning off down a hill to a village called Castello di Casola. Wouldn't it be more direct to stay on the *statale*, the state highway? I feel indecisive. I don't want to do extra walking, but a dry bone of a hunger bangs in my stomach, and I head toward the village to seek food and water, and then decide which way to go. It's one o'clock, perfect timing for a happy trattoria.

In the village, I eagerly ask the first person I see where to get food. The man in muddy boots responds, "There's nothing here. You have to go another four kilometers to Cassio."

I sink to a bench. Four kilometers (2.5 miles) sounds like the other side of the moon. How can I go another four kilometers without sustenance?

An old woman with a wooden pole walks slowly toward me. Her dark skirt falls halfway down her bare calves, her feet are tucked into navy slip-on shoes, and white tufts of her hair poke from under a blue cap.

I greet her, and she asks if I'm alone. I tell her I am. When she asks if I'm going to Rome, I nod. She asks who will know if something happens to me.

"I have a cell phone. And other pilgrims have done the route alone," I assure her.

"Ci sono bestie!" (There are wild beasts!)

"Um, well, just vipers and wild boar, right?"

"Cara, non puoi farlo da sola, non puoi!" (Dear, you cannot do it alone, you cannot!)

"I'll be okay, really." I change the subject. "Have you lived here your whole life?"

"Si cara, si, tutta la vita." (Yes, dear, all my life.)

I tell her that I'm from the United States, to which she responds that the United States is far away.

I wonder if she's ever ventured away from her village. She folds and unfolds her large hands in her lap and, giving me a worried look, warns me again about the wild beasts in the woods.

Wondering how to reassure her, I repeat that I'll be okay. Just to be sure the man hadn't been incorrect, I ask if I can find food in the village. She kindly offers to bring me some and walks to a nearby house while I stay on the bench.

I have visions of salami and cheese. Instead, she offers a prepackaged pastry with lots of icing. I'm grateful, but my body cries for protein.

She wraps her thick fingers around her long pole and admonishes me to not go into the woods. *"Ci sono bestie!"*

At the mention of wild beasts for the third time, I giggle. Why am I laughing? That's not polite! Am I light-headed from the lack of food? Am I dehydrated?

"I think it's best to follow the directions," I reply. From the pocket of my hiking shorts, I pull out my folded up pieces of paper with Alberto's directions for the day.

She points out that she cannot read it.

"Well, let's see." In Italian, I tell her that it says, from the village to go directly down, cross a cart track, and continue straight along a barely visible trail.

She cries out that I will get lost.

She's so sweet, I want to reassure her. "I will be okay." I pull out my phone and show her, as if to prove that this tiny plastic and metal device will protect me from wild beasts.

I look at her white hair emerging like mist from under her cap and I'm reminded of my grandmother. I suddenly want to ask for her life's story. Instead I tell her I have to go.

"ArrivederLa," I say, using the formal form to show her respect.

With my every step down the hill, I wonder if in fact I should be heading up to the statale. I've lost my intuition. Which way should I go? The German makes my decision for me. He comes around the bend up the hill toward me, his large belly heaving, sweat dripping down the sides of his face from under his woolen Bavarian hat.

"No good," he huffs. "Too steep. The trail. Too hard. I'm taking the road."

"Oh," I reply slowly. "Oh, I guess I should take the road then." I turn around and begin to trudge back up.

Before long, I pass the German, who has stopped, but I refuse to let myself rest. I slog back up to Castello di Casola and then up further to the statale.

I push my poles in front of me—feet one, two; poles one, two. I force myself to march, hoping the rhythm will keep me going.

At the top of the hill, a dirt road to my left looks as if it might be a shortcut to the statale. It appears to join a road above me, wrapping around the side of the mountain. Is that the statale? Should I take the dirt road? Now that I'm not following Alberto's directions, I'm on my own.

I see a farmhouse halfway up the dirt road and decide to head toward it.

The house is a cheery yellow with lace curtains and window boxes full of geraniums. Approaching it, I hear a dog barking furiously. Then a pleasant-looking woman in an apron comes around the corner carrying eggs. She greets me warmly. I surprise myself by asking her if the road is a *scorciatoia* (a shortcut) to the statale. From what recess of my brain did that word tumble? I grin at my intimate moment with the Italian language.

The woman confirms that, indeed, it is the statale above us.

"My husband often gives pilgrims rides from here to Cassio," she states.

"Really?" I hadn't thought about pilgrims taking rides.

"There he is now!" She points to a man walking out of the barn. "I'll ask him!" she exclaims.

"Well, okay," I say, following her.

The short man with a weatherworn face looks like the typical *contadini* (peasants) I've encountered in out-of-the-way places in Italy's countryside.

"No problem. I'll give you a ride," he says with a smile that shows a few teeth missing. I feel guilty at the idea of not walking the whole way. But the old lady's talk of wild beasts, the extra hike up the hill, and the lack of food have worn down my resolve.

I climb into his tiny, rusty car and off we go. He brings me to the front of the hostel in Cassio.

Oh, I want to say to him, "You've delivered me from the wild beasts, you've delivered me to a happy trattoria, you're the best little contadino in the best little rusty car." Instead, I say, "Thank you so much."

And I feel my glow coming out in my smile.

"No problem," he says, grinning back, and drives off.

Ah, my heart sings, look at how adorable that guardian angel was.

NINETEEN

Cat and Mouse

A small sign next to the gate of the hostel provides the phone number of the man in charge. I call, and he arrives after a few minutes, leading me into a large building with cement floors. I follow him up two flights of stairs to a room with a vaulted roof that almost touches the floor, leaving space for small windows about two feet high. He gives me a set of keys, takes my passport, and disappears. (Every place of lodging in Italy must take the guest's passport to fill out forms as part of Italy's antiterrorism laws.)

I shower in the bathroom on the landing and use my tiny travel towel, a chamois not much larger than a sheet of paper. After changing into my extra pair of clothes, I head eagerly to the restaurant/bar a few yards up the road.

The hostel stands at the edge of the two-lane Statale 62, which leads south to the Cisa Pass, where the region of Emilia Romagna gives way to Tuscany. On the other side of the road, I notice a hotel with a closed gate.

The tall stone restaurant and bar a few yards from the hostel is wedged between the statale and the steep downward plunge of the mountainside. Along with the three establishments, I take in the wooded mountains and the busy wind sweeping down the road like a broom, picking up pine needles.

A young blond woman is behind the bar. She says that a meal at the odd hour of four-thirty in the afternoon isn't possible, so I ask for tea and biscotti. To my delight, she offers Earl Grey tea. Italians aren't tea people. Being raised with British traditions, I'm used to drinking quality tea every day around four o'clock. I have to admit, in spite of excellent coffee, I still find myself seeking—mostly in vain—a good cup of British tea whenever I'm in Italy.

I share the details of my pilgrimage with the young woman, who turns out to be Romanian. She in turn tells me her story about coming to Italy to work as a hotel maid and then marrying a local Cassio man. I realize I've not chatted like this with a woman since beginning my pilgrimage.

After about half an hour, the sweating German walks in. He sits near me at the bar and asks me to translate a question to the Romanian woman. How odd to be an American in the position of translating for a German. They're always so good at languages. He wants to know why the hotel is closed.

"Because yesterday was a holiday," replies the Romanian woman.

I giggle. "That's Italy for you," I say to him. "Yesterday was a holiday; therefore the hotel is closed today!"

The German says he doesn't like hostels and requires a hotel. He has me ask the woman if the hotel owner might open it for him. She calls the owner, who agrees to open the hotel, and the German heads out of the bar.

The sun comes out and I move to an outside table to write in my journal. I take off my Keens and rest my feet on the edge of a chair. The wind has stopped and the sun warms my body. It's peaceful until two middle-aged Italian men wearing motorcycle leathers arrive, sit at a nearby table, and try to get my attention.

"We want to offer you a *caffè*," one of them says boldly in Italian when I look up. He has a large, square face, and his gray hair is cropped along the top of his flat head. He seems confident that I'll want his company.

"Thanks, but I just had tea, and Italian caffè is too strong for me."

"Let us offer you a glass of wine then," the bold one says. The other one looks down at the cigarette he's rolling.

I've enjoyed my chats with others I've met along the way. Maybe they'll be enjoyable to talk with too. But something makes me hesitate.

The bold one, taking advantage of my hesitation, jumps up.

"I'll get you a glass of pinot grigio!" He pronounces it *peanut grigio*.

When he brings the glass, he sits at my table. I notice his nicotine stained teeth, and as he launches into questions, I call him Chatterbox in my head.

"Where are you from? What are you doing here?"

"The United States. I'm on a pilgrimage."

"To where?"

"To Rome."

"Why would you walk to Rome if you can take a train? Or a motorcycle!" He chuckles and points to his motorcycle. "We are from Parma, and we ride our motorcycles up here for fun."

"Yes, a nice motorcycle ride," I say politely.

"How many kilometers did you walk today?" Chatterbox asks.

"Too many." I shuffle the journal in my lap.

"Oh! Are you going to write about me?"

"Um, well. . ."

"What kind of profession do you have?"

"History instructor."

This causes Chatterbox to go off on politics, telling me how the Americans saved the world from the Russians and the Muslims. "They would have eaten us all alive. If I were American, I'd be Republican because I don't like immigrants."

I shift in my seat. "I'm not worried about immigration."

"What are you worried about?"

"Health care."

He leans toward me. Fleshy lips curl above yellow teeth.

"You're a liberal!" he announces triumphantly, as if he's psychic. "Health care. Why is that an issue? You guys are a rich country."

I take a breath and keep my voice even. "I have to avoid going to the doctor because I can't afford it."

"If you are a professor, why wouldn't you have health care?"

"Because I work part-time. It's super hard to get full-time work as a historian."

"Where are you staying?" he suddenly asks.

This sets off an alarm in my head, so I say I'm staying at the hotel instead of at the hostel.

"Are you going to write about me?" he asks a second time.

I need an excuse to leave. It's my dad's birthday, and although I have no way to call the US, I find myself saying, "I need to go back to the hostel and call my dad for his birthday."

As I walk away, my heart sinks. I had said *hostel* instead of *hotel*.

The white-haired man in charge of the hostel walks up to the door the same time I do. He's come to give me back my passport. "Do you know about the vipers?" he asks as we walk into the reception area together. He shows me a photo of a viper to be sure I know what they look like.

"Yes, I remember being told about them when I first lived in Italy in 1985 and hiked in the Apennines," I say. "But I've come close to one only once—when I lived in India."

I was twenty-five years old when I lived in an international community in southern India called Auroville. One night, walking across the soccer field in flip-flops and shorts, I was pointing the beam of my little flashlight into the grass in front of me when a viper rose toward my leg. Its triangular-shaped head was half an inch from my calf. Luckily, the bright light caught its eyes. Momentarily stunned, it shrank back.

It had two dark stripes behind its eyes and its grey-colored body showed white diamond-shaped patterns. I believe it was a saw-scaled viper. I had heard the rubbing of its scales. These snakes are ill-tempered and attack quickly. Along with the Russell's viper, the cobra, and the krait, saw-scaled vipers are among the four most venomous snakes in India.

A good hospital was very far away, and I knew that a bite would cause gangrene, resulting in the need for amputation. Twenty-four years later in the hostel in Cassio, I notice how clearly the incident remains imprinted on my mind.

In Italy, I have to be concerned with the meadow viper, also known as the Orsini's viper. While death is rare from a meadow viper's bite, all kinds of freaky things can happen from its bite like abdominal colic, incontinence, vasoconstriction, loss of consciousness, and bronchospasm. It can take up to a year to recover.

"By the way," the man who runs the hostel says, interrupting my thoughts, "vipers are more dangerous when they emerge from hibernation—right now, in early June, rather than later in the summer."

Oh, great.

Taking off his glasses and rubbing them with his sleeve, he looks at me with kind blue eyes. "You have trekking poles?"

"Yes, I do."

"Good. Just stomp the poles vigorously to warn the vipers. Then you'll be fine."

I thank him and ask if I'll be in the hostel by myself.

"Yes, you'll be alone. No other pilgrims are due to come tonight. But it's perfectly safe here."

I tell him about the motorcycle guy and how it unsettled me when the man had asked where I was staying. He tells me to put his number in my phone and call him if I have any problems.

Thankfully, the motorcycle guys are gone when I return to the bar for dinner. It's comforting to chat with the Romanian woman again, and she serves me a large truffle risotto. I think about slowing down and savoring it. After all, truffles are a delicacy, which I never get at home, but I am too hungry. As my mother would say, "Prince Charles wasn't there," so I plow through it without so much as lifting my head. Then I walk back to the hostel in the dark—alone.

Unlocking the large door, I enter and bolt the door behind me. I pass through the cold and shadowy interior, climb the cement staircase to my room, put my sleeping bag on one of the single beds, and look around. I picture Chatterbox on his motorcycle on the road below seeing me through the small windows, so I push the bed to the middle of the room, away from the windows. Then I put my headlamp and pocketknife next to my pillow, turn off the lights, and get into bed.

My fear of stalking started with Mutton Head, the first guy I dated. I was fifteen; he was a year older. After dating him about three months, I broke it off. He seemed unbalanced, and I didn't feel at ease with him. One day when we were bowling with friends, he suddenly ripped up a photo of me and scattered the pieces on the bowling alley floor. I had no idea what had upset him.

When I broke up with him, he tried to convince me not to, over and over. He became enraged when I wouldn't reconsider. To my horror, he got in the habit of yelling that he was going to kill me across the quad on our high school campus, shouting my name and his threats for all to hear.

At that age, I knew absolutely nothing about women's empowerment or about harassment from an ex. Neither did my friends who, like me, were just barely starting to date. My parents had been married in the fifties and had not been exposed to any theories about how to raise empowered daughters. They did not talk to me about how to note the signs of an unhealthy guy or an unhealthy relationship. There were no self-defense classes for girls. No one talked about these things.

No grown-up at my high school took any action when Mutton Head screamed his threats across the quad with at least half the school body present at lunchtime. This was the eighties. Stalking wasn't made a misdemeanor in California until 1991. Since no one acted like I was being traumatized, I had no idea that I was.

Mutton Head made harassing phone calls to me for two years, repeating the threats. He also drove far out of town to my parents' house at least three times, destroying things on their property. On Christmas morning, he was waiting at the end of our driveway when my mother, father, siblings, and I headed out for our annual Christmas day beach walk. He tailgated us the four miles into town, nudging his bumper into ours.

Only then did my parents understand that the guy was whacked-out. My dad called Mutton Head's dad. But my heart sank as I heard my dad buckling, allowing himself to be convinced by Mutton Head's dad that it was not his son who had been tailgating us or who had been destroying things on our property. My father was readily supportive of my academic achievements, but with anything emotional in my life, he disconnected himself, which made him unable to be fiercely protective of me when I was being abused.

My mother transferred me to a different school. This was important and helpful, but the threatening calls continued. Uncannily, they always happened when I was home alone. I went to bed petrified every night. If I heard a noise outside, I feared it was him, trying to get in my window. For years after that, I believed that if I broke up with a guy, he'd want to kill me.

I was very wary of having a boyfriend through the rest of my high school years.

When I was eighteen, something similar happened. I had graduated from high school and was attending a community college. I started cautiously dating a guy, Walter, who seemed mature and put together. He was about five years older than me, from a different city, and had done a lot of international traveling. All of this made me feel that he was different from the untrustworthy guys in high school. The relationship lasted about a year.

Walter was a decent boyfriend, although he was prone to depressive moods. I was not in love with him, but it seemed important for me to have the experience of a decent boyfriend. Then he asked me to marry him. There was no way in hell I was going to marry anyone at age eighteen. Even if Richard Gere had asked me, I wouldn't have done it.

Walter and I broke up. He left town, and I didn't see him for quite some time.

Then one day when I got home from work, my mother said, "Walter called. He's in town and wants to see you."

I was living in a converted garage at my parents' house, working in a shop at the local mall, and saving money for my first European backpacking adventure. This was before cell phones and e-mail, and the only way an ex-boyfriend, or anyone, could reach me was to call my parents' number. I was readying myself to go out with my friend Deirdre, and I was already running late, so I did not call him before I went out. Later, my mother told me he'd called again and she'd told him I was out with Deirdre.

Suspecting nothing as I drove home, I headed my car up the long, steep driveway to my parents' hilltop home and entered my garage room without locking the door. Walter must have been parked somewhere in the shadows at the bottom of the drive, waiting to see me turn up the driveway. I hadn't been in the room long when I heard footsteps on the gravel. Thank God for the gravel.

But then I froze. Every inch of my body, every ounce of my senses, knew that something was very wrong with the sound I was hearing. I did not know that it was Walter. I wasn't yet thinking of my mother's mention that he'd called. I only knew that given how far from town the winding country road was and how long and arduous our driveway was, there was no way it was normal to be hearing footsteps on the gravel coming toward my room.

As I froze up, my mind went into overdrive, forcefully telling me to get to the door and lock it. It took all my willpower to unfreeze myself and walk to the door. A second after I locked it, there was the distinct sound of a hand on the other side, attempting to turn the handle. There was no voice and no knock.

I wanted to alert my parents, but the landline in my room was the same as the one in the house. I flipped on the radio so the person on the other side of the door would not hear me and called Deirdre, hastily and quietly telling her to call my house and tell my parents.

The phone started ringing while I sat rigidly at the edge of the bed, my chest so constricted by fear that I could barely breathe.

I heard the house door open and the sounds of our pudgy mutt, Muffin, being let out. A light was turned on. Muffin didn't bark, but I thought I heard the footsteps leaving. No one came to my room to see if I was all right.

In the morning my father said, "Muffin didn't bark."

"But doesn't that mean that she knew the guy? And since when is Muffin a watchdog?"

My mother agreed with me that it must have been Walter. Try as I might, I could find no reasonable explanation for what he'd done. This flung me completely off any fragile foundation I'd managed to cultivate in the few years I'd been free of Mutton Head's harassment.

I was not a sophisticated eighteen-year-old. I was inexperienced. Mutton Head had been my first dating experience and Walter had been my first "real" relationship. Had I been older and more experienced, I might have had good relationships to juxtapose against these aberrations. And I likely would have had resources for getting emotional help. But in my vulnerability as a teenager, something happened that morning. An imprint was sunk into my bones, like a really uncomfortable tattoo, like a sizzling brand on a cow's rump. I tried to wriggle away; I didn't want it. But it was no good. The brand was there, on my bones.

That brand carried with it the belief that I was not worthy of being protected and that some men abuse women and get away with it because good men do nothing about it. It was the way the world worked.

Solo travel has been for me a way of overcoming—overcoming the fear of violence against women that took root in me after those stalking incidents. Every time I sensed it disabling me, I wanted to roar at it like a lion, "You will not have power!"

Traveling alone has helped me insist to myself that I'm not disabled by this fear and that most people out there are good. But there are still times when the fear comes up. I'll start to feel disabled, and I'll have to dig deep to find my roar. It is a cat and mouse game I've learned to live with.

As I settle into my sleeping bag, I feel very small as the only person in this large cement building. My thoughts turn to Gertrude Bell, alone in a man's world and reliant on strange men to transport her across deserts and seas. I think of her hand grasping the cold steel of a gun, the sharp night air hitting her cheeks as she stepped from her tent, alertness to danger prickling over her skin:

> The desert was as still as death; infinitely mysterious, it stretched away from my camp and I lay watching the empty sands as one who watches for a pageant. Suddenly a bullet whizzed over the tent and the crack of a rifle broke the silence. All my men jumped up; a couple more shots rang out, and hastily disposed the muleteers round the tents…I picked up a revolver and went out to see them go. In a minute or two they had vanished under the uncertain light of the moon, which seems so clear and yet discloses so little. [iv]

TWENTY

Duty

When I began to date Darrell I was in my duty phase, which meant that I was letting my head lead, not my heart. I'd spent much of my twenties either in academic programs or traveling and living abroad, and when I came home at age thirty and looked around, it seemed that all of my friends had careers going and could afford Santa Cruz's high rents. I was suddenly mortified that I didn't have a career and couldn't afford a roof over my head. The jobs were in Silicon Valley, so I moved there and got in at Sun Microsystems through a temp agency. Tech companies were scooping up workers like spilled ice cream off the sidewalks.

"I have no tech background. I'm one hundred percent liberal arts," I'd told the two women interviewing me at Sun.

"Perfect!" they'd replied. "We love liberal arts people."

I wasn't thrilled to be working in a windowless cubicle all day, but I was glad to be making ends meet. And I had convinced myself that it was imperative to buckle down and face reality by age thirty.

Darrell fit this as if he had a sign on his head: I Represent Duty. He was four years younger than me, and he seemed sweet and gentle. He was also tall and handsome. Most of all, his eyes were impossibly kind. No one encountered him without noting this. The comments of the women around me about how he was the kindest man spurred me on.

My friend Robyn was the only one disaffected by this. "He doesn't even own hiking boots! And you, tramping around the Himalayas solo at age twenty-one! What happened to the *National Geographic* photographer of our imaginations we knew you'd end up with?"

"I bought Darrell hiking boots, and he likes going to the Sierras with me," I had replied.

"He's *boring*. He lives with his *mother*. He doesn't *fit* you."

There was something in me that knew she was right. But the something was so far away, I couldn't access it. To access it, I had to reach through my DNA, my cells, and my bones to the earth, then across the land and the sea, and finally stretch to a soft pink pearl on a beach on the other side of the world.

What I *was* accessing was my conditioning to be a rescuer. My mother was a rescuer and a giver. It wasn't so much about giving money as it was about exposure. Being exposed to ideas, culture, a good liberal education, the great outdoors, an organic vegetable garden, a cabin in the Sierras, quality literature—these were considered important not only for her children, but for anyone who came into our lives and didn't have these things. Plus, I was sure my father would not have seen a move to Italy on my part as practical. And I was trained to do the right thing, just like the meticulous way I had watered the corn all those childhood summers.

I wanted to rectify the fact that Darrell hadn't traveled abroad (besides Mexico with his Mexican mother), that he'd not hiked in the gorgeous Sierras (something I had done every summer since I was a child), and that he lacked passion.

Early on in our dating, he had said he liked my passion and wished he was passionate about something.

"Oh, but you can be passionate about something! There's a wonderful world out there!" I'd replied eagerly.

So I took him to our family cabin in the Sierras and he relished the secluded retreat where I'd spent many youthful summers. I shared with him my favorite hike at the end of the lake where I had scrambled up the boulders by the falls since I was a kid. At the top, deep green pools rested in the scoured-smooth granite river basin.

"Slow down," he'd said to me. "I've never climbed over rocks like this. I have to figure out my balance."

I remember wondering in that moment if I would be better off with a guy who was more experienced than me and who led me to places I hadn't been.

When Darrell said he'd never gone over Tioga Pass to Mono Lake—a trip I loved—I immediately set out to remedy it. We stopped just before Yosemite to swim naked in the Merced River—

mellow, and warm, and golden in the last light of summer. We slept in the back of my dad's truck, which I had borrowed, at a camp on the pass and at the hot springs in the Owens Valley near Mammoth. Upon waking in the Owens Valley, we slipped our cold bodies into the warm spring water.

We had moved in together by then, but after about nine months of living together, we began to talk about splitting up. I didn't have enough perspective on myself to understand that my rescuing behaviors were not creating the kind of teaming connection that would become paramount to me in a long-term relationship.

But Darrell understood something. "I haven't had enough experience," he said, in our breakup talk. "You're my first girlfriend, and I need more experience before I settle down. The best way to get experience is to travel in Europe, like you did, with a backpack and hostel pass, for like, a handful of months."

I agreed with him. At that point, I was so driven to help him find his passionate life, I cared more about that than I cared about finding a partner who suited me. I plunged into helping him plan his trip, overly caretaking the whole thing: buying his travel clothes, plotting his climb of Mount Olympus in Greece, shooting off e-mails to my friends in Europe who might host him, and booking the entirety of the tiny Italian restaurant in Capitola for his going away party.

We decided we would be open to dating others during the separation. We would keep in touch and just see what happened. After Darrell's departure, my friend Lucy called and told me about a guy who had just joined the board of the Santa Cruz Symphony.

"He's single and he's polished. He's impressing us all. And he must be into the liberal arts if he's joined the board. I think I should set you guys up!"

Mike and I met. He told me he was adopted and had recently moved to Santa Cruz. We began dating. For one outing Mike suggested picking me up in his jeep with bikes, driving up the coast to a redwood forest where we'd ride on a trail along a stream and have a picnic lunch. When he picked me up I asked if I could bring my dog.

"He'll ruin my jeep," Mike said.

"No, if I tell him to stay on the floor at my feet, he will,"

I explained, wondering how the bikes in the jeep weren't ruining it, if it was that precious. Mike would not relent to my dog, and I silently ticked off a box in my head. After our picnic and bike ride, he showed me photographs of an opulent home in Pebble Beach, the highest-end housing area in the Monterey Bay.

"I'm thinking of buying it. What do you think?" he asked. And then he explained that he'd invented a handheld device and was busy getting investors. He gave the names of investors in Silicon Valley. "It's gonna be big."

We dated for a few weeks, and I brought him to my parents for a barbecue dinner when my sister and her husband were visiting. Mike brought an expensive bottle of wine and told everyone about the wine cellar he would have in his future Pebble Beach home. I struggled to feel as impressed as it seemed he wanted me to be.

And then he said he had to go on a trip to get more investors.

After he'd gone, Lucy called me, with alarm in her voice. "Chandi, do you know where Mike is? One of the board members who invested in Mike's device thinks that Mike has skipped town. He's not answering calls, and there's some kind of suspicion going on."

"I know nothing, only that he said he's traveling," I replied.

And then I got a call from the district attorney.

"I understand you've been dating a certain Mike Green."

Jesus! My hand on the phone trembled. *What the heck?*

"Don't worry," the DA said in a kind voice. "You've done nothing wrong. I just need to see if you can help us."

"Okay," I said, letting out the air I'd been holding.

"Have you actually seen this device he says he's invented?"

"No, come to think of it. He never had me over to his house," I replied.

"We have reason to believe he's a con artist. That he's not who he says he is. What did he tell you about his life?"

"That he was adopted, and uh, lived in a lot of places. Uh, I don't know much really."

"We don't think his name is really Mike Green. He's likely conned the investors. Can you let me know if you hear from him, please?"

And that was the end of Mike Green and me.

When Darrell came back from Europe and asked me to marry him, I said yes. I was done with whack jobs. Darrell was neither a stalker nor a con artist. He had those impossibly kind eyes, and my head assured me he was the right guy. On a deeper level, my heart was troubled by the relationship even as we went into the wedding, but my head was in the driver's seat.

We moved to Colorado a few months after the wedding and bought the house in the cohousing community. Darrell got a job at Sun Microsystems and continued to start and stop businesses on the side. I had stopped working at Sun and had started my weddings in Italy business. After a few years, Darrell told me he was going to volunteer for the layoffs at Sun and that he was ready to go live in Florence for a year.

"It will get me out of my comfort zone and put the fire under my butt that's needed for me to get a business going," he said.

And so we went, and we stayed a year and a half. It was when we returned to our cohousing community that my unhappiness became too apparent for me to ignore, and I raised the issue of separation.

There were months of hesitation. There was a weekend when Darrell cried for two days and kept asking me if I was sure. And then I broke down and felt entirely unsure. Then we did an all-day private workshop with Gregg to figure it out.

When Gregg pressed me to recount memories of being in love from the time of the wedding, I caught myself wanting to pretend I could. Throughout the past eight years, I'd secretly felt shame that I had no memories of being in love from the wedding. But no one had made me admit it out loud until that workshop.

"I'm so ashamed of it," I say.

"Of what exactly?" Gregg asks.

"Of knowing I was disappointed during the engagement. . ." I gulp, afraid of my words, but I plunge on. "That I felt such a disconnect with him at the wedding."

I'm aware that Darrell is staring at me, and I'm crumbling now in words and tears, like one of those porous cliffs in my home town that fall into the ocean.

"It wasn't fair to him. I should have understood that my soul wasn't happy."

I sense Gregg leaning in with a soothing look on his face.

I look at my husband through blurry eyes. "I wanted to help you get your passionate life, and this compassionate thing you do with your eyes, I thought you'd always have my back, but. . ." Tears are running into my mouth, and I imagine that my face looks like a squished tomato.

"That time before the wedding when I broke down and cried because I wanted him to love my soul," I say, turning to Gregg, "I was almost in touch with it then. But I lost it."

"What do you feel right now?" Gregg asks, prodding.

"I'm confused."

"Tell me about that."

I look down and sense the cliff falling into the ocean, so I close my eyes and hold the edge of the couch. "I'm confused because I was raised to do the right thing."

"And what was the right thing?" Gregg asks.

I take a deep breath, quell the tears, and collect my thoughts. "To take care of others. And to be very practical, very precise, and use only my head to negotiate life."

"You didn't feel it was okay to follow your heart," Gregg states.

"We did what your heart wanted! We went and lived in Florence!" Darrell's voice flings itself toward me like a harpoon as I'm falling from the cliff.

"How did that go, in Florence," Gregg asks. "Did it make you closer?"

I gasp internally. *Oh!* I feel a large truth gathering in my belly. I know it will push through my throat and speak, even against my will. I desperately don't want it to be my truth—that I was miserable in my favorite place in the world with Darrell. My head shouts that it was all fine, but my heart is fed up and insists on speaking.

"I, uh, if you take the marriage out of it, I adored being in Florence." I gulp and feel my shoulders caving in. "But with Darrell, I was miserable."

I don't know if I've said the words softly or if I've shrieked them, but I know I'm afraid of them.

"Well, Chandi, that's quite a—"

"What the *heck?*" Darrell throws up his hands, his face hardens, and there's anger in his voice. But I see his lip tremble, and I know there's fear under his anger.

I'm afraid too, but there's a tiny stirring, like a far-off lantern that's been lit. It's a glowing orange space that holds an invitation: *Come join me.* I sense that this far-off flicker offers a reuniting with my soul, but first I have to figure out how to propel myself toward it, how to cross the rough waters and the dark stretches of inhospitable land to reach it.

TWENTY-ONE

Pack Up Your Troubles

The morning is cloudy and the air brisk as I leave the hostel. Pulling the huge door shut behind me, I head to the same bar I'd gone to the day before. About eight men are waiting outside as I walk up. The Romanian girl opens the doors and the men surge in. I press myself up to the bar with them and wait for their calls for espresso to die down before I order a glass of hot milk and mix my protein powder in it.

Gray clouds jostle each other for position over the empty road that's squeezed between jagged rocks and sharp forests, where the trees press together tightly like a fortress. Within the first mile there are aches in my feet, my shoulders, and my heart.

My pace slows to a stumble, and I note that the hillside is cemented over, perhaps to ward off a mudslide. Part of the cement is shaped into a bench, and I steer toward it. Taking off my pack, I sit, feeling defeated. I have barely begun the day's walk, yet I'm already wiped out and chilled. I put on my rain jacket and tuck my knees up to my chest. Lowering clouds turn a darker shade of slate over the black road.

I place my notebook on my knees. Maybe I should write. Writing is supposed to help if you're feeling crappy, right? A minute later, a gray car passes me, screeches to a stop, turns around, and pulls up next to me.

Chatterbox steps out of the car. He talks quickly as he walks toward me. I neither get up nor set my journal aside. He chatters about how he thought it would be cool to find me on the road.

"So, um, you drove up here from Parma?" I say, scrunching my brows and trying to keep my voice light.

"*Sì!*" he says, wiggling as if he has to pee. "*Ho fatto bene?*" (Did I do the right thing?)

No, non hai fatto bene! my mind screams. "Don't you need to work?" I manage to reply.

"No, I'm on holiday. And look, you're writing again! Are you going to write about me?"

I almost want to blurt out, "Oh for Christ's sake!" But I'm alone with him on a silent road. *Don't piss him off, but don't encourage him.* "Well, I'm just writing."

"You look tired. It's cold. Why don't I give you a ride?" He gives me a yellow-toothed grin.

No way am I getting into his car.

"No, thanks," I say, conscious of keeping my voice calm. "This is a pilgrimage. I'm going to walk."

"Let me give you some tips on walking then," he proffers, positioning himself in the road. He proceeds to explain how the foot should roll and how the knee should lift—amusing advice if I hadn't been alarmed.

I hold back from telling him I've already walked from Fidenza and already know how to walk with a pack.

As he hops from one foot to another, his belly flapping, the demonstration looks like dancing a jig.

"You see?" he says, coming back to stand in front of me.

"Yes, thanks. I'll try that."

"But really, it's going to rain. You should let me drive you. I'm much better company than this cold road."

I inwardly sigh, knowing I have to get rid of him somehow, yet remain polite. All the while, not a single car has passed.

"I'm committed to walking, and you know, since it might rain soon, I had better get going!" I busy myself with putting away my journal and pen.

He backs up toward his car. "Well, okay then."

Relief washes over me.

"Okay then, have a good day!" I say with false cheeriness.

I bend over my pack so I don't have to look his way. The motor turns on and I remain busy with my pack until I hear him drive away to the north. Picking up my trekking poles, I take to the road, heading south, in the direction of Berceto, the only town before the Cisa Pass.

Fear addles my brain as I walk. *What if he comes back and tries again?*

What if he's angry this time? Suddenly I want to get off the road, but how? The wooded ravine on one side of the road tumbles sharply downward, and on the other side, a rocky mountainside thrusts steeply up into dark woods.

I'll call the man from the hostel! This is exactly the situation he'd said to call about. The idea cheers me. But my phone has no signal. The big X through the reception icon taunts me. "Crap!" I say out loud, putting the phone back in my pocket.

Jabbing the trekking poles in front of me, I continue my march up the road. As the poles *click, click* on the road, my brain says *shit, shit.*

I assess my choices: stay on the road or flag down a car. It could be dangerous to flag down a car, but staying on the road feels worse. I remind myself of my early travels when I'd cultivated so much trust. I think of the Turkish man getting me to the bus stop in Istanbul when I was nineteen. *There is only one Chatterbox up here on this mountain,* I tell myself. *Most others coming along in cars are going to be great.*

Five minutes later, hearing a car behind me, I cautiously turn to look, wanting to be sure it isn't *him* and trying to feel out whether the driver is safe. But because of the way the light hits the car's windshield, I can't see who is in the car, and I let it pass.

Since I can't see the driver, I'm going to have to rely solely on intuition.

I let two more cars pass me, each time trying to "feel" their level of safety as I force myself up the inclining road. No car comes for another ten minutes.

This time, summoning my intuition, I step into the road and wave. The car stops, the passenger window slides down, and I lean to look at the driver—a man with a kind face. I immediately know he's okay.

"I'm a pilgrim with a bit of a problem. Are you going to Berceto?" I ask in Italian.

"Yes, certainly. I can take you there. You can put your pack on the backseat. My name is Mimmo."

He looks about ten years older than me and wears a wedding ring. As we start off, he tells me he often gives rides to Dutch pilgrims.

"Dutch? Are most of the pilgrims Dutch?" I ask, noticing I'm relaxing.

"They always seem to be Dutch. You're American though, right?"

"Oh, my accent!" I laugh. "It's horrible!"

"No, it's not. You speak Italian really well."

"Thanks so much for giving me a ride. I just had a bad experience." I tell him about Chatterbox.

"He's an imbecile," Mimmo states.

The road curves down to the town of Berceto, and Mimmo stops in the small square and hands me his card. "I run a hotel just beyond the Cisa Pass. Call me if you need anything."

I want to hug him.

"Mille grazie! Mille grazie!" I say, clambering out of his car.

As I enter a grocery store, I immediately relish the normalcy of the place. I walk around the aisles looking at the boxes of pasta, tubes of tomato paste, and bottles of red wine. How comforting it would be to buy groceries and go home to a little Italian apartment and cook instead of wandering on a cold mountain road, worrying about an imbecile.

Then I tell myself I can focus on being freaked out by Chatterbox or I can focus on having been helped by Mimmo, another guardian angel.

The world is a mirror image of your mind.

The sentence seems to unfurl in the grocery aisle like the banner message I'd received after throwing up in the bathtub.

After selecting bread, cheese, and salami, I think ahead to the next day. The route from the Cisa Pass to Pontremoli might not pass through towns with grocery stores or restaurants, so I ask the store owner to wrap extra cheese and salami in wax paper.

Outside, I sit on a bench in the square to eat, but it's too cold to remain sitting for long. As I hoist my pack, I hope the food has revived me enough to continue. At least the rain hasn't come and the cloud cover has partially lifted.

It takes me a while to find my way out of town. The directions say to find the Via al Seminario. After making some wrong turns and asking people who don't know, I find the *via*, which leads past a seminary and to the statale. The directions say to cross the statale and take a *mulattiera* on the other side. I pause at the word *mulattiera* and walk a few paces, wondering what it means.

As I cross the road, I see a dirt track heading up the hill into some beech woods, and I realize the word means *mule track*. On the high side of the path runs an ancient-looking stone wall covered in moss. Pale sunlight filters through the beech leaves overhead, sending flickers of light onto the path.

I notice that I pause and look behind me a few times, still sensing the rattle of Chatterbox. In response, I count how many guardian angels have helped me thus far. This is the balance: to thrust intuition into high speed but not be naively trusting, and to balance those things by keeping an open heart, cultivating love and not fear—knowing that my experience will mirror what's in my mind.

After about a kilometer, the trail turns onto a worn road, paved only in patches. I pass a dilapidated house and then an abandoned factory. The broken windows gape at me like the mouth of the ogre in Viterbo's Park of the Monsters. I'm developing a distinct dislike of abandoned factories.

After another hour on the statale, not only do my feet burn, but I feel close to throwing up. A car slows to a crawl beside me. It's Mimmo. The passenger window lowers and he calls out a cheery greeting. *"È vicino! Forza!"* (It is near! You can do it!)

I want so much to say, "Wait! Give me a ride! I'm too worn out!" but I don't. It's too embarrassing to ask for a second ride.

Mimmo pulls away, and I slow to a stop and lean on my poles. Why does walking on asphalt hurt my feet so much? A voice in my head taunts me. *Because you're not supposed to hike on asphalt with a pack. That's why cars were invented!*

A car scoots by, a shiny red one, and I imagine its occupant is bright and shiny too, loving the downshift as his car hugs the curves.

Twenty minutes after Mimmo passes me, I'm still walking.

Vicino? I don't think so!

I'm hobbling by the time I see the big red hostel at the side of the road, a replica of the one in Cassio. In the doorway stands a young man who looks about twenty-five years old. I can barely form the words in Italian to ask him about a room for the night.

"Yes, plenty of room," he replies, giving me a concerned look. He leads me up a flight of stairs to a large room full of bunk beds.

Each bed has a folded wool blanket and a flat pillow with no case.

"I'm Massimo. Max," he says. "The bathroom is down the hall. Will you want dinner? It's about two hours from now."

"Oh, dinner. Definitely!" I take off my pack and sink onto a bed. "Um, will anyone else be here?"

"I'm not expecting any others, but I live upstairs."

"That's a relief," I say, too tired to explain why.

He leaves, and I take off my shoes, climb to a top bunk, pull the wool blanket over me, and put my feet up on the rung at the end of the narrow bed. Intermittent chills tremble through me.

A shutter bangs against the window.

I open my eyes. The wind slaps the side of the hostel. I shiver and feel for my phone. Good, I haven't slept through the dinner hour.

Swinging my legs over the bunk bed, I drop to the floor. Holy crap! Pain fires through my feet. Having no idea why they hurt so much and no idea what to do about it, I try to ignore it. My long-sleeve layer isn't enough, and I wonder if it would be bizarre to show up at dinner with the wool blanket wrapped around me.

I am the lone diner. Max serves me lasagna. I'm pleased by the hearty *ragu* full of wonderful meaty flavors. I imagine it contains pancetta as well as pork loin and sausage, and the béchamel sauce is lusciously rich. Only in Italy would a hostel have such excellent food.

The meal has warmed me. I'm no longer chilled, and I hum "Pack Up Your Troubles in Your Old Kit Bag" as I rearrange my pack and fill my CamelBak. I want to be ready early. The next day is nineteen kilometers. That's six more than I've been able to do. Fervently, I hope to walk the whole thing, enjoying the view from the Cisa Pass and walking into Tuscany. I tell myself that the pain in my feet will be gone by morning. There can't be anything seriously wrong with them. There just can't.

I've never entered Tuscany on foot before. A tingle of excitement warms me. It's a region so familiar to me. It will be comforting and full of everything I love.

TWENTY-TWO

Trembling Bridge

Thunderous rain wakes me. I ease myself off the top bunk and try to stand. My feet curl and cringe in protest. Hobbling down the corridor to the bathroom, I note that the hostel is utterly silent. Is Max not up yet? I won't be able to get breakfast and pay until he is.

From the bathroom window, through the fog, I see glimmers of a meadow with tall lush green grass edged by a forest. The massive mist eclipses all land farther than about twenty feet away. A deer appears, stepping tentatively into the meadow. It's smaller than the deer at home. As a surge of wind blows the rain sideways, the deer's ears flicker, and then it kicks up its hooves and vanishes into the fog.

With my hands on the edge of the windowsill, I stare out, thinking about the charming villages and wonderful views I've heard are part of the walk from Cisa to Pontremoli. I won't see them in this weather.

The thought of caffeine brings me downstairs, but the door to the reception and dining area is locked. Reluctantly, I return to my room. Using the wool blanket from the bunk bed as a mat, I ease my body into yoga stretches. Every inch of me aches.

Do I really want to walk nineteen kilometers to Pontremoli in the profuse fog and rain? The alternative—staying in the hostel all day, hiding from the downpour—seems silly. Surely, the pilgrims centuries before me walked in all kinds of weather, and they didn't even have Gore-Tex or microfiber.

I lie on my back on the blanket and do a long twist to each side, like I learned in an Iyengar yoga class back when I was a student at UC, Santa Cruz. Then I hold my feet in happy baby pose. The pose reminds me of the way the gynecologist had displayed me in the hospital.

An argument had erupted when I was wheeled into San Giovanni di Dio, a hospital on the outskirts of Florence. The man outside had rebuked the ambulance driver for not taking me to Santa Maria Nuova. "That's where she belongs," he had shouted.

"Santa Maria Nuova was full," the ambulance guys shouted back.

"But she doesn't belong here!" The man at the foot of my gurney waved his arms as if swatting gnats, but the ambulance guys won, and I was wheeled into a room with four other patients. A young male nurse had asked the level of my pain on a scale of one to ten.

"Between eight and ten," I said, gasping in my effort to speak Italian through the pain.

"Ten?" he asked incredulously. "Ten is really off the scale. Let's say it's a six."

From midnight until five the next morning, I was wheeled around, up and down elevators, off to the X-ray room, and then to the ultra sound room—with no pain meds. In the last room, three male doctors were sitting in chairs near the end of my gurney. A gynecologist was called in. He quickly pushed aside the sheet that covered me from the waist down. I was splayed in front of the doctors with a view fit for *Hustler* magazine.

"*Fa male qui?*" the gynecologist inquired, abruptly pushing what felt like a knuckle toward my cervix.

"*Sì, fa male!*" I cried out. Then he jabbed hard over to the left side of my cervix. "*Qui?*"

The worst pain yet.

I screamed, but it wasn't a scream—it was the sound a dog makes when hit by a car.

The doctors all jumped in their seats. Everyone in the room except me leaped into action. Two female nurses were shaving me. Someone else was pulling off my bracelets. A catheter was inserted, and someone said I was peeing, but I felt nothing.

I comprehended that I was headed for emergency surgery, but if the doctors and nurses suspected what my problem was, they didn't inform me.

Unlike the time when I'd had a month to mentally prepare for the removal of my thyroid, I had only moments to prepare. But my mind focused quickly, leaving no room for fear. I had only trust, gratitude, and surrender. My body experienced pain, but I sensed something beyond the pain, something larger and more permanent than the pain: trust.

The anesthesiologist asked my weight, but the effort to remember my weight in kilograms was too much.

"I can tell more or less," she said, looking me over.

In the operating room, I briefly saw the surgeon and four others. *"Ho molto apprezzamento per voi,"* I found myself saying. (I really appreciate you guys.)

The surgeon replied, *"Ma, è il nostro . . . "* and I knew he was about to say *dovere.* (But it is our duty.) I was out before I heard the word.

It is close to eight when I hear Max walking down the stairs. I throw my pack over one shoulder, grab my trekking poles, and scoot down the staircase after him—ignoring the pain in my feet.

"The weather is really bad. You won't be able to see anything. In fact, you might want to stick to the road instead of the trail," he says as he serves me bread and jam and a hot cappuccino.

"A trail sounds nicer, and the asphalt seems to be hurting my feet," I say.

"Yeah, and on the road, in this fog, the drivers won't see you. But on the trail, if the fog stays like this, you could lose your way. And it'll be super muddy."

I remember that Mimmo's hotel is at the pass and that he told me to call if I need anything. I'm not sure what I'll ask him if I reach him, but it might help me make a decision.

Mimmo's wife answers and says he is gone for the day.

Max then says he'll drive me to Mimmo's hotel, about ten minutes away, where people might be coming and going, and where I might get a ride. I don't really like this turn of events, but not seeing a good option, I go with what he suggests.

As Max inches the car over the pass, I can barely make out a huddle of stone dwellings through the window. I want to read the historic stone plaques, take photos, and mark the passing for myself.

"Tutto chiuso," he says. (Everything is closed.)

"I'll come back on a sunny day."

I tell myself that the day is unfolding as it should.

We get to Mimmo's hotel, and like everything else, it is tutto chiuso. We realize that Mimmo's wife had answered the phone from home, not the hotel.

"I'd better drive you to Montelungo," Max says.

We travel down some sharp turns and arrive at Montelungo. I exit the car into the unruly fog and rain and see the blurry forms of buildings hugging the edge of the road. I wonder if there's a bar where I can have a cappuccino and wait out the bad weather. No. Tutto chiuso. Montelungo is silent and startlingly cold.

"Someone will come along soon. It'll work out," I say to Max.

I think of the Greek man in the hut when I was lost in the woods outside Thessaloniki. *Remember that world?* my heart says to me. *That's when your heart is truly open, when your trust is stretched so wide—that's when you have your glow.*

After ten minutes next to the silent road, I hear the noise of a vehicle. Because of the fog and the road's curves, I'll have to stick out my thumb before I can see who it is. I decide to go for it because there is no way to know when another car might drive by. And who wants to stand in the rain for very long?

A small and dilapidated truck stops. A man who looks rough around the edges peers at me from behind the steering wheel.

"I'm a pilgrim," I say. These words are my protection, as if a nun's habit is dropped over me when I say them.

The truck is cluttered inside, and the thought crosses my mind that most Italians don't own trucks. They have small, tidy cars.

A definitive hit on whether he's safe doesn't come as it had with Mimmo the day before. I get in. Mimmo had said that Dutch pilgrims hitchhike in this area. There hadn't been any reports of decapitated Dutch pilgrims, had there?

Out of the corner of my eye, I see the driver scratch his crotch as we start moving. At least I think he did.

Oh God, here we go. I'll have to poke out his eye with my trekking pole.

My confidence that I can do this if necessary stops me from being afraid. Then I make a concerted effort to speak with him in a tone of confidence. But more than that, I summon all the power I might possess in order that every Italian word I say and every gesture I make shows a masculine energy—so that he won't completely register that I'm female.

I comment that I'm sorry to miss seeing the stone villages I'd heard about en route to Pontremoli.

He mentions a small road off the main statale that leads to some of those villages where he can drop me. From there, he explains, a lower road leads to Pontremoli.

Even though I have the option to ride with him straight to Pontremoli, and even though my body aches, I believe I should walk as much as possible. So I have him drop me at a narrow road leading to a hamlet called Cargalla. I begin walking down a path under green, dripping tree bows. The rain stops and patches of sun come through the misty sky. Along the banks of the roadside hang vines, while rambling roses and tall foxgloves with wet eggshell-colored petals reach for the sky. Large trees curve their branches gracefully over the road.

I'm now in Tuscany—the part of it called the Lunigiana.

The tiny village of Cargalla is perched on a hillside. Outside a little church, I notice a woman in slippers sweeping the entrance. The church has a rustic façade of sand-colored bricks and the stand-alone bell tower has chunky square sides of rough, grey stone.

When I approach, the woman stops sweeping and invites me inside the church. She points out the statue of Saint Lawrence (San Lorenzo) wearing a red robe and holding the spit upon which he was roasted. Outside, on the front door, is a bas-relief depicting his roasting process. I recall that in the legend, he'd said to his persecutors, "Okay, guys, I'm done on this side. Time to turn me over."

Thinking of San Lorenzo's legend reminds me of the Church of San Lorenzo in Florence. In the fifteenth century, it had been the main church in the *quartiere* where the Medici family, de facto rulers of Florence during the Renaissance, had lived.

I think of Lorenzo de' Medici and my grad school discussions about him with my professor. When I suggested that I focus on humanism, her emphatic response was, "Impossible! You'd need to be fluent in Latin!"

In spite of her initial reaction, I focused on the Neoplatonic humanism of Lorenzo and his circle—one of the greatest intellectual circles in European history.

At the side entrance, I note two plaques to the *caduti* (the fallen), one for men from the village who had died during WWI and another for those who perished in WWII. I ask the woman how many people lived in Cargalla during the wars.

"Oh, many more than now. Now there are about fifteen, but back then, about five hundred."

There are eight men on the WWI plaque and six on the other. I remember my grandmother telling me that after WWI, there were no young men for her older sisters to marry in the small English town where they grew up. She had been eighteen when WWI ended.

"Germans!" the woman says, pushing her broom vigorously into a corner. "What they did here!"

I hold my breath and nod, waiting for her to say more.

"In Zeri, they killed everyone, *tutti!* Every man, woman, and child. Took them out and shot them. They burned villages, churches, animals . . ."

"War seems to twist people's minds so they become capable of committing horrible acts," I reply.

"*Ah, si,*" she says with a sigh and then asks where I'm from.

At that moment, I'm glad to answer that I am from America, thinking of the Americans and their allies pushing back the Germans on this very turf. I leave her and travel down the peaceful road, soon coming to the turn where a slightly wider road points toward Pontremoli, about ten kilometers (6.2 miles) away. I sit down to eat the salami and cheese I'd bought the day before in Berceto. It isn't enough, but it will have to do.

The surprisingly dense terrain seems like a jungle. On one side of the road, rising at almost ninety degrees, is a steep mountain with rivulets of water coming down through trees and vines. The other side drops down sharply, with the same dense, wild foliage.

After an hour of walking, I need to pee. But since one side of the road has a sheer drop and the other side has a sheer ascent, it's impossible to move off the road and relieve myself in privacy. After holding it for far too long, I finally squat next to the road and hope no car will come along—which would have been molto embarrassing.

As the steep mountains recede and the valley widens, the small road deposits onto the larger SS62 that comes down from the Cisa Pass. These last miles on asphalt almost cause my teeth to grind as I try to bear the pain in my feet.

Nearing Pontremoli, I come to a tributary that meets with the Magra River in Pontremoli's center. The Magra cuts through this northwestern part of Tuscany and empties near the border with Liguria. A characteristic medieval stone bridge beckons as a resting spot. Removing my pack, I sit on the wall, and realize that Pontremoli means "trembling bridge." Centuries ago, how many hands had lifted these stones to make this arch?

The water below embraces the rocks in its path and moves with ease over them. The key to contentment is to be like that river. When would I get there? Would I have moved on from the divorce more quickly if the medical disaster hadn't happened?

An acupuncturist friend had suggested a Mayan abdominal massage to restore and reposition my abdominal organs. I'd never heard of this type of massage, but I had given it a try. During the treatment, the massage therapist pronounced, "Your divorce is stuck in your body."

I don't believe *all* woo woo stuff I hear, but the "divorce stuck in my body" phrase rang true.

Sitting on the bridge, I feel impatient. I don't want to be the person with a divorce stuck in her body who obsesses about things that are water under a bridge.

These things will pass before me on this pilgrimage. I have to witness them and then let them wash on by. My pilgrimage is a trembling bridge.

TWENTY-THREE

Partisans

The twisting streets, stony riverbeds knitted with bridges, and jumbled grey buildings of Pontremoli confuse me after the singular road cutting between mountain and ravine.

I stop to take out my list of accommodations and begin to make calls. The Capuchin friars have a voice message about being closed for restoration. I ring a B&B and I'm told no singles are available. I then phone a B&B called Ai Chiosi. A young-sounding woman, Adriana, answers in a cheery voice. Yes, she has a room, and she gives discounts to pilgrims. Great!

When I enter the comfortable room with Adriana, the impact of my relief takes me by surprise. As if Adriana has fished me out of the Magra River, I hug her, my weariness causing my body to go limp.

Her startled expression changes to a smile. "Come over to the main house after you've rested. Have some tea."

After showering, I lie down and elevate my feet. Why do they hurt so much? This doesn't seem normal.

Slightly rested but famished, I cross the courtyard to Adriana's house. She offers a tomato and mozzarella salad, and then she scrambles an egg for me as well. Food, glorious food, and Earl Grey tea. What joy.

Adriana tells me about her decision to run a B&B. She had been living with her husband in Genoa, where they had careers, but she kept thinking about her vacant family house in Pontremoli. She'd quit her career and moved back to Pontremoli to turn the old home into a B&B.

"My husband and I travel back and forth to see each other. It's a sacrifice and not traditional, but I needed to follow my heart, and he understands that. We're making it work, and I'm so happy," she tells me with a grin.

On her computer I check e-mail. This gives me a chance to e-mail the Via Francigena Yahoo Group, describe the symptoms in my feet, and ask, "Is this normal?"

"There's a wonderful museum here, in the castle," Adriana says as I return to her kitchen. "It's got these statues called stele, made by strange people who lived here way back in the bronze age. We don't know who they were."

"That sounds so cool." I sigh and sit down. "I know I can't do a museum; my feet are in too much pain. I kind of feel like a bad pilgrim not going there."

"Oh!" Adriana says and laughs. "You can take my bike if you want to get off your feet and still see the town."

I perk up. "Awesome! Thank you!"

"And have dinner with my husband and me tonight. 9:30."

Dinner with wine in a home instead of a panino in a youth hostel room? Fantastic! Although I usually go to bed by eight o'clock because of exhaustion and the need to get up early, I eagerly accept her invitation. Maybe I'll stay in Pontremoli another day.

The rain lets up, and I cycle to a grocery store and buy a bottle of Vernaccia to bring to dinner. Then I bike on to a *farmacia*, where I buy inserts for my shoes—squishy blue gel-like ones. They are expensive—the cost of a meal in a trattoria. I feel a slight sense of panic about funds, but then I get on the bike. And there's nothing like bouncing along cobbled streets on a bike, without a helmet and with a wine bottle at my side. It's like being back in Florence.

That evening, I enjoy a typical dish of the Lunigiana: *testaroli al pesto*.

"It's an ancient dish," Adriana tells me as she mixes flour, salt, and water and pours the batter onto a cast iron pan. "It was known back in the Roman Empire."

On the plates, the testaroli are layered with homemade pesto and sprinkled with freshly grated parmigiano. I'm glad the wine I chose is white.

Digging into a rustic Tuscan dish while the rain pounds outside and chatting in Italian—about history, no less—is my recipe for perfect contentment.

I tell Adriana and Lorenzo about the woman I'd met at the church in Cargalla and what she said about the Germans.

"You know the famous Gothic Line was there?" Lorenzo asks me.

"Yes, the Germans established it in the Apennines," I say, "when the Allies were coming from the south, liberating towns."

"That's right!" Lorenzo says, looking pleased.

"Any stories about the partisans?" I ask. "They were big in this area, right?"

"Lunigiana was the most important area for the *partigiani*," Lorenzo says enthusiastically. "A chaotic scene resulted because Germans would sometimes dress as partisans to escape the Allies."

"The horrible reprisals against villagers that the woman in Cargalla talked about, those were due to the counterattacks of the partisans?" I ask.

"There's confusion about that," Lorenzo explains. "It was because Italy had capitulated to the Allies. Italy wanted out of the war, which was a shock to the Germans. In fact, it pissed them off. So the Germans exacted all kinds of senseless reprisals."

"Like blowing up Florence's bridges when they left Florence," I say.

"Absolutely!" Adriana chimes in.

I tell them about Hugh Evans, my eighty-five-year-old friend in Boulder who had been with the Tenth Mountain Division and was part of the assault on Riva Ridge and the decisive battles on Monte Belvedere in the Apennines. When I teach US History at the community college in Boulder, I have Hugh visit my class.

"So," I continue, "the partigiani helped the Allies break through the Gothic Line. But where were the partigiani when the Germans came into these villages?"

"When the Germans were coming," Lorenzo replies, "the men of the village would leave and hide in the hills. Everyone was sure the Germans wouldn't harm women, children, and the elderly. After all, they were not partigiani and had little to do with the war or with Italy's withdrawal. But the Germans killed entire villages of people and set everything on fire."

"That's like a scorched earth campaign," I comment, my mind flashing on the El Mozote massacre in El Salvador—the dreadful details of which I dredge up when teaching Reagan Era policies in Central America.

"Oh, yes," Lorenzo agrees. "I believe those orders came from Hitler or someone high up. The massacres became worse as the defeat of the Nazis became imminent."

"A horrific massacre took place in the village of Sant'Anna di Stazzema," Adriana adds.

"Oh, where's that?" I ask.

"South of Aulla by Pietrasanta. I think the pilgrimage route goes near there. After killing everyone, the Germans then killed all the livestock and set fire to everything. They shot the priest at point-blank range and used the church pews for a fire to burn the bodies. . ."

"And in Vinca," Lorenzo adds, "everyone in the village was massacred: women, children, and the priest. The same story."

"Can I get to Zeri and villages like that where this happened? Are there monuments to see?" I ask.

Adriana replies, "There's a bus that goes to some of them, but it doesn't stop long enough for you to explore and see the monuments. It's just a transit bus. Then you'd be hanging out in the rain, waiting a full day for a bus going back."

"Oh. I'll have to come back with a rental car at some point."

We fall into sharing our favorite places in Italy while Adriana opens a bottle of Vin Santo. "Homemade by my dad," she says as she pours the amber-hued dessert wine into simple tumbler glasses.

Lorenzo cuts the *Torta della Nonna*, a pastry cream-filled tart with pine nuts on top, and rattles off the merits of five of Italy's twenty regions.

"Where would you run a B&B if not in Tuscany?" I ask Adriana as I relish my first glass of Vin Santo and my first Torta della Nonna in four years.

"Oh gosh. Liguria, I guess."

"There are a lot of spectacular places in Italy," I say, "but I think the Tuscans are the luckiest people on earth."

"You really love Italy!" Adriana exclaims.

"*Italia,*" I notice I say the word as if Italy is a person I'm immensely proud of. "The world would be so much poorer without Italy."

TWENTY-FOUR

The Fastidio

Checking e-mail at Adriana's the next morning, I read two responses on the forum about my feet. Both say that I must have developed plantar fasciitis.

What the heck is that?

After Googling it, I learn it's a condition that occurs when the fibrous plantar fascia ligament along the bottom of the foot tears, resulting in pain and inflammation. It's caused by an overload of physical exercise or a sudden increase in exercise (possibly with ill-fitting shoes), and to cure it, one must stop doing the physical activity that caused it. I read that icing the fascia ligament is important.

Crap.

My heart sinks. I don't want to quit the pilgrimage.

Had I chosen the wrong shoes? Would it have happened if I'd taken my sturdier day hikers? They'd have provided more of a buffer between my feet and the pavement. I hadn't thought about all the asphalt walking.

My mind whirls. I'm only on the seventh day of my pilgrimage, and I'm supposed to walk for forty days.

Yikes.

I flash to the third night in the farm stay outside of Fornovo when I first hobbled due to painful feet. I'd developed plantar fasciitis in only three days? How much asphalt remains between Pontremoli and Rome?

I look at Alberto's directions for the next stretch. Pontremoli to Aulla is 32.9 kilometers, more than twenty miles. He says the first part, leaving Pontremoli, is on a heavily trafficked highway. He suggests skipping it and taking public transportation to Filattiera.

Then he says that the end of the route, into Aulla on the statale, is very dangerous. So which part am I going to walk, if I can walk at all? I resolve to walk what I can from Filattiera and leave it up to the gods.

I set down the papers. If I want to rest my feet for a few days, where would I like to be? The next destination of Aulla, which the Americans bombed to smithereens in WWII, would be the least charming town on the entire route. Although it had been rebuilt in the 1950s, the builders didn't pay attention to aesthetics.

The sea. That's what I miss. That's where I was supposed to go last summer after arriving in Italy with so much anticipation. Why not go to the Cinque Terre—the collective name for five villages on the Italian Riviera—to rest and enjoy a coveted swim in the sea? After all, those lovely villages are only a short train ride from Aulla.

I call the owner of a B&B in one of the villages where I'd booked many clients over the years and where I'd stayed a few times. I'm disappointed when his wife says her husband doesn't deal with bookings any longer, meaning I wouldn't get to talk to him. I had hoped for a "welcome back" greeting. And of course—in June, high season—they're full. Then she mentions a little apartment owned by Donatella, an employee of hers.

"It's at the far back of the town. It has a bedroom and a kitchenette," Donatella explains when I call her.

I briefly tell her about my pilgrimage and past business relationships with the B&B.

"I can do fifty euros a night," she offers.

It's a lot for me, but half of what I'd pay anywhere else in Cinque Terre. I splurge and book *two* nights. It's not worth traveling the extra distance there to stay only one. Even though I have learned that it can take a year to get over plantar fasciitis and I know that two days of rest won't solve the problem, I still feel optimistic. The sea will be rejuvenating, no matter what.

Adriana kisses me on each cheek at the train station. "Take care of that *fastidio* in your feet," she says.

Fastidio: annoyance; nuisance. Yes, I'll refer to it as a fastidio and try not to give it power.

Filattiera is a small medieval town all in grey stone. Thick homes stand shoulder to shoulder with narrow brown shutters and wide doors edged with brick. Next to the piazza is a castle, now just a private residence minding its own business in a peaceful town. But I bet it bristled with feuds in the thirteenth century.

It is almost eight kilometers (five miles) to Villafranca. It should be nothing—chicken feed; smaller than small potatoes. It should be little green peas easy. But it's hard. Alarmingly, stupidly, hard. In the train station of Villafranca, waiting for the train that will take only ten minutes to arrive in Aulla, I eat my last three energy nuggets, drink all my water and take an ibuprofen. My feet are screaming at me.

In Aulla, I walk, and walk, and walk from the train station to the center of town. How can it be this far? I'm gasping, stumbling, and wincing. Oh, but at the end of the war, the train tracks through the city's center were targeted by the Americans to cut off the German's supply lines, I tell myself. That's why the station is now so far from town.

On uneven roads with no sidewalks, I make my way to the Abbazia di San Caprasio. The abbey, founded in 884 AD, has offered beds to pilgrims ever since. Sigeric, the Archbishop of Canterbury, whose route I'm following, mentions Aulla in his diary, calling it Aguilla.

Inside, I'm greeted by a friendly man with an enormous nose. I hand over my pilgrim passport and sink into a chair. My exhaustion is over the top. *Esagerata*, as the Italians would say. I don't catch the man's name so in my mind I refer to him as *Il Naso*. I answer his questions about where I'm from and how my pilgrimage has been.

"There's a museum connected to this abbey that you must visit," he tells me as he rises to take me to the accommodations. I follow him outside and across a piazza to a gigantic wooden door, then up a series of flights of stairs. We pass through a disarray of doors, landings, and small rooms until we come to a hall with two dorm-style rooms.

"There are two French cyclists in that room," Il Naso says, waving his hand toward one of the doors, "so let's put you in the other one."

The door creaks as he pushes it. There's no handle. We enter a large institutional room with a row of rickety cots and a grimy-looking floor.

"Thank you," I say, setting down my pack and poles.

"Whatever bed you want," Il Naso says.

Scanning the long rectangular room I see a few tall windows with no curtains at the far end. The cots are pushed against the walls, head to toe, lining the edge of the room all the way around.

"Do come by the museum and abbey before the day's end," Il Naso says. "It's one of the most important structures on the Via Francigena!"

"Certo!" I reply with a small wave as he backs out the door.

"Oh, are there any keys?" I ask, following him.

"No, no keys. There's the bathroom, by the way." He points to a narrow door off the landing room. "See you later."

I peer into a dark, narrow space and see two stalls with hole-in-the-floor toilets. "Well, look at that," I say out loud, "a real Indian-style squat toilet!"

The flood-the-floor shower looks equally unappealing.

The French cyclists emerge from the other dorm room.

"Buon giorno," I say. Goodness, they are sweaty. Super sweaty. They wear biking clothes and hold tiny traveler towels and soap.

"Bonjour," they say as they pass me and go into the inglorious bathroom.

Back in my room, I choose a mattress, put my sleeping bag on it, and look at the pillow dubiously. I examine five other pillows. None have cases. My friend Kat, who travels with her own pillowcase, comes to my mind. I search my belongings for what might suffice as a pillowcase and settle on the rain cover I use to keep my pack dry.

Had I been with a friend, we could have laughed at this room that looks like the Italian state mental hospitals of the 1960s depicted in the film *La Meglio Gioventù*. If yesterday's cold rain and crotch-scratching truck driver hadn't rattled me too much, why does this room bother me? Part of me wants to run out and find a hotel room. A debate ensues.

Voice one says, *It's a free room, you nincompoop. Pull yourself together. You've slept in worse places. Remember India?*

Voice two says, *Yes, but that was over twenty years ago. You crave comfort now. You were darn uncomfortable in the hospital, and you're pushing your shattered body on this cockamamie pilgrimage.*

Voice one replies, *Tomorrow you're treating yourself to the Cinque Terre. For heaven's sake, take the free room tonight!*

Okay, I'll stay, I say to voice one.

Since the door doesn't lock, I collect my important things into my small shoulder bag: camera, passport, money, cell phone and journal. Then I gingerly step into the streets. After stopping at a bar for a panino and a caffé, I go to the abbey to see the museum. My feet are killing me, but Il Naso was so keen that I see it, I tell myself I can ignore my feet.

"The settlement of Aulla goes back to 884, when this abbey was built on the order of Marquis Adalberto of Tuscany," Il Naso explains as we stand at the church altar. "Now, are you ready for something marvelous?" His eyes sparkle.

I follow him behind the altar. In the dim light, I step up to a railing. Below me, lower than ground level, is an archaeological excavation. White rocks come into focus, along with a white marble coffin, its lid half off. The bones of a skeleton nearby seem to thrust themselves up from the powdery brown earth.

"This," Il Naso proclaims with a sweep of his arms, "is the tomb of the great French saint, San Caprasio, who was buried here in 433 AD. He was the patron of this part of the Via Francigena that goes through the Lunigiana."

Il Naso talks quickly, not moderating his Italian for me.

"So," I say, my brows furrowed, "the tomb is empty, and there's a skeleton over there in the dirt. Did he crawl out of his tomb or what?"

"Ha! No!" Il Naso chuckles. "We found the remains during the excavation a few years ago. The skeleton is from the Middle Ages. It was buried in the wall of the apse. The bones were determined to be the saint's. You see how wonderful it is?" Il Naso grins. "The saint was hidden from us for a thousand years!"

In spite of my love for history, I'm having trouble focusing on the story. The fastidio in my feet seems to travel up through my legs, into my torso, and to my head. Desperation to sit down overcomes me.

"Did you know," Il Naso continues, "the pilgrims in the Middle Ages stopped here to visit San Caprasio's tomb, just like you're doing now? Look." He touches my elbow and steers me along the railing. "See that hole?"

I peer down. I don't really see the hole, but Il Naso is continuing. "In 1944, when the Americans were bombing Aulla, a bomb fell right into the apse, but *it didn't explode.* Imagine! Finding an unexploded bomb during our excavations!"

"An American bomb?"

"Yes, yes, an American one. It's in the museum. I'll show you. And do you know why it *didn't* explode?" His words come at me quickly. I shake my head. "Because of the saint!"

"Because of the saint?" I echo, feeling dense.

"The bomb didn't explode because the saint was protecting the church! You see?"

"Yes. Wonderful." I shift from one foot to the other. I *do* like these stories, I just wish I'd taken another ibuprofen.

"Now, the museum!" Il Naso makes a grand gesture toward the entrance as if he's a prince opening palace doors for me.

In the museum, I see the American bomb, the remains of the wooden coffin that transported the bones of Saint Caprasio from France to the abbey in Aulla, and a replica of a pilgrim from the Middle Ages. He has a black cape, a tall staff, leather, slipper-like shoes, and a gourd for water. These things are pretty cool.

Il Naso talks nonstop. I take in about half of his rapid Italian. Every time I thank him for the fascinating time, he launches into another story. He completely loses me on a long narration about the Marquis of Aulla. Sadly, it's impossible to ignore the fastidio, and the cry in my head to get off my feet is all I can hear.

I'm walking over nails, hoping to see a welcoming trattoria. A town Aulla's size is sure to have some, but oddly, I can't find any. Then I see a sign for a pizzeria that leads me across a long bridge, spanning the Magra River. At the end of the bridge is one of those blue highway signs that mark entrances to towns. It says Podenzana.

I've walked to a different town?

To my relief, right on the other side of the bridge I see a jolly looking pizzeria called Gli Elfi. Salivating, I enter.

"Ha prenotato, signora?"

"Um, no, I don't have a reservation," I say, realizing it is Saturday night.

"We're fully booked," the lady says apologetically.

I tell her I'm a pilgrim and only require a small table and quick meal.

"Well, if you order immediately and don't linger, we can accommodate you."

"Oh, that's fabulous! *Mille grazie!*" I say with relief, promising to decide quickly.

When the young waiter hands me the menu, I scan it quickly. Any pizza from the wood-burning oven will be the best thing that's happened all day.

"I'll have the porcini one . . .and a small beer."

"Benissimo," the waiter replies.

As so often happens in Italy, it tastes like the best pizza I've ever eaten.

Where else on earth could I find such a succulent porcini mushroom pizza for only €6? In the US, it wouldn't happen. Not only would pizza that good cost a lot more than eight dollars, but it would be rare to find fresh porcini mushrooms at all.

I think of Kat's obsession with porcini when we traveled around Tuscany one autumn, years ago. Every day she ordered anything with porcini mushrooms. I vow to someday bring her to this hole-in-the-wall town and to Pizzeria Gli Elfi to share a porcini pizza. It really is to die for.

After my meal, I cross the long, unlit bridge. I'm aware of being alone, in the dark, and heading to the eerie psych-ward room. But I manage.

No ghosts of psychotic patients clutch my throat, and I somehow avoid the hole-in-the-floor toilet.

I get up early to take a train to La Spezia. On this beautiful new day, I'm going to the sea. Fastidio be damned.

TWENTY-FIVE

Next to the Sea

It is doubtful that any place in Europe has changed so radically in a relatively short time as the Cinque Terre. These five seaside villages, a few miles apart from one another along a ruggedly beautiful coastline, received only a small number of tourists a year when I first went in 1985. Tourism increased steadily in the next ten years, and then rapidly after the mid-1990s when guidebook writers began promoting the area as a kind of undiscovered Shangri-la.

The number of visitors rose exponentially in the early 2000s, and about ten years later, mega cruise ships docking at La Spezia added the Cinque Terre to their shore excursion options, creating a new channel of tourists, which fed into the already unsustainable numbers.

The price of a simple *pensione* style room shot to over a hundred euro, restaurants had waiting lists, long lines developed outside gelato shops, elderly locals became unable to pass through the crowds to reach the train station, and with a dearth of public bathrooms, tourists were accused of urinating—or worse—in people's yards.

I first went there in 1985 when I was living in Florence, attending language school. One of my teachers told me about these charming fishing villages linked by trails on the cliffs. "Take a train to Pisa, then one to La Spezia. From there, get on a local train that goes through tunnels in the mountains and get out at Vernazza. You'll be approached by elderly village women who will offer you a room in their house," she had instructed.

Indeed, I followed a woman in a shapeless black dress and black headscarf who had approached me with one word: *"Camera?"* (Room?) Along narrow paths through the village we went, and then up steps cut into the mountainside, past pink walls, and through a green doorway, where I was shown to a cramped bedroom in her house.

She pointed to the numerous framed photos of her deceased husband. *"Mio marito,"* she said with a trembling voice, wringing her hands. I was worried she would start wailing.

The room was less than ten dollars, and a dinner of the local seafood soup, including a pitcher of white local wine cultivated on the impressive terraces, came to about five dollars. I learned that the footpaths over the rocky promontories and sea routes were the only connections between the villages before tunnels were blasted into the mountains for the railway line. I wandered along the footpaths with the Tyrrhenian Sea below, spreading to the horizon. The Mediterranean *macchia* delighted me—the tall stalks of the agave shooting up from the rocks below me with bright yellow pom-poms against the blue water and the jumble of flat, green mitts of prickly pear, looking like they were vying to bat at the clouds.

No other hikers came my way, but I recall arriving above the village of Corneglia and walking behind a white-haired local woman. Between her dress and sturdy shoes, I could see short muscled calves hewn from a mountainous life. In the crook of her arm she held a great curving bunch of calla lilies.

The next time I went was with Diego in 1993, when I was living in Lugano, Switzerland. Diego, a Colombian who'd been a guerilla in his native land, had come to Switzerland as a refugee. I didn't speak Spanish, and he didn't speak English. We had Italian in common.

Before the Cinque Terre trip, we had a conversation about Italy in my studio apartment. Diego was at the table making *arrancini*. I watched as he whisked an egg, applied it to a glob of risotto, and rolled his brown hands deftly over the balls of rice.

"You always travel to Italy," he said.

"Because it's right there," I said, poking my thumb over my shoulder in a southerly direction. "It's just across the border, and it's the most fantastic country in the world."

"I have never bothered," Diego replied, picking up a tumbler glass of wine. "Switzerland seems pretty good to me."

"Oh, Diego! Everything is better in Italy!"

"Tutto?" Diego raised his eyebrows.

I flung my arms wide. *"Tutto! Ti giuro!"* Everything. I swear.

One weekend in March, Diego and I took the train over the

border into Italy, down to Genoa, and then east along the Riviera—
our first weekend away together. When the sea came into view,
Diego jumped up, rushed across the aisle, and pushed open the train
window. I ran after him and, like children, we hung out the window
shouting, *"Favoloso! Stupendo!"*

"I can't believe it was so easy to leave Switzerland and be at the
sea!" Diego had said, his coffee-colored cheek touching mine.

There, in Vernazza, I was charmed to be approached by a
woman in black, just as I had been eight years before. She took us
to a top-floor room with a window that opened onto a tempestuous
sea. It was fabulously stormy. We were so in love with each other—
and with being in the charming Italian seaside town—we would
have loved any kind of weather the gods threw at us.

We were the only tourists in the restaurant next to Vernazza's
harbor, and as we consumed a briny seafood spaghetti by candlelight,
Diego couldn't get the grin off his face.

"You're right," he said, "everything is better in Italy!" Then he
told the waiter that the seafood spaghetti was so good, he wanted
another helping. And he ordered it all over again.

The waiter exclaimed, *"Mai capitato!"* (Never happened before!)

It was the last time I saw it that way, before the hordes of
guidebook devotees burgeoned into impossible numbers and the
prices skyrocketed. In 2003, when Darrell and I were living in
Florence, I was surprised to learn that a fee had been instated to
hike the Cinque Terre trails. On the one hand, the fee helped the
maintenance of the trails, but it also was a clear sign that times were
changing.

I was running my wedding business then, and I had been hesitant
to accept requests for weddings in the Cinque Terre, knowing the
toll tourism was taking on the region. So I'd gone knocking on the
Vernazza town hall door to check things out with the mayor.

Without much prompting, he lamented to me about the changes
the tourist boom had brought to his village. "The Cinque Terre
are losing their culture, their traditional way of life. Hardly anyone
works the land anymore. The vineyards are owned by cooperatives
now, and the locals no longer cultivate the special wine of the region.
The youth are concerned only with making money."

"They aren't interested in preserving local traditions?"

"They're oblivious. They're ignorant about the original culture of the villages." He told me he was born in Vernazza, and in his younger days, only a handful of tourists came—and only in July and August. "Now, the prices are ridiculous in the restaurants. I keep hoping those prices and the new fees to use the trails will deter tourists, but the problem only gets worse each year."

In the end, I did only one wedding there because it was just the couple with no guests.

Now, on a detour from my pilgrimage, I step off the train in Manarola at ten-thirty in the morning. The station is swarming with Americans. Sixty-something couples in zip-off hiking pants turn maps in their hands and point toward the trails. College girls in tiny shorts and flip-flops talk loudly about the party in the youth hostel the night before. Hearing English all around me is a shock. I've not heard or spoken my language in a week. Disoriented, I fall in step behind the crowds, heading through the tunnel and into the village.

Donatella leads me to the far top of the village, then through a door in a wall and into a patio. The apartment has a small kitchen, a bedroom mostly filled by a double bed, and a bathroom. The patio contains a tree full of lemons, a few cats, and a plastic table. It's a sanctuary, removed from the crowds.

I unload the few groceries I bought at the co-op in Aulla, planning to save money by eating in. After making a snack, I put my bikini on, wishing I had something a bit cuter than baggy hiking shorts to wear over it.

Taking the pedestrian road toward the sea, I arrive near the harbor, stunned by the crowd. I can't see past it to the sea. But I know how the obsidian-colored rocks rise straight from the blue water like many little monoliths, how the tallest rock flattens itself against the edge of the village, as if keeping the homes from toppling, and how the sea sloshes in and out of the little harbor below.

Standing by the last house—a pale peach one with green shutters that nestles its back into the rock, as if for warmth—the flesh in front of me presses together like a large pack of sponges. Finally, I wedge myself to a spot where I can look over the wall to the concrete-topped rock where the bright yellow and cobalt blue boats are resting. Short bursts of rain intersperse with the sunlight. At the far horizon, a line of sky is deep violet.

I breathe the familiar salt and rosemary on the air and try to ignore the masses of bodies, the elbows, the sweat, and the roar of voices. On the hillside, a steady stream of people tread up the path and another comes down, reminding me of worker ants.

After being in the quiet woods and near-empty mountain towns, I reel at the commotion. It's as if I've been on a weeklong silent retreat and then gone straight to Disneyland.

I think of the pre-internet age when I'd shown up in the Cinque Terre, or Istanbul, or Kathmandu. No booking sites, no travel forums, no enhanced photos with saturated color leaping out at me from a screen. I didn't even take a Lonely Planet guidebook with me. This allowed for true wonder on arrival, my senses lit up by all that was truly new. I used instinct to find the way, honing it more each time.

I meander into the bar Enrica and nab a table at the edge of the glass-enclosed patio. There, I rest my feet, gaze at the sea, and watch the multitudes pass by. I recklessly order a Limoncello, light gold and potent, in the middle of the afternoon. Perhaps it will ease the fastidio in my feet.

At the table next to me, an Italian couple—handsome as can be—dine with their baby. I watch the beautiful man kiss the baby's face over and over. He murmurs, "*Caro mio,*" between his kisses. The woman's eyes are bright and happy when she looks at him.

My aloneness distances me, as if I'm watching them on a screen and I'm the only one in the theater.

Here in the Cinque Terre, everyone is with someone.

Well, I tell myself, I've got my Limoncello and my yellow saint, the one from my dream on the first night, the same one that's the symbol on the signposts.

Coraggio!

The clouds part and a warm, honeyed light bounces off the mountainsides. Telling myself my feet can handle a wee walk around Vernazza, I head to the train station. The patch of sand at Vernazza's harbor is chock-a-block with bodies. So are the rocks beyond the beach. But I manage to settle into a spot on a rock and have a dip in the glorious water.

On the main street, I'm surprised to see many gelato shops where there had once been only one. I begin to climb the multitudes of steps that twist around the homes, leading up through archways between thick walls mottled red and pink, until I pop out at the tower.

Now, instead of hiding from pirates in the fortified tower, people climb up for the stupendous views and to dine at Belforte. I can't imagine a more exquisite setting. On this high terrace, the tables overlook an unparalleled vista of the sea—better even than Big Sur in California near where I grew up.

I walk across the terrace, past the empty tables with white cloths fluttering, to the railing on the cliff edge. The sea undulates below— dizzying and electrifying. I picture myself there, dining with a lover, enveloped in cerulean light, and sharing a bottle of *Sciacchetrà*.

Back in Manarola, I exit the train tunnel and turn toward the sea instead of up the hill to my apartment. At six o'clock, the air is warm. I have to get into the sea again.

Setting my clothes on the wall, I drop into the gentle water.

After my swim, I perch on the wall, slowly detangling my hair with my fingers. Oh, to be on the warm stone wall at the end of the day, when the sun closes in on the horizon and time hangs suspended. In these moments, sitting in silence with the sensation of the last warm rays on my bare skin, my mind floats like a cloud. Every cell seems to relax, as if I'm nothing but water.

I walk trance-like through the village and up the hill to my room.

Could it be next to the sea? The place I long to buy in Italy, could it be next to the sea?

TWENTY-SIX

Fatal Flaw

I head out early, ignoring my foot pain, to walk the short path to Riomaggiore. At this hour, the ticket booth at the trailhead is unoccupied. I can't believe the Via del Amore is empty. Through the thick cactus leaves that have names carved into them, I look to the expanse of sea that frolics and blows kisses to the sky.

Arriving in Riomaggiore, I stop for a cappuccino and overhear the elderly Italians talking about the American college kids who'd partied through the village the night before, sending their beer bottles rolling loudly down the steep streets. At the harbor, I read a sign in English that clearly shows me the old days are gone: Do not accept rooms from people who approach you. The rooms will be dirty and unsafe.

I've never been in the Cinque Terre National Park shop, and I want to see it. In 1999, the national park was set up to preserve the ecological balance and protect the distinct landscape there. Locals, lured by tourist dollars, had abandoned the labor-intensive farm work their ancestors once did on the mountain terraces. The mountain terraces testify to the agricultural and engineering prowess of medieval Italians, but if neglected, they risk collapsing. That's why the Cinque Terre has been included in the World Monuments Watch.

In the shop, three American girls mutter to each other that they want to use the e-mail service, but the woman behind the counter is busy. The girls start to go up the stairs to the computers without following the protocol of checking themselves in and leaving their passports, which is part of Italy's antiterrorism law.

"Where do you think you're going?" the woman shouts at them in English.

"We've waited long enough!" one of the girls yells back.

"Documenti!" the woman shouts angrily.

Two of the girls come back and flip their passports onto the counter. As they re-climb the stairs, the third girl begins to follow them.

"You can't go up there!" the woman yells.

"I'm not going to use the computer!" the girl protests. "I only want to sit with my friends."

"Impossible!" the woman booms.

Heads turn toward the girl on the stairs as she rolls her eyes and retorts, *"You're* impossible!"

I make a quick departure, my heart aching.

In the apartment, I lie down with my feet raised. I'd like to hike more of the trails, but I must prioritize resting my feet. I try to nap, but my mind begins to obsess. In his book *The Art of Travel*, Alain de Botton said that travel on trains, ships, and planes is highly conducive to internal conversations. I'm starting to think that a long-distance solo walk is even more conducive. Maybe too much so, because now I'm obsessing about my wedding, when this tortuously looping CD in my head started.

When the time came to decide on a wedding location, Darrell said he didn't have a particular image of where we'd get married and was open to my idea of marrying in Florence. So I began to wonder if it might be possible. My many months of researching included a trip to Florence to figure out how I could marry in Italy as a non-Catholic.

For a while, it seemed we'd only be eligible for a civil ceremony. But then I discovered that with Darrell's baptism and confirmation certificates, we would qualify for a blessing in a church if we did the civil paperwork first. After a lot of dead ends, I finally found, to my delight, a charming church in the Florentine hills where the priest was willing to provide our blessing, even though we weren't part of his parish.

Naturally, the planning of the wedding landed on my shoulders. I was the one who spoke Italian and had experience planning trips in Italy. Neither the priest nor various vendors had e-mail, and frequently, I had to wait until midnight to call them due to the time difference, which didn't help me manage my job at Sun Microsystems.

Because all efforts had been lopsided in my direction, I anticipated Darrell would willingly do a few tasks that he *could* do. That included sending invitations to his family. He had no siblings and told me he did not know his cousins. His father lived and traveled in a trailer with no fixed address. I gave Darrell the five invitations and envelopes he said he would require. Naively, I figured that within a week he would tell me the task was done and ask if there was anything else he could do. After ten days with no update, I asked him for one. He got silent and withdrew. His reluctance to respond to my request left me confused. Had I asked at a bad time?

Another week went by with no update. Having to ask again made me uncomfortable. Was I supposed to step in and take on the task? Just blow it off? He didn't seem to want to let me know if he'd done it or not. I blamed myself and decided I must be approaching it wrong.

I asked him if he liked the idea of writing our own vows. He did. That was better than leaving it up to the priest, he said.

"I was thinking we could have two poems read too. Do you want to each choose one?"

Yes, he thought that was a good idea.

But despite the nearness of the wedding, and despite my attempts at arranging an evening for us to look at poems and craft our vows, I couldn't get Darrell to join me.

I thought maybe he wasn't finding a poem he liked in the books we owned, so I went to the library and got more.

"These are good ones," I said enthusiastically on a Saturday morning, patting the place on the couch next to me. "Let's have a look."

"Just leave them there. I'll look later."

"What about the vows?" I said, trying to keep my voice upbeat. "We should get those done."

"Maybe later. I'm having lunch with a colleague."

In the end, I wrote the vows and chose the poems myself. As incidents like this piled up, the sense of "team" I was craving was nowhere to be found.

The night before the wedding, we were all at the church, and my guests had fallen into a poetic state as they admired the hillside setting with the shiny olive orchards and view of Florence's dome far below.

"Beautiful," my friends said in hushed voices as I led them into the Romanesque stone church, dedicated to Saint Mary of Antioch.

"It's small, and perfect for our group of twenty," I said as we walked toward the altar. I left them and went with the priest to his office to finish paperwork. As I struggled to decipher the paperwork in Italian, Darrell walked in and told me his mother was crying because she didn't like the church. I fervently hoped the priest's English was too limited to understand what my fiancé had just said.

"When I told her there would be no flower decorations, she cried even more. What are you going to do about it?" he asked me.

Why was he not sparing me his mother's bad behavior? Why did he interrupt the priest and me to ask me to take care of it? Why didn't he have my back? My mind raced through questions, but I didn't dare reply to Darrell. Whether or not the priest understood the words, he would understand that I was hurt and tense, if I replied.

I had been sure that Darrell's mom, a Catholic, would be thrilled we were getting married in a Catholic church, never mind which one. She also knew of our surprising good luck; we were the last foreigners allowed to have a blessing there. The next morning, before I headed to my hair appointment, I asked Darrell if he'd go to his mom's hotel and figure out the flower problem with her. I tried to ask softly.

"No, I don't want to do that," he replied.

I had a foreboding that his mother's upset about the flowers would bite me in the butt if it wasn't dealt with. I tried again. "It would be easy to do. There are two terra-cotta vases already in the church. You could pick out two bouquets, and she could take them when she heads up there this afternoon."

He shook his head. I sensed his heels digging in to the bricks of the apartment floor.

In a frazzled state, I forgot to ask my mother and my friend, Kat, to help me get dressed. Thinking I wanted only my friends Martha and Nadine, my mother and Kat went ahead to the church with everyone else while I was at the hairdresser.

On returning from the hairdresser, Martha, Nadine, and the makeup artist were the only ones there. But as I sat with the makeup artist, Martha and Nadine left the apartment unexpectedly. When the makeup girl departed, I found myself alone.

With time ticking, I became anxious to get into my dress and call a taxi. I tried to put my dress on, but I couldn't get the corset over my head. With anxiety mounting, I stood in my bra and waited. Finally, with no time to spare, Martha and Nadine burst in with bouquets in their arms.

"Oh, my *gawd!*" they exclaimed, breathless and laughing. "We were running around trying to find a florist, trying to explain what we wanted in Italian!"

"But why?" I asked weakly.

"Because Darrell's mom wanted them!"

"Oh," I replied slowly, feeling my face redden and my voice falter.

"Wasn't that…?" The enthusiasm drained out of Martha's face as she looked at me from behind the bouquet.

"Let's just get me in this dress."

My dress was thrown on in a rush, and I forgot to check myself in the mirror before we clattered down the stairs and into the street to get a taxi. Later, in the professional photographs, I was mortified to see that half of my breasts were falling over the top of the corset in two unseemly lumps as I walked down the aisle.

As I doze in the Manarola apartment, I chide myself. Are you obsessing? Come on, think of something happy. But wait, my mind insists, remember that therapy session? And down the rabbit hole I go.

This therapy session after the wedding had high stakes for me. I needed it to broach the subject of my disappointment about the wedding with Darrell. But I was scared. Who wants to tell their new spouse that they were disappointed at the wedding? But then I thought, if I don't share how I felt left out in the cold and ask what behavior on my part caused him to withdraw and be obstructive, then this same kind of thing could keep happening.

I was still sure we could come together as a team. I believed he could be my man. There were times when he still had the impossibly kind eyes and earnest voice. I could learn to bring that out in him more. Growing up, I'd received the idea that women were bossy and critical and that men were long-suffering because of it. So I was pretty sure that most of the problem lay with me.

There was a family narrative about my mother's female relatives, the Isherwoods, that went like this: "There is no privacy with your grandmother. She rearranges my T-shirt drawer!" "Your great aunt is so bossy, she backseat drives like crazy. Don't get in a car with her or you'll be sorry."

Growing up, I was ill at ease when I heard my female ancestors being referred to as bossy. When I was a teenager, I was told, "You're so Isherwood." I knew that the label had stuck well into my twenties because it had been applied to me when my sister and her boyfriend had visited me in Colorado. He had wanted to see a particular town, and when I'd offered to show him where it was on a map, his reply was, "Don't be such an Isherwood."

Sometimes I got the impression that I was bossy by default, even if I'd said nothing, like the time when my mom and I were doing a video project and my dad walked in unexpectedly. My mother asked him not to come in because we were filming. I remained silent. Then my brother also walked in, and my father called out, "Watch out! They're being bossy!"

These warnings that I heard periodically, I translated as, "Watch out! A woman might devour you!" I began to think I was fatally flawed—flawed from being in a line of bossy women who had marched down from that British isle and into my prepubescent blond head in California.

Even if I set the Isherwood narrative aside, I had surely screwed up. Had I even explained to Darrell what would feel supportive to me as we began to plan the wedding? After all, I was his first real relationship. He just didn't know.

I went to the therapy appointment full of resolution. I was going to be vulnerable. In a gentle way, I was going to share what hurt my feelings. I was going to ask him to share what I did that made him withdraw. The therapist would help us open our hearts and explain to each other what we needed, and we'd come out stronger.

At the therapist's office, Darrell sat at the other end of the couch from me. As I began to explain what I hoped to get out of the session, I wanted to hold his hand, but he seemed out of reach in more ways than one.

"He doesn't seem to want to have my back. I feel left out in the cold," I said.

The therapist turned to Darrell, asking for his reply.

"She has to fight her own battles. I don't want to have to do that for her," he said.

"I've *been* fighting my own battles," I said. "I don't shrink from doing that. What I want is to feel a genuine energy of supporting each other."

"Yes." The therapist nodded and turned to Darrell. "Show her that you have her back. It doesn't mean she's not going to fight alongside of you. But you don't abandon her if she's surrounded by arrows."

Darrell stated flatly, "I don't get it. I don't relate to that."

"Can you give an example, Chandi, to help him see what you're talking about?"

I nervously began to give an example from the wedding. Worrying that I would be told I was wrong, I softened the example, not giving the full brunt of how it made me feel.

But I was only halfway there when Darrell said, "I ban any discussion of the wedding."

I looked frantically at the therapist. *Tell me I didn't just hear this.* I was afraid to take a breath.

"If he has banned it, there's nothing I can do about it," the therapist said.

"Oh." The word escaped in a small gasp. I felt like a ladybug shut in a jar, unable to get enough air.

I walk to the patio of my Manarola apartment and do the foot exercises for plantar fasciitis, telling myself to fling these downer memories over the cliff.

Manarola doesn't have a place to check e-mail, so I take the five-minute train ride to Monterosso. At the internet café, a young Italian guy with carefully coifed hair and an expensive watch asks, "Why would you walk to Rome when you can take a train?"

It was the exact question Chatterbox had asked. "Um, there are spiritual reasons for walking."

"Silly," he says, waving his hand dismissively. He responds in English no matter how capable my Italian is.

I check my e-mail quickly and then head to the beach. I don't want to walk much; I am aware of the need to stay off my feet. But a swim would be lovely, even if it's raining lightly.

The lounges on the curving beach are empty due to the rain, but the promenade is full of people eating gelato, pushing strollers, buying trinkets. I pass a man selling apricots from a truck, and I'm tempted to buy some. Instead, I turn onto the beach.

The rain lets up, and although clouds block the sun, I strip to my bikini and set my clothes on a dry patch of a lounge chair. In the slightly cold water, I have to urge myself to walk all the way in.

After swimming alone in the dark sea, I huddle on the lounge, watching children dig in the sand and contemplating the e-mails I'd received. New responses had come in regarding my feet: Get a tennis ball and roll your feet on it. Avoid asphalt. Consider coming home and doing the pilgrimage another time. A message from a German woman suggested I skip the part between Aulla and Lucca. "It's all on the periphery of cities, and it's all asphalt," she wrote.

A young Italian man speaking English interrupts my thoughts. "Miss, you have to pay for this lounge if you want to stay."

"I'm sorry. It was empty due to the rain. No attendant."

"Yes, well, it's stopped raining now."

I pull my shorts over my wet suit and walk across the brown beach.

The last time I'd been in the Cinque Terre in the rain was when Darrell and I lived in Florence and some of my family and cousins were visiting. We'd taken them to the Cinque Terre in March, and at the end of a cloudy hiking day, it started to rain. We were in Cornelia and decided to trot down the long staircase to the train station and train back to Manarola instead of walking.

The temperature dropped, and as we waited on benches in the deserted station, I noticed how my cousin wrapped his arms around his girlfriend to keep her warm. I hoped Darrell would do the same, but he didn't. Everyone was tired, cold, and hungry, and I felt responsible. It was my Italy I was showing them. Why was the train not coming? Trains usually came through these towns every ten minutes. I perked up when Darrell said he'd walk back to look at the timetable.

He returned eating a bar of chocolate and made no pronouncement about the timetable. "I didn't look at it," he said.

"You didn't look at it?" I asked, my frustration showing. That moment became tangled with the other times he had said he would do something and then didn't. It became tangled with the fact that we'd been in Italy six months, and he'd not yet done laundry or cooked a meal. I had said nothing, worried that I'd appear bossy and critical. But those things now rose in me like a swarm of wasps. "Why, why can't you be helpful?"

He chewed his chocolate bar, his eyes expressionless, looking through me.

"Stop! I hate it when you do that," a family member said sharply to me.

I'd done it. I'd enacted the fatal flaw. I'd sucked the life out of my husband by wanting him to look at the train schedule and being sharp with him when he'd not done it.

In that moment, I realized how much I wanted a family member to really see me, to look deeper, to offer a safe place for me to talk about my unhappiness with Darrell.

I cried all night at the apartment in Manarola while the rain gnashed its teeth against the roof tiles. All night long I told myself to get up and sneak out of the apartment, get on a train, and take it all the way down to Sicily. The urge to escape was consuming.

I will train to Sicily, I repeated to myself. *And in the morning, I'll keep going, get on a boat to Malta, and then one to Tunisia. I'll paint my face blue and walk and walk and walk across the desert until I either die or get my joy back.*

But if I had done that, there would have been all the proof in the world that I really was whacko. That I'd left my husband, who people saw as the kindest man, in a bizarre fit. So I held myself back from running to the station in the dark and dolorous rain.

There were so many shades to the Cinque Terre: Here at the carefree age of twenty, before I'd ever been truly in love. Here with Diego, a great love. Here during a painful time in my marriage.

And now, here as a divorcée on a pilgrimage.

TWENTY-SEVEN

The Most Fly-in-Amber Little Town

Following the advice in the German woman's e-mail, I take the train to Lucca. I hate to miss towns like Pietrasanta and Massa Carrara, but my feet hurt more than I care to admit. At the same time, I'm unwilling to take the advice of the person who suggested I go home and postpone the pilgrimage.

Since I'm not walking into Lucca, I think about Hilaire Belloc, an Anglo-French writer, who did. He walked from France to Rome in 1901 and wrote a book about it titled *A Path to Rome*. In it, he mentions his arrival in Lucca after walking through the Garfagnana Mountains.

> Then, it being yet but morning, I entered from the north, the town of Lucca, which is the neatest, the regularest, the exactest, the most fly-in-amber little town in the world, with its uncrowded streets, its absurd fortifications, and its contented silent houses—all like a family at ease and at rest under its high sun. . . Everything in Lucca is good. [v]

It's a cliché, of course, to say that Lucca is heartbreakingly beautiful. When I'm in Florence, I say the same thing. But how I love Lucca on this trip!

Entering Lucca's huge walls through the Porta San Pietro, I follow my nose to the Via Fillungo. I remember the left turn into Via degli Angeli where the B&B San Frediano is. I had stayed there nine years ago. Ilenia, the young manager who responded to my call earlier, had cheerily offered a pilgrim discount.

Wandering Lucca's narrow cobbled streets on a sunny, quiet June day delights me. The people of Lucca languidly pedal past me down the shady side of the street, without helmets. The shop windows sport inviting displays of Tuscan products. I admire the amber-hued Vin Santo bottles on top of old wine barrels, the packages of biscotti, the luscious green olive oil of Lucca (considered one of the best), and baskets full of old-style straw-covered *fiaschi* of red wine.

Lured by the scent of aged cheeses and prosciutto, I enter a cheese shop. There, gigantic yellow rounds of parmigiano are stacked three feet high. On top of them are rounds of pecorino. Labels stuck in their sandy-colored sides state *stagionato* and *semi-stagionato*. On shelves, smaller white rounds of cheese are stacked between jars of olives in a precise pattern. I note *accasciato* cheese from the Garfagnana with its reddish-colored rind.

"Che bel negozio!" (What a beautiful store!) I say to the signora.

"You speak Italian so well," she says after chatting with me. "Particularly for an American."

"I miss shops like this," I tell her.

"You should move here and marry an Italian! Are you married already?"

I have never said the words in Italian, *sono divorziata*. I have to push them out.

The signora doesn't miss a beat. "That's perfect then! You can marry an Italian!" I smile and buy a small piece of accasciato, even though I want a very large piece.

Bidding her a *buona giornata*, I make my way to the farmacia that Ilenia recommended for buying arch supports. Apparently, the squishy, expensive inserts I'd bought in Pontremoli aren't the right solution for plantar fasciitis.

"Are you really walking all the way to Rome?" the pharmacy clerk asks incredulously.

"Well, I'm going to try," I reply with a smile.

A shopper joins the conversation and states, "But you're not alone."

"Yes, I'm doing it alone."

"Coraggiosa!" she and the signora both exclaim.

"Do you mind if I try on these arch supports?" I ask, knowing my shoes are dirty.

"No problem, go ahead!"

I buy them and then wander up the Via Fillungo. A wine bar called Vinarkia draws me in. It has two wide doors open to the street, black-and-white photos of 1950s Italy, quaint wooden tables, no other patrons, and the loveliest girl behind the counter.

I take a stool at the bar and chat with the lovely girl, telling her she has a *faccia stupenda* (beautiful face). A song in French by Edith Piaf wafts out the doors and into the street. A woman bicycles past with a cherub-faced baby in her basket. German men with long legs stroll by carrying toddlers on their shoulders.

I want to run a wine bar in Italy.

If I worked here, one day my man would walk in. I'd serve him a glass of Tignanello, and within a week, we'd be traveling to the Island of Elba together.

Two men enter and warmly greet the beautiful girl. One is the owner, the other an Iranian doctor. Immediately, she introduces me to them as a pilgrim. They ask if they can sit with me and hear about the pilgrimage. We move to a table, and the owner brings out his laptop to proudly show the doctor and me photos of his daughter, born the day before. "Do you have children?" he asks me.

"No, I forgot. And then it was too late," I spontaneously reply, and they both laugh. The doctor asks the reason for my pilgrimage, and I tell him about my burst appendix.

"It's really amazing you lived," he says. And then he says something that plagues me later that night. "The appendix shouldn't have burst, there must have been a lot of missteps."

"You must be Catholic if you're doing the Via Francigena," the owner adds.

"I'm not, exactly," I reply lamely.

"But you *must be* Catholic if you're doing this!" the Iranian doctor insists.

Suddenly, I feel ridiculous, an imposter. I try to explain that when I went around the world in my twenties, I focused on absorbing the good in all the religions I encountered.

"God saved you when your appendix burst, so you're walking to Rome as a promise to God," the Iranian offers.

Walking back to the B&B, I ponder his statement. If God had saved me, why would he have let my appendix burst and sepsis rage through my organs in the first place? If I had prayed to God instead of taking the ambulance to the hospital, it's unlikely I'd be alive. When does God enter one's life? Is it when one has nothing left?

The darn fastidio in my feet keeps me awake, and worry sets in. And then the Iranian doctor's statement about missteps rolls over in my brain, causing me to recount the steps leading up to it.

The day after I arrived in Florence, I was walking to the Cascine Park with Sydney. She had a part in an outdoor play at an American July Fourth event. It was god-awful hot. In the full clutches of jet lag, I struggled to stand upright, never mind walk.

The heat from the pavement seared through my thin sandals. My hair felt like a wet bunch of straw on my neck. I wished I'd worn a sun hat. At the park, I conked out on a bench. But after a short rest, not wanting to be a party pooper, I walked around with Sydney.

We came upon the food area where bags of burgers and chicken pieces from a popular American fast food chain were being handed out. In this gastronomic capital, the Americans had chosen *this* for their July Fourth event? But I accepted a bag of the greasy food that I'd never before eaten.

"How bad can it be?" I said to Sydney as we sat down with a group of her friends at a table. The burger, in fact, tasted okay. But when I bit into a chicken piece, I wanted to spit it out. It was disgusting.

Every ounce of my intuition told me to spit it out, but that meant abruptly leaving the table and walking through the crowds to find privacy. Not heeding my intuition, I ate it. Late that night, we returned to Sydney's apartment. Ecstatic about going to the beach with Sydney at Castiglione della Pescaia the next morning, I packed my beach bag before going to sleep on her couch. Very early, something woke up me, and it wasn't excitement. There was a terrible pain somewhere below my chest and above my stomach.

Feeling the need to throw up, I got out of bed, walked to the bathroom, and placed my hands on the sink edge. I didn't feel myself falling. I didn't feel the crash of my head on the hard tile floor. I had no idea how long I was passed out before I regained consciousness. I looked up at Sydney and Antonio standing over me, calling my name, and I wondered where I was and who the hell they were.

I threw up all morning, feverish and in pain. But I kept telling Sydney that any minute, it would all be out of my system, and we'd still make it to Castiglione della Pescaia. By afternoon, Antonio called a doctor. It was Sunday. The doctor made a house visit and proclaimed it a virus. Through my feverish haze, I saw heads nodding in agreement.

"People always pick up bugs on airplanes these days," someone said.

The next day, I was no longer feverish and the pain had subsided, although I had an odd knotted feeling somewhere in my organs. Sydney went to work. I spent the day lying on the bed in the stifling heat, a fan aimed at me.

What had been the fateful misstep? The fact that I'd not wanted to go to Santa Maria Nuova?

When Sydney called to check on me, I told her that although I felt a bit better, an odd pain persisted, which didn't seem congruent with having a virus.

"It might be wise to call the doctor, just to ask if these symptoms still sound like a virus," I said. "He must have left his card, right?"

"No," Sydney said. "He didn't. We really should get you to urgent care at Santa Maria Nuova. I'm worried about you."

"I don't know, yeah, I'm maybe being too stoic."

Clicking off the phone, I curled on the bed in a daze, and before I fell asleep I wondered how I'd get down the steep stairs from the apartment and walk through the inferno of a city to get myself to Santa Maria Nuova. Plus the hospital freaked me out. Ex-pats called Santa Maria Nuova a Frankenstein place. Amazingly, it had been operating in Florence since the Middle Ages. In fact, Beatrice Portinari's father (the Beatrice with whom Dante Alighieri was in love) had founded it in 1288. And there was my friend's story about being in a hospital in Rome. She'd gone in for stomach pain. They'd put an IV in her arm and left her on a dirty cot for hours. Everyone else in the room was worse off than her. She had walked around the room pulling the apparatus that held her IV as she gave attention to the other patients. No nurses were heeding their moans and cries.

If I only had a virus, did I really want to be trapped in a scene like that?

When Sydney came home from work, I tried to eat something with her. We talked about going to a pool the next day. I'd be better by then.

But then I tried to pee and I couldn't. Oddly, I told Sydney I'd be able to pee if I could squat on a bucket. I was in more pain than I cared to admit, and as I sat doubled over on that red bucket, I had one of those surreal moments when you know something that you shouldn't technically know. I understood that my organs were shutting down.

That's when Sydney called an ambulance.

In the B&B in Lucca, I finally fall asleep. Hours later, I awaken with a start and sit up in the middle of the bed, crying hard. I'm shocked by how forcibly the trauma has been reignited. It's been eleven months! How long does trauma stay in the body?

I e-mail a friend back in Colorado to ask him. Apart from my sister, he is the only person I can think of who has had emergency surgery for a life-threatening situation. Knowing my sister is struggling daily, I don't want to worry her. My friend's message back only asks if I'm okay.

In fact, yes. Because I'm in Lucca, the place where "everything is good," as Hilaire Belloc said.

Ilenia suggests I rest up another day, and she offers me a free night. I accept her offer. I'm boosted by the generosity. The generous Italian spirit will keep me going.

Churches should be a good antidote to a night of relived trauma, I think, as I make a morning plan. Lucca is called *la città delle cento chiese*, the city of one hundred churches. Some of the churches, with their connection to Saint Fredianus (San Frediano), directly relate to the Via Francigena. Saint Fredianus, of Irish origin, made a pilgrimage on the Via Francigena to Rome in the sixth century, after which, he took up the life of a hermit in Lucca. Pope John III subsequently elected him bishop of Lucca. During his episcopate, he founded the monastery of San Frediano, and Lucca became a stop for pilgrims—particularly Irish ones—on the ancient Via Francigena.

I head to the Church of San Frediano, consecrated by Pope Eugene III in 1147. On its façade is a beautiful Byzantine mosaic depicting the Ascension of Christ. I wander through its cool interior, noting the impressive baptismal font and the tomb of Saint Zita. She lived in the thirteenth century and was mentioned by Dante in the *Divine Comedy*. According to legend, she was a noble family maid who got caught stealing bread from the kitchen to give to the poor. When asked what she was carrying, she said flowers. Upon investigation, the bread had miraculously turned into flowers. Apparently, Saint Zita worked miracles in her afterlife too. Stories from the Middle Ages attest to miraculous healings for those who prayed in front of her tomb.

The priest stamps my pilgrim passport, and then I make my way to the other side of town, to the Cathedral of San Martino. The current cathedral is modeled on an earlier version, which is believed to have been founded by Saint Fredianus. This version was consecrated in 1070 by Pope Alexander II, formerly the bishop of Lucca.

The bas-reliefs over the entrance doors catch my attention. One depicts a woman in what appears to be a hospital bed with men surrounding her—doctors, presumably. It's as if my own experience in an Italian hospital is depicted on this church. I take a photo of it to remember that my life was saved in Italy.

Although much of the interior is crowded with scaffolding, I can still admire the Gothic stained glass windows, especially the one representing Saint Zita. It depicts her as a dark woman, seemingly Middle Eastern. Her long purple robe falls to her bare feet. At her waist is a scarf filled with flowers. I love her dark face, the contrast of her purple robe with the red flowers in her scarf, and her bare feet. These attributes make her seem like a primordial earth goddess full of summer sun, abundance, and strong femininity—like Gaia herself.

After getting my pilgrim passport stamped in San Martino, I walk back up the Via Fillungo and stop in at a bar for a *caffè macchiato*. I wait as two German couples with six young blond children place their order. When the two families are ready to leave, the proprietor calls to them. "Wait!" He collects six lollipops and gives them to the kids. Everyone's eyes light up, and I again witness the Italian spirit of generosity.

That evening, I return to Vinarkia, remembering how inviting it was during happy hour the night before. I order a lemon soda and the owner greets me as if I'm a regular customer. When it comes time to pay, he says, *"Va bene così, un regalo."* (A gift.)

As I prepare for bed, I'm full of the warmth of the people I've met in Lucca. Ilenia at the B&B, the signora in the farmacia, and the wine bar owner. They all expressed a genuine interest in my pilgrimage. I go to bed happy to have had two days in "the most fly-in-amber little town in the world."

TWENTY-EIGHT

The Race Is Not to the Swift

The streets of Lucca are drowsy—quiet except for the sounds of a street cleaning truck. I make my way toward the huge walls and pass a sign for a cooking school. When Darrell and I had lived in Florence, he'd made plans to offer cooking classes to tourists. He wasn't a cook, but he was going to be a middleman. Thinking it might be useful for Darrell, my business associate Angelo—who managed an elegant hotel in Florence—offered to take Darrell and me to the opening of a cooking school that a friend of his was launching.

As we stood by a table of appetizers, Angelo suggested we go out to dinner with him and his wife after the event. I happily accepted, but when Angelo turned away to greet friends, Darrell sternly said, "We are not eating out until you make more money, Chandi."

A black stain of "I'm not good enough" prevented me from responding. "There are lots of ways you could be making more money with your business, but you're just not doing it," he continued. I sensed anger below the surface of his voice.

"Please, not here," I said as Angelo came toward us. I formed my face into something bright as best I could and tried to hear what Angelo was saying, but the tension between Darrell and me pounded too loudly in my ears. I was sure Angelo could hear it too. Mortification clapped shut like a cage around me.

I take a big breath as I exit Lucca's immense walls. A cascade of things I want to do better next time rain into my mind so quickly that I struggle to sort through them. Gregg had referred to a divine balance. When I had some sessions with Gregg during the divorce, he'd said I had attracted a man with weakened masculine energy. It seemed to have started with my fear from the stalking.

"You've not found a balance," Gregg said. "In choosing guys who feel safe, you choose ones who aren't in their masculine."

"In their masculine?" I rolled the words around my head, sensing that a door was unlocking.

"There are different types of masculine, and there's one in the middle, where the guy is in his healthy masculine. That's what you didn't understand. You decided that if a man was very masculine, he had the potential to become aggressive, dangerous. So you jumped to the other extreme and chose men who weren't in their masculine at all."

"Oh."

He was so right—so goddamn right.

"Plus you developed a coping energy that was masculine," Gregg added. "And a woman who has strong masculine energy will attract, and be attracted to, a wobbly man—one with weakened masculine energy. Then your masculine energy comes up and tries to save the day."

Saving the day. This role had become so normal for me over the years—like what I did about Darrell's aborted business ideas.

On our first trip to Italy, Darrell had gotten the idea to start a business buying the large handcrafted leather albums that are prevalent in Florence and selling them in the US. He brought boxes of them home with a plan to find stores that would buy them.

If my husband was going to start a business that was related to my favorite place in the world, how cool would that be? I spent weeks planning with him, helping design the website, and brainstorming names for the business.

But the beautiful albums remained in our closet. Month after month. He stopped talking about the idea and became reticent when I asked about it. I couldn't imagine leaving all those huge embossed leather albums in our closet. Could I help? Would he like me to go with him to the stores? He shrugged and said nothing.

I tried again in a week. "The albums are so gorgeous, we can find a buyer. We don't want to leave them in our closet, do we?" I offered to find stores for us to go to in Denver. "I'll make a list of them. We can go this Saturday."

He acquiesced, but in the first store, he placed himself behind me and didn't say anything to the proprietor. I wasn't comfortable being the only one to talk, but I tried my best to be an enthusiastic salesperson.

As we left the store, Darrell said, "That's not the way you do sales."

"But I'm not a salesperson. You're the one with training in it," I protested. I asked him to show me how it's done as we went into the next store. But again he said nothing, and I was obliged to do the talking. The albums were never sold.

"Do other women in your family do this?" Gregg asked.

"Way overboard caretaking? Oh God, yes! This is what women in my family do. Don't cut your losses and move on. No. Stay and keep rescuing." My breath and words came quickly. "That's probably why I kept plowing on with Darrell when I was already unhappy, even at the wedding."

"Chandi, you are so used to saving the day and having no one at your back, but it doesn't have to be like that. To choose a man who has your back doesn't mean you're not capable on your own. It's a divine balance."

Divine balance? Like Shiva and Shakti?

I'd bought a Tibetan tanka painting of Shiva and Shakti with limbs intertwined on my first trip to Nepal, and I had hung it in all the places I'd lived for the past twenty years. I'd obviously not learned the painting's message.

He's right, I think, as I walk along the side of the road. Relaxing into my feminine with a man doesn't mean I'm not empowered. I try to imagine it. How would it feel? Like Sierra granite that holds up a pine tree so it reaches higher toward the light? Like a ship that supports the figurehead of a woman as she opens her heart over the sea?

A car comes to a stop and a woman about my age jumps out. She runs over to me. "Are you a pilgrim to Rome?"

"*Sì.*" I lean on my poles at the road's edge.

"For cultural or spiritual reasons?" she asks quickly, with an eager voice.

"A bit of both," I reply, relieved she hasn't asked specifically about my religious persuasion.

She points to the sky and says, "*Ti vedo lassù.*" (I'll see you up there.) And then she scuttles back to her idling car.

Capannori is six kilometers (3.72 miles) from Lucca. It takes me two hours to get there, and it's all on asphalt. Without plantar fasciitis and without a pack, I would have done that distance in half the time. My slow progress reminds me of the fable of the tortoise and the hare. Identifying with the plodding but successful tortoise makes me feel slightly better.

A biblical line seems to drop from the sky: "The race is not to the swift, nor the battle to the strong." I'm not a swift pilgrim, and my body does not feel strong. Yet these are not crucial attributes in spiritual traditions.

My body almost cannot bear to have this pain in my feet— daily pain again so soon after last summer. But this is the trial I must walk through.

I'm okay, I'm okay, I'm okay.

Soon after Capannori, I can't continue. I find a bus stop and manage to comprehend from the weatherworn schedule that a bus for Altopascio will come in an hour. I sit on a patch of grass and eat the bread and cheese I'd bought in Lucca the day before.

During the bus ride, I'm astounded by how far we travel to reach Altopascio. *I could never have walked all this way.*

The free accommodation in Altopascio is listed as a *palestra comunale.* I know *palestra* means gym, but what's a communal gym? A basketball court with tents in it?

The streets are crowded with market stalls and knots of people. I edge toward the shade, my skin prickling. I find my way to the library, where I need to check in. A young librarian stamps my pilgrim passport and says to wait for her colleague, who will take me to the palestra. She lets me use a computer.

I welcome the opportunity to check e-mail. It makes me feel less alone. Besides, the library is cool and quiet. I open an e-mail from my mother. My eyes tear as I read the first sentence: "Your sister is back in hospital."

I scan the e-mail, hoping to find something reassuring, but my mind only registers distressing fragments: extreme sudden bleeding, passed out, urgent care, transfusion, a pill with a camera. My vision blurs, and I turn from the screen to fumble in my pack for a Kleenex.

The last time something similar happened, I was also in Italy. When Darrell and I lived in Florence, I'd received the news that my sister had colon cancer. That was spring. She appeared to be recovering well by summer, after her surgery, but on a certain day before Christmas, I was prompted by a premonition, and I called my parents' house. My dad answered and said they were rushing out the door to take her to the hospital.

I considered taking a last-minute flight to California, but airfare prices were prohibitively high. For the week leading up to Christmas, I was anxious about my sister and increasingly aware of my unhappiness in my marriage. But I resolved to make an effort for Christmas Eve. On the morning of December 24, I pulled myself together, looked up what Italians eat for Christmas Eve, and went to the market. Fish, apparently, was the thing to eat. The fishmonger suggested *nasello*. I looked dubiously at the whole fish with its head and tail intact and then bought it.

I walked back to the apartment with the nasello, imagining how Darrell and I could laugh together as we figured out how to cook a fish with a gaping mouth and glassy eyes that stared at us. I pictured us drinking wine, cooking together, and managing to feel festive.

Darrell stayed at the computer while I cooked the fish by myself. I wanted him to notice my effort, to help me cope with my anguish about my sister, and to realize the best thing to do on our lonely Christmas Eve was to be together. But he remained at the computer—as unreachable as if he was in Siberia. Emptiness stung my soul.

My mind is brought back to the present when a group of children come into the library full of chatter. The librarian hushes them, and I manage to write a response to my mother just before a young man comes to escort me to the palestra.

We walk a few blocks and enter a nondescript building. Up a flight of stairs and down a hallway, he shows me to a small room with two narrow beds and a table. He tells me a male pilgrim who is biking the route is in the next room. Across the hall, I notice a dining room of sorts with folding tables and plastic chairs. The garbage is overdue to be dumped. If a gym exists, I don't see it. Perhaps it's downstairs, or perhaps palestra comunale means something else entirely.

The shower down the hall is bruised by grime, so I opt out of a shower and wonder instead how to relieve the pain in my feet. There's no ice. I lie on a cot with my feet up on a table. As I rest, my mind goes back to my sister. I wonder if having children helped her, mentally, to get through the traumatic hospitalizations.

During my hospital stay in Florence, I'd wondered who to hang on to in my mind for comfort. Having children would have provided the image I needed.

The most fascinating book talk I'd ever been to was given by Beck Weathers, who had been left for dead while hiking in a horrendous, and subsequently famous, storm on Everest. With his brain mostly shut down and much of his body frozen, he had summoned up the image of his kids needing him, and against all odds, he stood up and walked through a blinding storm to miraculously find the tents.

I had no children, and I was raised without God. These two things had never been a problem until I was in the Italian hospital, experiencing physical pain beyond anything I had ever imagined.

A few weeks into my hospitalization, I received a call from my Unitarian minister friend. She told me that her children had been asking when I was coming back. Back home, whenever they saw me, they'd shout my name and run toward me with outstretched arms. When I held that image in my mind's eye, I knew I'd get better, I would go home, and they would run toward me with outstretched arms, shouting my name.

As I fall asleep, I picture my sister with her two children in a garden. Then I think of Saint Zita in Lucca, and I envision her in the same garden. She tosses flowers from her apron, and my sister and her boys catch them.

TWENTY-NINE

Divided Memories

I've walked three kilometers out of Altopascio along the edge of a busy road that's frequented mostly by truckers, and already my body aches. As I stop near a field looking for a place to pee, my mind is in contortions. Why the heck didn't I do a spa vacation instead?

Abruptly, my tangled thoughts disappear as I notice a man in the field about twelve yards away beating off.

"You're freaking disgusting!" I want to shout, but I don't.

Instead, without allowing myself to pee, I go back to hugging the white line at the road's edge under the eyes of the passing truck drivers.

A few minutes later, two Belgian pilgrims quickly walk up behind me. Thank God! After the gross behavior I just witnessed, I welcome the idea of walking with others.

But the Belgians don't share my enthusiasm. The woman marches brusquely by. Her man slows and quietly says hello, but I have to pick up my pace to walk with him. He says they've walked from Lucca that morning, leaving at six.

Oh my, it's only 10:00 a.m. All that distance in four hours! They must be walking at five times my pace. The woman is way ahead already, marching in her big hiking boots down the highway like a Roman legionnaire off to conquer Gaul.

We come to a junction where the route leaves the highway and continues on a historic Roman road. My directions call it a magnificent ancient Roman road. To my surprise, the Belgians choose not to take it.

Me? I'm not staying on that highway if I have a chance to get off it. I step onto flat, wide, black stones. Trees touch one another overhead; grasses and earth cover most of the stones. It is cool, green, and silent.

At the end of the Roman road, there's a marble plaque set into an ivy-covered stone wall. Inscribed on it is part of a poem by the Italian poet Giovanni Pascoli.

Walking the 25.3 kilometers (15.7 miles) to San Miniato is beyond my capabilities. I have gone twelve kilometers (7.4 miles), which seems to be my maximum. My arch supports are sliding around, failing to provide the support I need. Duct tape would keep them in place, and I used to travel with it, but I didn't this time.

It occurs to me that it's not normal for me to get up and immediately exercise. I'd love to be like friends of mine who, at five every morning, rain or shine, go on a run. But I'm not. If I don't absolutely have to get up early, my desire to sleep longer always wins. My best morning is a leisurely one when I don't have to rush off anywhere.

I have some hiking in my background: backpacking in the Sierras and trekking in Nepal in my twenties. More recently, in my first years in Colorado, I'd snowshoed with a pack into huts at eleven thousand feet, sometimes in a blizzard—albeit with people who knew mountaineering well. But when the concept of the pilgrimage had wafted romantically into my head, I'd not had a clear image of what it meant to get up early *every* morning and get on the road *first thing* to walk for hours, often without breakfast.

The twelve kilometers brings me to a town called Ponte a Cappiano where I find a bus to San Miniato Basso. When I arrive at the accommodation, called the Misericordia of San Miniato Basso, I'm shown to a room containing four single beds, two of which are occupied by the Belgian couple.

The man gives me a quiet hello as the woman comes out of the bathroom with a towel around her. I want to engage her somehow, but when I ask if the shower is good, she gives a tight-lipped one-word affirmative in Flemish.

Even though it's not far from Florence, I've never visited the hill town of San Miniato Alto. Its history is rich, and after a shower, I find the minibus that loops between the *basso* (low) and *alto* (high) parts of the town.

Like many small Tuscan towns, San Miniato Alto was colonized by the Romans. Centuries later, Saint Francis of Assisi traveled to San Miniato on his way home from Pisa and founded a convent there in 1211. By then, the town had become an important stop on the Via Francigena.

Fast forward to World War II, when in July of 1944, San Miniato came under siege due to clashes between the Germans who controlled the city and the partisans who were assisting the advancing American army. The Germans had rigged the village houses with mines, causing much of the town's population to flee. On the morning of July 22, they locked the remaining citizens in the cathedral. An explosion and a collapsed column inside the cathedral killed fifty-six people. This kind of setup—herding a village population to one location—usually preceded a massacre, so the villagers first believed that the Germans had placed a time bomb in the church. Later, evidence pointed to an American shell hitting the cathedral.

In 1954, a plaque was placed on the outside wall of San Miniato's town hall commemorating the deaths. Yet, divided memories remained, and a debate continued. Historians revisited the incident, and a commission in 2004 stated that the bomb had indeed been American. An article I read by John Foot, a history professor in London, explained that a conclusion for how to deal with the divided memories was achieved by placing another plaque that respected the anti-fascist memories of those viewing the Germans as responsible for the war itself.

And so, only eleven months before my visit to San Miniato, a second plaque had been placed next to the first. The new one called for shared responsibility for the deaths. vi

Standing in front of the town hall and looking at the plaques, I begin to relate the concept of divided memory to my marriage. There was the feeling of caring for Darrell and the feeling of being disappointed in him. There were the red flags I saw, and there were my choices not to heed them, choosing instead to keep trying to create the marriage I had envisioned.

I wonder whether the two plaques, honoring two truths, had been cathartic for the citizens. It makes me think of how I'd often not felt confident in the marriage about speaking my truth. In my divorce support group, the facilitator had explained that speaking our truth is different from having an opinion. Opinions contain judgment, whereas our truth is how we feel. It's not about being right, it's about expressing our emotions in an authentic way. Every woman in the group admitted she'd never been able to confidently state her truth to her husband in her marriage.

Like the others, I had been hesitant to voice my truth in my marriage. A while after we got married Darrell told me that he didn't like French kissing. He said it so matter-of-factly that I was taken aback, not only by the news, but by the way he said it, as if he was saying he didn't like butter on his toast.

"But this is a big deal," I managed to say. "What about all the times—"

He jumped in with a quick, dismissive tone. "Oh, I did it because you seemed to like it."

My mind raced around the information like a cat around a ball of yarn, trying to unravel it. So he'd lured me into thinking he liked it before we got married? I felt cheated, duped, rejected. I didn't know which way to turn. I was angry, but I was also deflated. I felt almost unclean, as if there was something wrong with me, as if I wasn't worth kissing.

I didn't know where to begin with telling him how it made me feel, so I didn't begin. I felt ridiculous letting it drop, but I couldn't find a way to voice my truth.

As I walk away from the town hall, down the shady side of a narrow cobbled street, I wonder why so many women are reluctant to speak their truth. The phrase *the truth will set you free* comes to me. Did the plaques set the citizens of this town free from their conflicting memories? Will the pilgrimage relieve me of mine?

It's only five in the afternoon, and I'm starving. The restaurants won't be open for hours. I notice a *gelateria* and my body angles toward it, realizing I've not had a single gelato on this trip.

Instead of the fruit flavors I usually choose in the summer, I'm drawn to the yogurt one. Outside on a bench, I delve into its rich texture—almost like sinking into silk sheets.

I had talked to one of my doctors in the hospital about gelato as he ran an ultra sound device up and down my legs because of my swollen ankles and feet.

Over my distended stomach, I'd barely been able to make out my strangely swollen feet. *"I miei piedi sono gonfiati!"* (My feet are swollen!) I'd said to the doctor, realizing that I loved saying gonfiati—it's one of those wonderful Italian words that sound exactly like the thing that the word is for.

"*Sono gonfiati!*" I announced to the doctor a second time, just to hear the word.

Then we started talking about gelato.

"I guess you probably go to Vivoli," the doctor said.

"I like Gelateria Carabe," I replied.

"Where's that?"

"In Via Ricasoli. It's Sicilian and has the best pistachio and *mandorla*. And I also love the gelateria in Settignano."

"You know the one in Settignano?" The doctor turned from peering at my legs to look at me with a sparkle in his eyes.

"Yes! In summer, they have the best fruit flavors!"

I imagined what it would be like to go there instead of being in the hospital. I'd see if the same guy ran it, see what fruit flavors he had. Maybe he would tell me the plums weren't good this year but the peaches and apricots were. He would have only the flavors of the fruits in season. He'd talk to me about his gelato as if it were a work of Renaissance art, and I would soak up every word.

Here on the bench in San Miniato, I look across the street to a beautiful palazzo. Its façade is an improbably clean, creamy white, the same color as my gelato. Two rows of windows—four across with green shutters and flower boxes, each with bright pink blooms— add a burst of color across the façade. The town is so pretty that, for a moment, it's hard to imagine it crawling with armies, blotched by bombs, and strewn with rubble. And yet, the war always seems so close in Italy. I encounter reminders of it in most towns I visit.

I rise from the bench to return to the Misericordia to sleep early, without dinner. How important it must be for these people here, I muse as I walk in the quiet cobbled street, that their town has been a peaceful place for over fifty years now.

THIRTY

Education for Sanity

In Alberto's notes, the day's route is marked as *impegnativa* (challenging). It will be almost twenty-four kilometers (fifteen miles) from San Miniato to Gambassi Terme. Even in my twenties, when I was young and strong, I couldn't hike more than twelve miles with a backpack—and that was on soft trails with no plantar fasciitis.

Before taking the route out of San Miniato Alto, I decide to start the day with some spiritual sustenance by going into the Church of Santi Jacopo e Lucia. The man who checked me in yesterday told me it's worth seeing.

After the plain façade, the inside of the church is an eyepopper. It looks like a drawing room in a Renaissance palazzo with its mint green walls. Along the top fourth of the walls are frescoes, each one a square shape, contained by baroque cornices in white, giving the impression that a cake knife with frosting had been flicked along the top of each wall. The roof is unusual too. It's a trussed roof, but it's been whitewashed and painted in a light gray—a perfect ceiling for a shabby chic home.

I examine the Madonnas on the blue roof of the apse. My grandmother had a glass-blue Madonna statue that I inherited. She must have loved the churches in Italy. She had passed to me her tiny black-and-white photos from her trip to Florence in the 1930s, which I examined intently, trying to recognize streets, trying to imagine what her experience of Florence had been.

I wonder about my grandfather, who did not believe in God. Would he have sat with her in a church such as this had they visited Italy together? When pressed about his views, he stated that having a sense of the sacredness of life is key, and that nonreligious people can have this as much as religious people can. He found his sacredness of life in Bach's music, saying, "It satisfies my religious emotions without requiring me to assent to any propositions from which my intellect would revolt."

My grandmother was born in 1900 in Victorian England, the daughter of an Episcopalian minister. She became a passionate teacher during the progressive educational movement of the 1920s. The man she married was a renowned educator who was hired as the headmaster of Dartington Hall School in Devon at age thirty—a fact in our family lore that was akin to him winning the Nobel Prize. He codified his thoughts on education and pacifism in his book, *Education for Sanity,* which he wrote in reaction to the two world wars.[vii] He died before I was born, but when I arrived in Dartington as a nineteen-year-old backpacker, within minutes of meeting me, people there told me how he'd changed their lives. In the school archives, I read praise of him by the school's founder saying that in the school world, there wasn't another mind as creative, positive, or courageous as his.

My grandfather claimed Bertrand Russell among his closest friends. Russell, a prominent British political and social activist and one of the founders of analytic philosophy, sent his children to Dartington. He and my grandfather shared the same goals for education and for international cooperation and they shared the same despair about WWI.

My grandfather quoted Russell often—to the point of his students saying, "There is no God but Russell, and Curry is his prophet."

My grandmother regaled me with stories of her English childhood, of boarding during WWI, when food was scarce, and how, after divorcing my grandfather in 1940, she took the last boat out of Genoa bound for the United States. With her was my mother, age ten.

She told me how one of her sisters was traumatized after being forced to sleep in the underground passages of London's subway system while the Germans bombed the city. And how another sister, Margaret, never married because she was in love with Gerald Heard—a British intellectual who wrote thirty-eight books, including pioneering works on the evolution of consciousness—and who, my grandmother hinted, might not have been heterosexual. At any rate, Aunt Margaret and Gerald Heard had a real meeting of esoteric minds. Aunt Margaret wrote books too, with titles like *Searching for Meaning* and *Faith Without Dogma*. Because of the two world wars, she and Heard saw the world in crisis, a crisis of spirit. To them, the solution was to focus on the inner world, to evolve spiritually.

For my grandfather, the solution was education.

These thoughts about my ancestors make me feel much less alone. As I leave the church, I recognize that in the contemplative nature of walking each day, my mind scans my known world, looking for a sense of comfort, and it comes up with my ancestors. Just like the message I received in the Church of Santa Maria in Trastevere in Rome: *We have been here all along. You only have to turn to us.* And just like in ancient Rome where every woman had a Juno, a spirit of an ancestor who guided and protected her.

In the quiet streets I keep alert for an open grocery store, wanting to heed Alberto's warning about the lack of food shops and restaurants on the day's route. Happily, I see displays of colorful fruit and vegetables coming into view, stacked outside a small *alimentari* (foodshop).

The shop owner greets me warmly and slices salami and bread for me. I tell her I'd like some cherries, but I'm worried they will squish in my pack. She enthusiastically puts the cherries in a plastic container inside a puffed-up plastic bag. Then she ties a ribbon around the bag, leaving a length of it to tie to my pack. "You can hang them off your pack and they won't get squished!" she declares with a grin.

Touched by her effort, I head off in good spirits, following the directions out of town. I walk on a pleasant country road with infrequent traffic and leafy trees providing shade. After an hour, I turn onto a dirt track that runs next to some woods along the top of a hill. Already, my shoulders hurt. The fastidio in my feet is a constant problem. Not having found a way to stop the arch supports from sliding around, I experiment with a new approach.

I had been placing the arch supports on top of the slippery inserts, but they'd not stayed in place. And I'd thrown out the original inserts because a pilgrim shouldn't carry nonessentials. So my choice is to either use the squishy inserts and no arch supports or use the arch supports on their own. I opt for the latter and have support for my arches. They stay in place, too, but the rest of my feet have zero padding. This is not ideal, and darn it, why hadn't I hiked around San Miniato looking for duct tape? Perhaps it hadn't occurred to me because I'd wanted to relax with a gelato and go to bed.

Needing rest, I sit in the shade under a few pine trees. It's only 10:00, but I'm famished. I can't help it; I eat everything I bought at the store, down to the last crumb. This seems to be a pattern—starving by ten in the morning. I rise regretfully from my shady spot under the pines to confront the trail where the sun poises overhead like a hammer ready to pound me into the dust. I walk on the dirt trail, losing track of time and becoming too weary to look at the views.

Stumbling up the last bit of hill and crossing a narrow paved road, I plunk down on a low wall near a building. I figure I've arrived in Pieve a Coiano, a hamlet that Alberto's directions indicate is at 11.6 kilometers (7.2 miles). I don't see dwellings in Pieve a Coiano. The one building I see looks empty, more like a warehouse. But somewhere nearby is the parish Church of Coiano.

Sigeric had noted it on his pilgrimage in 990, but it wouldn't have been the one that stands today. That one was built in 1029. I should get up and find it, have a look at it. But I can't get off the wall.

Even if I were to hitchhike, I have no idea on which side of the road to stand because this road runs east and west, while Gambassi is south, through the fields beyond the warehouse.

Everything is quiet. I remain sitting. Weariness and hunger settle over my body. Ants move over my hand that's placed on the wall. I watch them absently. I have no idea how I'll go any further today. "No idea, no idea, no idea," I say to the ants.

A car pulls out from behind the warehouse. I suck in my breath. *Now or never.*

I slide off the wall, leaving my pack, and trot as best I can on my maimed feet toward the car. A lone male. Of course. Every ride thus far had been from a single male. But he looks nice and at least five years younger than me.

"I often encounter pilgrims here," he says to me as I set my pack in the backseat and get in beside him. "At this point on the day's route, they can't go any farther."

"Veramente?" I reply incredulously. After my encounter with the

marching Belgians, I was sure I was the most pathetic pilgrim ever to traverse the Via Francigena. I feel much better knowing that other pilgrims have crashed and burned in the same spot.

"I'm going to Castelfiorentino. From there you can get a bus to Gambassi Terme."

"Perfect. Thanks so much."

"I understand the Via Francigena is hard—harder than the Camino in Spain. My wife and I like to hike," he says.

"One challenging thing is that I often arrive in towns after the lunch hour, and you know, I can't cook myself a big American breakfast."

"Eating well is essential," he says emphatically.

"Yes. Where do you and your wife hike?"

"We hiked in Australia recently."

"You'd love Colorado, where I live."

"The Wild West." He smiles and does the gesture meaning *wonderful*—twisting an imaginary mustache with index and middle finger on the thumb, the other two fingers pointing up.

He pulls up in the town of Castelfiorentino. "That was a gigantic help," I say as I collect my pack. *Really gigantic.*

I merge into the crowds gathered for the Saturday market. Dodging market stalls and the North Africans with their tarps full of Gucci knockoffs, I arrive at the train station, where I see a *Punto Informazione.*

"There might be a bus to Gambassi across the bridge," the girl behind the information desk says with a shrug. Back outside under the bright sun, I make my way across a long bridge and see a large bus idling. Please let it be to Gambassi!

Moving as quickly as I can, I get to the front of the bus and, low and behold, it says Gambassi Terme. I climb the bus stairs in the nick of time. What a relief. I'm as thrilled to get on that bus as I would be to fly first class on Emirates.

My eyes get wide with astonishment as the bus climbs the hill—a very long, very steep hill—to Gambassi. And I wonder if the pilgrimage route stays on top of ridges so pilgrims aren't climbing such a momentous hill at the end of the day.

Off the bus, the first thing I see is a hotel. I walk straight in and ask about a room.

"Yes, we have a room. Thirty-five euro," the proprietor says.

Music to my ears.

She shows me up narrow stairs to a simple room—my own room *and* with its own *clean* bathroom. Heaven! Even better, a restaurant is attached to the hotel, and I've arrived in time for lunch. Jackpot!

I shower quickly and make a beeline for the restaurant patio, where I happily dive into a large pile of *garganelli con porro, pecorino e pepe*— egg pasta with leeks, pecorino cheese and pepper—a marvelous new experience.

More marvels await. I ask the proprietor if it might be possible to have a *bascinella con ghiaccio* (a tub with ice). Yes!

I sit in my hot room with my belly full and my feet in a tub of ice water for the first time since the plantar fasciitis began to afflict me. These are the best things in life: Garganelli con porro and a bascinella con ghiaccio.

THIRTY-ONE

No Chance or Accident

Leaving Gambassi by six in the morning is my earliest start yet. San Gimignano is my destination today, and I imagine it's about halfway between Fidenza and Rome.

I'd called the convent in San Gimignano the day before, and a nun had explained that they close daily from noon until three thirty in the afternoon, so I had made myself get up at five fifteen in an effort to arrive at the convent before noon.

A dirt track leads me down to a vale where vineyards in bright spring green spread around old stone barns. A sign, *Agriturismo La Torre*, points to an attractive stone farmhouse. Since the 1980s, it seems everyone and their uncle who owns a farmhouse in Tuscany has turned it into an agriturismo.

After climbing a hill out of the little valley, I follow an overgrown, narrow path through a field and into some woods. My steps are hesitant in these unfamiliar woods at seven in the morning. I imagine wild boar and vipers being active at this hour.

Poking my poles vigorously in front of me each time I take a step, I make it through the woods without incident. I then begin to climb a yellow hill. Toward the top, I instinctively look back and see a guy pushing a mountain bike up the hill toward me.

When he reaches me, we exchange greetings and begin to chat. An Italian from Milan, he has blue eyes and fair hair pulled into a ponytail. He says he's doing the pilgrimage alone and he has no photos of himself on the route. Would I take some? I take several as he bikes up the hill. Then he goes back to pushing his bike, and we walk together. At a fork in the trail, we are indecisive and chat about which trail to take. I notice how pleasant it is to decide with someone else. When we reach a paved road, he says ciao and takes off on his bike.

The shaded road brings me to a hamlet where red stone farmhouses with spruce-green shutters show off pink roses climbing up their sides. Through a gate is an inviting swimming pool. Alberto's directions indicate it's an agriturismo called Fattorie San Pietro.

In a few more kilometers, I arrive at the sanctuary of Pancole, *Santuario di Maria Santissima Madre della Divina Provvidenza* (Sanctuary of Maria, most saintly mother of divine providence). The loggia, with its white arches framing the green landscape, draws me in. I sit on the low wall between the arches next to the church and eat two bananas. It's not quite nine o'clock. I have time to visit the sanctuary and still get to San Gimignano before noon.

In the fifteenth century, a little temple had been on this spot containing Pier Francesco Fiorentino's fresco of the Virgin Mary and infant Jesus. Later on, the temple became covered with vines and, by the seventeenth century, no one knew it was there.

As the story goes, in 1668, the Virgin Mary appeared to Bartolomea Ghini, a young deaf-mute shepherdess, after which Bartolomea could hear and speak. The townspeople went to the spot of the apparition and miracle, cut back the vines, and found the little temple. After that, the first Sanctuary of Pancole was built in 1670 with the Virgin Mary fresco at its center. During WWII, the Germans destroyed the sanctuary, but the fresco remained intact. Another miracle. The sanctuary was rebuilt after the war.

At the high altar, I view the fresco. The Madonna is blond and has a fair complexion, thin arched brows, and a long narrow nose— as the Madonna was typically depicted by Florentine painters at the time. The blond baby Jesus is feeding from a breast that awkwardly pops out of the Madonna's robe, and which she holds in her right hand. It looks like a Christmas snowdrop cookie that she offers to her child.

Outside on the wall, I take off my shoes and stretch my legs along the wall. The garden, with its scent of jasmine and roses, is soothing. I feel a mesmerizing tranquility, like I did on the sea wall in Manarola.

In my twenties, I decided I wasn't good at being spiritual. When I was wandering around India with Ted, other travelers repeatedly asked us if we'd done a vipassana retreat.

"If we've been asked so many times, it must mean we need to do it," Ted eventually said.

I agreed, sensing that everything that happened in India had a heightened meaning. We joined a silent ten-day vipassana retreat outside of Jaipur. We were instructed not to read, write, or talk for a whole ten days. I had my own cell-like room in the women's quarters, while Ted stayed in another part of the compound in the men's quarters. We lined up silently for meals, our stainless steel plates outstretched, to receive lentils, rice, and bananas.

During the course of this retreat, I decided I was a failure at meditation. First, getting out of bed at four in the morning was nearly impossible. If I did make it to the meditation hall, I'd get my body into a semblance of the right position on a thin cushion with a wool blanket around me. And then I'd try to follow the instructions and stay awake, which I could do for five minutes or so if the swami kept talking. But if he left us to our own practice, I'd always fall asleep.

Then there were the distracting antics of a Canadian guy. As soon as he caught my eye one morning, he threw me a Canadian flag pin and winked. What was he thinking, flirting with me when I'm trying to be serious about meditation? Then I smiled back. Being thrown a Canadian pin was more entertaining than meditating.

Ted was a good boyfriend, solid, unflappable. He was an easygoing traveler and a great backpacker, strong as a Sherpa. Once when we were hiking in the Dolomites, I couldn't get down a scree-covered slope without taking off my pack. I was mortified because it was the first time I'd not been able to carry my pack. But with ease and grace, Ted hoisted it to his shoulder and carried it down the mountain along with his own pack.

Ted came from an unbroken family and had no discernible baggage. I met him when I was twenty-two, once I was back in Santa Cruz after living in Florence and London and roaming around India and Nepal. We stayed together for six years.

Those years of my twenties, I was hippie-dippy, and Ted fit that. But when I was twenty-seven, I started spending summers in Italy as a group leader for a cross-cultural exchange organization. The first summer I had twelve sixteen-year-old girls.

One night in a medieval Tuscan town with them, I realized I loved myself more in Italy than I loved myself with Ted.

A buzz began to build as people emerged from the stupor of the hot day. Next to me, the long manes of my girls lifted in the air like incense. Nearby, young Italians converged outside a gelateria. Boys straddled their scooters like young Marlon Brandos. White shirts set off rich tans, the red of a cigarette flickered near their smiles as they posed for their girlfriends.

I shepherded my girls as they approached the piazza like fillies stepping out of a barn. A Pino Daniele song wafted from a screen-less window with green shutters flung open. There was nostalgia in his voice and a shiver over my warm skin as I felt passion spill like Tuscan linden blossom honey from the rooftops. And in that moment, I knew Italy had my heart more than any man ever had.

Those steps through that piazza on that summer night, how many times I replayed them in my mind when I went home.

I was distraught, bereft even, to have left that passion behind. Ted began to feel like a reliable friend, but not like a lover. And while I wanted a guy who hiked and who knew how to hang food high in a tree away from bears like Ted did, I also wanted a guy who was at home in European wine bars. If I could have been happy living in a yurt on an organic farm, Ted would have been a good choice.

Ted and I lived for four months in the international community of Auroville in southern India—founded in 1968 by "The Mother," a French follower of Sri Aurobindo. Its goal: to realize human unity in diversity and a transformation of consciousness in which "the greed and blindness of the ego will no longer exist."

We knew little about Auroville when we decided to go. As on my prior international travels, this was pre-internet. We arrived in Auroville in September of 1989. The internet was to become available in homes two years later, even though I didn't hear of it and start using it until 1994. One of the few things I knew about Auroville was that it was considered "the city the earth needs." Those words beckoned me like the siren's song enticing Odysseus.

Upon arrival, I went to the library to check out books on the founder, Sri Aurobindo. Since it was much easier for me to be academic than spiritual, this was my way of enlightening myself. As I read about his evolutionary metaphysics, I realized his vision was uncannily similar to the one shared by my grandma, my great-aunt Margaret, and Gerald Heard.

My grandmother shared her sister Margaret's belief that people had to evolve spiritually instead of technologically, and she gave me a sense that the world of the mind wasn't the only worthy world.

It was no accident that I ended up in Auroville.

As my grandma used to say, "There's no chance or accident."

From my perch on the sanctuary loggia, I watch Italian parishioners arrive at Pancole for Sunday morning mass. Soon the sound of singing emanates from the open door of the church. Voices rise and fall on the fragrant air.

Lifting on my pack, I wonder if there might be just as much spirituality in my family background as hyper-intellectualism. Perhaps I'm on this pilgrimage renewing a spirituality that had importance to women in my family a few generations before me.

THIRTY-TWO

The Procession

Six kilometers (3.75 miles) later, I arrive in San Gimignano, the most touristed hill town in Tuscany. Three million tourists a year flock to this town of tall towers. Because most visitors are day-trippers who make the town crazy-crowded by day, I've always preferred San Gimignano in the evening when the tour buses heave off with their cargo, arduously negotiating the tight curves of the road out of town.

San Gimignano's original prosperity was directly linked to its position on the Via Francigena, a fact I didn't know until this visit as a pilgrim. As my route takes me further into Tuscany, the towns now consistently display Via Francigena information, usually in the form of large maps of the route in glass cases and information about how the towns developed during the Middles Ages as a result of their location on the Via Francigena.

Sigeric recorded San Gimignano as *Sancte Gemiane* in his diary as he passed through on his pilgrimage. Somewhere between the end of the ninth century and the beginning of the tenth, hospices opened for pilgrims in San Gimignano, and the town grew in size and became prosperous. The prosperity encouraged a flurry of art production, much of which still adorns the town's churches and monasteries. The pilgrims of the Middle Ages took a route through town from the Porta of San Mateo to the Porta of San Giovanni, and this became the town's main road.

I check in at the nunnery called *La Foresteria del Monastero San Girolamo*. A rather businesslike nun shows me to a small room that includes a private bathroom. I note the real towels—a welcome change from my tiny travel chamois. The single bed with crisp sheets looks heavenly, and out the window I gaze over a stone wall and into the Tuscan landscape—an abode of peace.

"*È perfetta!*" I can't help exclaiming to the nun.

"*Bene,*" she replies and asks for my passport. I tell her about the fastidio and ask if I might have a tub with ice.

"I'm too busy now, but I can help later," she says, taking my passport and dashing from the room.

After showering and putting on my one change of outfit, I venture up the cobbled street in search of food. Following an instinct, I turn up a side street that brings me to Piazza Sant'Agostino. There, an inviting trattoria with tables and umbrellas outside waves at me.

The cool interior has exposed stone walls decorated with a multitude of framed, old-fashioned paintings of roses. Colorful bunches of dried flowers hang in rows from the ceiling. I order a salad and a focaccia with sun-dried tomatoes and melted mozzarella. Both turn out to be huge. Happy to be off my feet, I spend a long time eating, enjoying the tranquility and knowing I can sit for hours. No one will care.

Toward the end of my meal, two Dutch pilgrims named Gerda and Ruud come into the restaurant, and we strike up a conversation. They're sympathetic about my plantar fasciitis.

"When I did the Camino in Spain," Ruud says, "I had a lot of pain."

I don't know if he means he had the same ailment or something else.

"I called my doctor," he continues, "and he said I could keep walking, even with the pain. So you can do this, with pain, if you choose to."

Gerda nods and smiles encouragingly at me.

"I've heard that continuing the activity that caused the problem will make it worse. I'm wondering about getting a donkey for the rest of the pilgrimage," I say. I'm only partly joking.

"Oh, I don't think a donkey is a good idea," Ruud firmly replies. "They are very stubborn. If they decide to sit down and not move, that's it. You're not moving."

"He's right," Gerda chimes in. "Look, everyone's pilgrimage is their own. People go at their own pace. It's totally okay to take the bus when you're in pain."

"I've done that, but I feel a bit guilty about it," I say.

"Oh, don't feel bad!" Gerda says quickly. "To get to Gambassi, we took the train from San Miniato Basso to Castelfiorentino, and from there we walked to Gambassi. We knew that route would be too much."

"Oh really?" I remember my crash and burn that day and the ride I took.

Ruud wags a finger at me. "Bus yes, donkey no."

"Don't be hard on yourself," Gerda says.

After my two-and-a-half-hour lunch, I wander into the nunnery, down the silent halls, hoping to find a nun who might get me some ice. But I don't hear a sound, and I find no one. Disappointed, I go back outside and head to the center of town, joining the crowds in the two adjacent squares, Piazza del Duomo and Piazza della Cisterna.

An abundance of red-faced tourists, many licking ice cream cones, sit cheek by jowl on the steps of the cistern while toddlers frolic on the herringbone-patterned piazza floor. I amuse myself by trying to catch a photo with no one on the cistern.

Then I head to the Church of San Agostino. In this church is a fresco cycle by Benozzo Gozzoli. He's the Renaissance artist that did that very cool *Procession of the Magi* fresco in the private chapel at the Medici palace in Florence.

Augustinian monks began constructing the church in 1280. About two centuries later, Benozzo Gozzoli came to San Gimignano from Florence to avoid the plague, and here at the high altar of the San Agostino Church, he and his assistants painted a fresco with seventeen scenes of the life of Saint Augustine.

I make my way eagerly to the chapel to view the frescoes. The bottom left begins with a representation of Augustine starting his education as a child in the town of his birth in North Africa and then at the University of Carthage. The point here is to show that he was a learned man.

In grad school, because I had to examine influential figures from periods prior to the Renaissance, I attempted to read Augustine's thousand-page tome, *City of God*. My struggle with it, apart from its daunting size, was that Augustine didn't intend to write unbiased history. My graduate program trained me to examine all sides in an unbiased way—the opposite of Augustine's approach. His purpose in *City of God* was to defend the Christian faith against all objections.

In *City of God*, he attempted to answer this question: Why had God allowed Rome, the center of the Christian faith, to be sacked by the Visigoths in 410? The pagan claim that the disaster had befallen Rome because the traditional pagan gods had been abandoned in favor of the Christian God, was a gauntlet thrown at Augustine's feet.

While Augustine's writings had immense influence on the history of Western Christian theology, I found I wanted to say to Augustine, "Just know that the faith is right for *you*. Don't spend fourteen years and over a thousand pages attempting to convince others of the superiority of your faith."

My eyes jump to the fourth and fifth scenes in which Augustine has left North Africa and moved to Italy. In the fresco of him disembarking at Ostia, in the Italian region of Lazio, the background is more reminiscent of the Tuscan hills than the coast of Lazio. Perhaps because Tuscan landscapes were in vogue for the Renaissance paintings of Gozzoli's time.

Scene six strikes me with its similarity to the *Procession of the Magi*, Gozzoli's fresco in the private chapel of the Medici palace in Florence. The scene depicts Augustine setting out on his journey from Rome to Milan. It is reminiscent of Gozzoli's *Procession* fresco in Florence, with the depiction of a journey where men are on foot and on horseback, coming in from the left side of the picture. Both contain recognizable contemporary figures, and in both, Gozzoli has inserted himself as one of the participants in the scene.

The procession fresco in Florence uses a biblical story to make a statement about the Medici's political and financial power. So you've got the story of the Magi (the three kings) traveling to Bethlehem from somewhere in the east to visit Jesus after his birth, but Gozzoli adds Pope Pius and male members of the Medici family as part of the procession. The idealized landscape doesn't depict the Near East but rather the Mugello region north of Florence, the provenance of the Medici.

In this way, the fresco makes a strong statement about Florence being the new Jerusalem and the Medici, who have no royal background, having status on par with the biblical kings. The Medici were members of the Brotherhood of the Magi, an important congregation that organized processions in Florence on Epiphany, the feast day of the Magi. The procession Gozzoli portrays alludes to those Magi processions in Florence as much as it does to the biblical story. The fresco also alludes to the Great Ecumenical Council that Florence hosted in 1439. Financed by Cosimo de' Medici, it aimed to reconcile the Byzantine Orthodox Church with Roman Catholicism. Thus, the fresco highlights Cosimo's role in the reconciliation between the churches.

The delegates who attended the Council came from far-flung places in Africa and Asia. They brought their exotic costumes and never-before-seen animals to Florence, which is where Gozzoli received the inspiration to include giraffes, leopards, and monkeys in the fresco, as well as his wonderful rendering of lavish costumes. The fresco literally glitters because Gozzoli used gold leaf and ultramarine, costly pigments that demonstrated Medici family wealth. It surely wowed viewers of the time.

What captures me most about the fresco in San Gimignano is that Gozzoli depicts Augustine's journey as a medieval pilgrimage. Back then, the impoverished masses made their pilgrimages on foot, while the upper classes undertook theirs on horseback. In this fresco, Augustine is astride a beautiful bay horse while a young man in the role of protector walks next to Augustine's horse. It shows me how a pilgrimage by a well-to-do person in the Middle Ages might look.

Despite my lack of Catholicism, I'm plugging in, in this moment, to a place of deep roots. The question comes to me, what do I begin to understand here that I cannot learn anywhere else?

Looking at these frescoes within the context of being a pilgrim, I begin to understand the people who moved across this land centuries ago and how the very bedrock beneath my feet was transformed into things of significant purpose by those people.

I begin to know the hands that laid the Roman roads here and to sense the sandaled footsteps of the Roman legions when this land was not yet Christian. I begin to feel the life of the stones, and how they were used first for roads to control a continent, and then how they were molded into churches, to worship a new god.

I sense the northward march of the Romans over these hills, sense the strength of their sturdy legs and the single focus of their minds. Then I feel how the new religion of Christianity spread over these hills. I feel the hands of the people who built the first small Romanesque churches and the way the stones were pulled from the earth and shaped into a place where humans felt safe.

I begin to understand the stride of the medieval pilgrims and sense their legs, shorter than mine. I sense how their fingers wrapped around a staff that was taller than their heads, like the one I saw in the museum in Aulla with the teardrop shaped gourd tied to it. I begin to understand how the world was mysterious to them and how they hoped for a miracle.

Down the side aisle, thin angles of sunlight come through tall Gothic windows. I pause at the wrought iron stand of votive candles and light one for my sister and one for Kari, who is still digging herself out of the "damn hole" back in Colorado.

After finding a priest to stamp my pilgrim passport, I step into the piazza, its stones amber-hued in the late afternoon light.

THIRTY-THREE

True Spirit

Locally referred to as Colle, the town of Colle di Val d'Elsa is situated above the valley of the river Elsa, nine kilometers (about five and a half miles) from San Gimignano. Much less touristed than its famous neighbor, Colle has a medieval, well-preserved *alta* (high) part of town, while the *bassa* (low) section lies on the banks of the river Elsa. Alberto's directions indicate a day's walk of thirty kilometers from San Gimignano to Monteriggioni, skipping over Colle.

The nine kilometers to Colle is probably considered too short for many pilgrims, but no way can I do the thirty kilometers to Monteriggioni. When I wake up in San Gimignano, I can barely walk. The fastidio in my feet roars like a dragon, impossible to ignore.

I take a bus to Colle, reluctantly giving myself another day's rest. Yes there's history to see in Colle, and yes it's a pleasant town, but I want to be rolling over trails on happy feet, swinging my poles, singing a tune, my face lit by the fresh green light glancing off the vineyards.

From the bus, I call a B&B. The proprietor says a room is available, but I'll have to wait until she returns, so I sit for forty-five minutes in the bassa part of town on a bench in a small piazza. I take off my shoes, massage my feet, and watch a woman slowly circling the piazza pushing a baby pram. Her long ebony hair falls like a curtain next to her round, white face. She reminds me of someone, but I can't put my finger on it. Then I remember Josette, the French communist at the Volunteers for Peace work camp in Poland.

In 1985, I joined a work camp at the former concentration camp of Majdanek in Poland through an organization called Volunteers for Peace that created projects around the world designed to both prevent and resolve conflict while helping meet local needs. In the heart of the Cold War era, VFP was particularly involved in the exchange of volunteers between the former USSR and the US.

Among our international group in Poland was Josette, a committed communist who, I quickly learned, was angry at the United States. To her, Americans were blindly patriotic and chose disastrous "cowboy" presidents who felt entitled to police the world.

While the rest of us did gardening work at the museum of the former concentration camp, Josette would often remain on her bunk bed, unresponsive to our invitations to join us. She especially refused to speak to me, presumably because I was an American. In fact, the only time I heard her speak at all was during the evening discussions.

I was full of youthful curiosity about the world. It was only a year after my first backpacking journey around Europe, which had opened my mind to history and politics and had piqued an awareness of my country's role in the world. I listened eagerly as the young Polish guys leading the camp told us about daily life in Soviet-controlled Poland and as the two Dutch participants recounted how 550,000 Dutch citizens had flocked to The Hague to protest the planned deployment of American cruise missiles in Holland. I was fascinated when the Danes in the group described how many peace groups had sprung up in their country since 1980. Grinning, they ticked off on their fingers, "Fishermen for peace, teachers for peace, doctors for peace, trade unions for peace. . ."

If Josette joined the discussions, it was to accuse the United States of being imperialistic and escalating the arms race, thanks to the election of Ronald Reagan as president.

"He's putting us at the brink of nuclear war!" she stated, her eyes hard with anger.

"The Russians are playing this game too," a Danish girl replied.

"How can you not back me up? The Americans are pushing us to have bases for their missiles, and we don't want them."

"Well, there's a perception that we're being pushed to take them," a German participant replied. "But your President Mitterrand pressured the Germans to take American missiles."

"The point is," the Danish girl interjected, "apart from what the governments are doing, the average people in Europe are upset about being between these two superpowers who have so many weapons pointed at Europe."

I had listened to these discussions for a few nights without making any statement about my country. My knowledge was nascent; I was still formulating my thoughts on these topics. They were being formed in an emotionally tumultuous way, not in a studious way, which made me unsure how to articulate them.

The month before this work camp experience in Poland, I had been on the peace walk in Germany with fellow Americans who cared deeply about promoting goodwill between the US and the Soviet Union. And I'd spent a few days at a women's peace camp at the American cruise missile base at Greenham Common, England. Time and again, I heard Europeans complain about Reagan and US foreign policy. Was my country a bully? Why was it spending a fortune on more weapons when we already had enough to blow up the world ten times over? Could I trust my president to keep the country—and the world—safe?

One evening, Josette glared at me and said, "The US started this Cold War! The Soviets are only reacting to US threats!"

"I'd like to say something," I said hesitantly.

The discussion stopped and heads turned my way. A palpable curiosity hung in the air. What would the American say? Everyone wanted to know.

"It's not easy being an American. You're all here in Europe, in the middle, between the US and the USSR, in an out-of-control arms race. It scares you." I stopped and took a breath. "I feel a lot of guilt."

My hands twisted in my lap and I felt everyone looking at me.

"It's like I'm carrying around this weight, this sense of responsibility."

The Dutch girls nodded, urging me on.

"You're all freaked out by Reagan, and even if I didn't vote for him, I feel a certain responsibility." My voice cracked. I was on the verge of tearing up. "I'm as appalled as you are that Reagan called the Soviet Union an evil empire."

The Danish girl gave me a hug, and I noticed Josette get up, her straight black hair falling forward and half covering her impassive face. It was impossible to tell what she was thinking.

Four days later, I took a night train out of Lublin, west across Poland. The train would cross East Germany in the middle of the night, and I would get out in Berlin in the morning. The only other person from our group on that train was Josette. She sat a few rows up from me and never acknowledged my presence. Two plump Polish women wearing headscarves sat across from me and a younger Polish woman sat next to me. None of them spoke English, so I buried myself in a book. Then the train light went out. I put the book away and managed to fall asleep. Just past midnight, the train's jolting stop at the East German border awoke me. When I saw the Polish women pulling out passports, I did the same.

A large, bellicose East German woman wearing a border guard uniform burst into our car with sharp German commands that slapped us to attention. She took my passport along with the three Polish ones. Apparently, she found something wrong with mine. She shouted at me. I didn't understand a word. I was alone at midnight on the strictest border in the world, confronted by a large, pissed-off guard.

I told myself not to panic. "English? Anyone speak English?" I managed to ask.

No, the Polish heads tipped apologetically. The East German guard shrieked, *"Nein!"* and waved my passport so vigorously, I thought she'd rip it.

I had no other language but Italian. God willing, it had to help me. *"Italiano?"* I queried without much hope.

"Sì! Italiano!" the young Polish woman next to me said, startling me with her miraculous words. How on earth did a Polish woman who wasn't allowed into Western Europe speak Italian?

Quickly, she told me what the border guard was shouting about. "You don't have a transit visa to cross through East Germany. Your visa is only for Poland."

"Oh, I didn't know. Can I pay her?"

"Yes, perhaps. I'll ask her what the visa costs."

As I recall, after the guard shouted at me for a few more minutes, I paid her the equivalent of ten dollars. But what came next was even more miraculous. When the helpful woman next to me left her seat, Josette appeared, sat on the edge of that seat, and haltingly said, "I want to tell you something."

I remember how the moonlight came through the train window,

how Josette's shoulders rocked as the train rattled across the forbidden countryside of East Germany, and how her round face was illuminated as she struggled to find her words.

"Before you, I hated all Americans. I was so angry at Reagan and at capitalism. I stereotyped all of you." She paused and grasped the back of the seat. "What you said that night, about the guilt . . . I never heard an American say that. I didn't know."

Her hair swung forward, and I looked at her with compassion. She was clearly struggling.

"It's okay," I began, but Josette wanted to continue.

"Because of you, I have changed. I've had a window open. I won't see the world so black-and-white anymore."

She paused, and I gave a nod of encouragement.

"You have . . . opened my eyes." Even as her voice faltered, her eyes were clear.

"Thanks, Josette."

She stood up, said, *"Auvoir,"* and disappeared down the darkened train corridor.

In Berlin a few days later, after catching up on sleep (and after the pleasure of using real toilet paper wore off), I felt curiously content in a way I'd never experienced before. My hopes of promoting better international relations through my travels had, in fact, come to fruition.

I'd not thought of that night on the East German border for twenty years—not until now in the piazza when the woman with the round moon face and dark curtain of hair pushed a baby pram into my view.

How could I have forgotten Josette and her halting words that bridged a gap between us? How could I have forgotten about the brutish East German border guard and how the Italian language had rescued me?

On the bench, I rub my feet, contemplating that younger me. Is this part of the magic of the pilgrimage—reliving memories that remind me of my own true spirit? My true spirit was my twenty-one-year-old self watching funeral pyres on the banks of the Ganges, it was my twenty-year-old self discussing international relations with European peers at the peace camp in Poland, it was my nineteen-year-old self lost in the woods at night in Northern Greece, trusting a man in a hut and accepting yogurt from him in the morning. It was the self that strove to replace fear with trust, the self that found she could love the world and it could love her back.

I realize clearly now that my marriage was a deviation from my true spirit. The marriage had been an outgrowth of things I'd unwittingly absorbed: the need to play it safe in choosing guys so I wouldn't be stalked; the need to rescue; the familiarity of no one having my back; the tendency to steer by my head instead of my heart.

No wonder I'd cried that morning before the wedding, saying, "I want to know that you love my soul." I was, in essence, admitting to myself that he did not fit into the world of things that represented my true spirit. And if he did not fit into that world, he could not love my soul.

The memory of Poland has come back to me now, helping me reclaim my story. I'm reminded of the red balloon of my spirit, of the way I hold the string as it bounces above me, leading me to interactions with people like Josette and the others at the peace camp in Poland, leading me to meaningful adventure.

I'm welcomed into the B&B by a chatty proprietor. Accepting the bottle of water she offers, we go to sit in the lounge and chat. When the problem of my plantar fasciitis comes up, she's a fountain of ideas.

"Do away with the pack and get a suitcase on wheels!" she suggests.

I visualize pulling a suitcase along single tracks through the woods and over the hills covered with chunks of claylike earth. "I wouldn't be able to use my trekking poles. I ward off vipers and angry dogs with them," I explain to her.

"Oh, but it's a solution, I'm sure of it. I'll take you to the suitcase store!"

"Well, I'm trying to picture it," I say wrinkling my brow. "I'd have one arm pulling a weight behind me, and while that's fine at an airport, I think twelve kilometers of it isn't ergonomic for my body."

"Ergonomic?"

"Like I could get a torn shoulder or my hand that's got to grip the suitcase handle for so many kilometers could become cramped."

"But you have to get the weight off your back! Really, this is the solution. We'll go to the store when they open at 4:00!"

"Getting the weight off my back could help, but once you have plantar fasciitis, it hurts to walk even without weight."

She looks so crestfallen that I promise her I'll think about it.

"And for your inserts, there is a specialized shoe shop," she says.

Now this turns out to be very useful. At the shop they glue my arch supports to my squishy inserts.

Glue! Why hadn't I thought of that?

Leaving the store, I wander through Colle alta in search of lunch. On Via Campana, which grandly stretches on the ridge, I walk over flagstones the colors of amber and ebony. The *via* leads to Palazzo Campana, a sixteenth-century Tuscan Mannerist villa that straddles the road by way of an arch. Through the arch, I arrive in the oldest part of town, where there's a castle.

I imagine the Guelph and Ghibelline troops scrambling over the castle walls, loading their crossbows. The Guelphs (who supported the Pope) and the Ghibellines (who supported the Holy Roman Emperor) perpetually clashed in these parts during the late Middle Ages.

In June of 1269, the Ghibelline troops of Siena and the Guelph troops of Charles of Anjou and Florence confronted each other inside Colle's walls. Even though Florence had only 1,100 troops compared to Siena's 9,400, the Florence army was victorious and captured all of Siena's territory.

By evening, heading into the B&B for an early night, I think of the dolce vita scene of wine bars where the Tuscans take pleasure in the fruits of their land. I want to join in, but the dolce vita isn't conducive to my pilgrimage.

I remember standing with Darrell outside a wine bar in the Sant'Ambrogio quarter of Florence and spying an outdoor table at which a couple were leaning toward each other over a bottle of wine. I had playfully nudged Darrell and said, "Wouldn't it be fun sometime to order *a whole bottle?*"

"Not until you make more money," he'd replied.

The culture of deprivation is gone now, I tell myself as I enter the B&B. Curling into bed, I allow myself to express what I really want. It's like I've been given permission to pick flowers in the queen's garden.

> *I want to eat pasta and drink wine with people who believe no one should eat alone.*
> *I want to laugh more and take myself less seriously.*
> *I want a variety of languages around me.*
> *I want to be by the sea.*
> *I want another chance to live in Italy when the natural glow and joy I was born with once again rings jubilant like the bells of Giotto's tower.*

And then I feel like I'm underwater, swimming toward the surface in that moment when the mind questions whether the breath will last.

I know what I want, what I've wanted since I first fell in love with Italy more than twenty years ago. All the passion and joy that Italy sparks in me, I want to share it with others.

In some capacities I've done this—when I teach a course on the Florentine Renaissance, or when I ran the wedding business—but I want to live in Italy for real. Not for a stint and not with a bad marriage shadowing me like a Stasi officer.

I don't know where in Italy this place will be, or how I'll own it, or what exactly it will be, but I want to welcome travelers, I want to offer to them the special richness of Italy. I want to serve it to them on a plate, and say, "Here, here are the best things in life." And I want it so much that it creates in me that under the surface moment, where fear and hope are combined.

THIRTY-FOUR

Sprezzatura

The B&B owner suggests I take a bus for the first few kilometers of my route to Siena to avoid asphalt. She tells me which stop to ask for and where the trail, with its softer ground, begins. The bus driver nods when I ask him to alert me when we come to that stop. But he forgets, and I end up in Siena.

I had plans to stay with Adam, an American friend. But he was expecting me much later in the day. I usually don't call friends at seven in the morning, but luckily, he's up and not bothered about my early arrival. He tells me to get off the bus at Porta Camollia.

Porta Camollia, the traditional entrance to Siena for pilgrims, is the most beautiful of Siena's eight entrances. Its arched opening in the city's medieval red-brick walls is adorned with marble ornamentation. An inscription in Latin over the *porta* reads "Siena opens its heart to you wider than this gate." I like to think of it as being there for the pilgrims of the Middle Ages to read, but it was added in 1604 for the visit of Grand Duke Ferdinando I, who served as Grand Duke of Tuscany from 1587 to 1609.

"Eccomi!" (Here I am!) I say as I step through the historic porta as a pilgrim, just like all those others hundreds of years ago. I try to imagine them. Were they bedraggled, with feet as painful as mine? Were their bodies aching with hunger and fatigue but their spirits full of the strength of their faith? Were their eyes eager to take in the beauty of Siena?

And there's Adam a short distance away on the other side, looking expectantly at the porta's opening.

He leads me a short block to his apartment, and before he goes to work, he gives me yogurt, granola, and English tea—my first real breakfast since beginning the pilgrimage. A feast.

I wash my clothes by hand and hang them on a rack in the postage-stamp garden at the back of the apartment. As any expatriate living in Italy knows, washing a load of laundry in an Italian washing machine can take up to two hours because the machines heat their own water. In addition, all the odd symbols and unusual dials on them stump me every time. Much easier to wash my lightweight clothes by hand.

Sigeric had called Siena *Seocine* in his diary. When he entered the city in the tenth century, it was flourishing economically, thanks to its position on the Via Francigena. Numerous inns and hospices sprouted up on the Via di Camollia that heads to the city center from the Porta Camollia. With its Gothic-style architecture and all its ties to the Via Francigena, it's so clear that Siena is a product of the medieval era.

As I make my way to the library to check e-mail, my thoughts pass from Sigeric to the Americans and Europeans on the nineteenth century grand tour. The grand tour was popular with the privileged classes from the 1600s to the 1800s. Typically, young English men with a liberal arts education made the trip. The aim was to broaden their horizons and help them learn about the roots of Western Civilization. Italy was considered the essential place to do this.

The poet Robert Browning set out on the grand tour in 1834 and fell in love with Italy. In 1846, he married Elizabeth Barrett, and they ran off to Italy together a week later.

I think of Elizabeth now as I walk down the shaded side of the Via Camollia. She had fallen in love with Robert Browning, but her father had forbidden her to marry. She married Robert (six years her junior) in secret and scandalously absconded with him to Italy. Her poor health improved in Italy's climate, and they both wrote their best poems in Italy. Her husband called her sonnets, "The finest sonnets written in any language since Shakespeare's."

Believing in education for women, she was mostly self-taught. She pushed for gender equality, and her poems went beyond the prescribed themes of love and religion set for women poets. They lived in Florence, and she died there in her husband's arms at age fifty-five. She was buried in Florence's English Cemetery.

I am happy that she had Italy. Her father disowned her after her elopement. But in her poetry, she found an outlet to express her passions. She had Robert, Italy, and her poetry. That's quite a lot for a Victorian woman to have. Heck, even for me to have. Do I really want more than an outlet to express my passions, a wonderful love, and Italy?

At the library, I post on Facebook so that everyone who donated to my journey can learn how I'm faring. I read messages from friends encouraging me not to quit the pilgrimage in spite of the plantar fasciitis. Feeling buoyed by the messages, I think about how I had inadvertently skipped the route that morning. Tomorrow I'll bus back and do that stretch without my pack, leaving it at Adam's.

Thrilled with the idea of a day's walk without a pack, I duck into a bar and savor a mozzarella and tomato panino. My agenda in Siena that afternoon? Visit the famous Enoteca Italiana (wine cellar) located in an imposing sixteenth century fort.

The entrance on the ramparts leads into the vaults of the fort and to an elegant, large space with a soaring brick ceiling. Feeling self-conscious in my hiking clothes, I head to the sleek bar tucked under a hefty brick arch. That's where I meet Franco.

Franco's shiny black hair curls at his shoulders and is styled to swoop from his forehead in a seemingly effortless wave. The word *sprezzatura* comes to mind—something complicated that appears to be without effort. The term was coined by an Italian named Baldassare Castiglione. In the 1500s he wrote *The Book of the Courtier*—a guidebook of sorts for the model gentleman wherein he uses the term sprezzatura to mean mastering something difficult and making it look effortless. Today, Italians apply this to the idea of looking beautiful or fashionable without seeming to have tried hard.

Franco sports a crisp black button-down shirt and a black-and-white tie. To make up for my less than posh appearance, I quickly mention that I'm a pilgrim.

"Welcome!" Franco says, flashing a white smile. "A pilgrim deserves a drink! What would you like?"

"How about something from the south, a *passito*?" I say, smiling back, relishing the thought of a sweet dessert wine. Just then, a large group enters the bar.

"Why don't you take a seat on the *terrazzo*, and I'll bring it to you," Franco says with a nod toward the large group.

On the terrace, where only a few other visitors sit, I'm delighted when Franco brings me a generous glass of a Sicilian passito, which he considers a "tasting."

"Is it a Moscato?" I ask.

"Yes, *Moscato di Siracusa*. Enjoy!"

Moscato di Siracusa might possibly be Italy's oldest wine, and it almost disappeared. It was brought to Syracuse by the ancient Greeks when they colonized Sicily a few thousand years ago. In the 1700s, before the Protected Designations of Origin (DOC) laws were passed to protect regional products from imitation, other wine producers took advantage of the prestigious name. They used it to label cheap dessert wines, causing the Moscato di Siracusa name to be devalued. In 1983, when it was recognized as a DOC wine, only half a hectare was given to its production. Moscato di Siracusa was about to go extinct.

Franco returns and pours me another generous glass.

"How did this wine get revived?" I ask him.

"By a family named Pupillo. Today, they produce mostly Moscato di Siracusa on a vineyard outside of Siracusa."

"I'll have to visit the estate next time I'm in Sicily," I say and thank him for the liberal pour.

"Figurati!" (No problem, don't mention it.) He pulls up a chair next to me. "Tell me, what's the reason for your pilgrimage? You must be very religious."

I explain about my divorce and illness, and I tell him that I desire to do something positive to heal.

"Most people would become depressed," Franco says thoughtfully, "after these problems and not confront them in the way you are."

"I'm trying. The pilgrimage can be pretty hard sometimes."

"You're confronting life!" Franco replies.

"Thank you for your compassion," I say.

"It's not compassion, it's esteem!"

That night, I go with Adam to his choir practice, which is in a tiny green and white marble church. Talk about sprezzatura! I think of the word for a second time and of Baldassare Castiglione's words, "Everyone knows the difficulty of things that are exquisite and well done, so to have facility in such things gives rise to the greatest wonder."

That's me, in wonder at Adam's seemingly effortless fluency in Italian, which is at odds with his Alabama drawl in English. It's as if he becomes the very courtier that Castiglione was talking about when he speaks Italian. And there he is, singing in an Italian choir, as mellifluous as a Raphael cherub.

A memory surfaces as I listen to his choir practice, a memory of another time when Adam was singing. It was on the terrace of the apartment in Settignano that Darrell and I were renting.

It was a modest place with a galley kitchen and only a single small armoire for all our clothes. But it had a terrace. In the insufferably hot summer of 2003, people were dying from the heat. The basin of Florence was an inferno. We invited our friends to come up to Settignano to drink, eat, and sing on the terrace.

Our guests included our neighbors Donatella and Ricardo—who swooned over the gin and tonics I made—and a jolly group of expats. The owner of the wine bar where we had our Friday expat gatherings came bearing endless bottles of wine. Two Italian boys, both named Marco, followed me with a string of compliments when I went to the kitchen to pour more gin and tonics, making me laugh. Bodies were sprawled on the terrace, savoring the slightly cooler air after the burning sunset.

Adam and his Italian friend brought guitars. They knew all the songs I love to sing by Simon & Garfunkel, the Rolling Stones, and Crosby, Stills & Nash. They sang "Sweet Home Alabama," and Adam, with a nod to me, changed the words to "Sweet Home Settignano." My face lit up as I turned to Darrell and called out, "This is our song! This is for us!"

I jumped up and went to him, reaching for his hands, asking him to dance. He pulled his hands away and remained seated. Had he forgotten how dance lights me up? Had he not noticed that I'd approached him with so much joy? Why did he not want to join that? Who was he? Why had I married him?

I turned away in confusion, seeing the eyes of my guests on me and feeling my spirit fall away as if it had been slapped.

Adam and I walk to the Piazza del Campo. I'm happy to be with an American who shares the inextinguishable love for Italy. I don't even have to talk to him about Italy. It's enough to know that he gets it.

"This," Adam says, making a wide sweep of his arm, "is a UNESCO World Heritage Site." We stand at the top of the Piazza del Campo, which is the shape of half a church dome turned upside down. Teenagers sprawl on the piazza floor in groups, their cigarettes glowing like fireflies and their laughter echoing across the scoop of the piazza.

Heading uphill toward home, Adam points out Siena's McDonald's, tucked into the bottom of a large, square palazzo. "It's somewhat obscured, but still . . ." Adam says and puts an arm around me.

"Yes." I nod, distracted by his arm. "Luckily, the one in Florence is in the train station."

We enter his apartment.

"Chamomile tea?" he asks.

"Sure." I take off my Keens and tuck my feet up on a chair.

He pours hot water over tea bags in little white teacups and joins me at the small table. Fingering the label of the tea bag, he says ever so casually, "Would you like a massage?"

I pause, teacup halfway to my mouth. I sense my eyes widening. A massage is a euphemism for something else, isn't it?

I try to compose myself and imitate his casual stance. He's ten years younger than me, yet I don't feel like a confident older woman. I've been celibate for two years. For the past year, the more-painful-than-I-thought-it-would-be divorce and the interminable weakness of my body has had me feeling incapable of dating. But even before that, the year prior, I'd not dated. It was my first year of teaching college, which was a killer, as others told me it would be. Any energy I didn't put toward that, I put toward personal growth. I wanted to take time off from relationships and see what I could learn about my choices. And if no one wonderful came along, I didn't want to grab at just anyone to be my Band-Aid.

I sense a tensing in my body, and I'm sure I'm not ready. I fear that if I'm intimate with Adam, the feelings stuck in my body might come flying out—like opening Pandora's Box. Adam would have a sobbing mess in his bed when he might be expecting a Wisteria Lane cougar.

I decline the massage, and we go to our separate rooms.

THIRTY-FIVE

Absolution

To make up my walk to Siena, I take a bus to Abbadia a Isola, a Romanesque abbey that became a powerful force in the region in the eleventh century and began offering lodging to pilgrims in the year 1050. The abbey sits in one of those tiny, charming Tuscan stone hamlets called a *borgo*.

This borgo was built on the only piece of solid ground in what was once a swampland. Today, the flat fields are full of golden wheat and terracotta earth baking in the sun.

Along with the abbey, there's a church, a restaurant, and a few homes, all knitted together by an encircling stone wall. I pause to read the plaques about the Via Francigena placed outside the abbey. One plaque has a map of Italy with pilgrimage routes outlined, while the other is of Europe with an orange line from Canterbury, across the channel, and into France at Guines. It's marked *Itinerario di Sigeric*.

Another plaque states that European identities were formed by the cultural comparisons that the pilgrims and merchants made as they encountered people from different parts of Europe en route.

I take the dirt track from the abbey toward Monteriggioni, passing fields sprinkled with periwinkles and poppies like drops of blue and red paint on a wheat-colored canvas. At the end of the track is a farmhouse. A long line of white linens wave next to a vineyard, its bright, spring-green leaves shining in the sun. A fenced-in area of mud and pigs comes into view. I recognize the pigs as the Cinta Senese breed.

They come over snorting when they see me.

"Buon giorno!" I call to them.

Known as the Tuscan heirloom pig, this breed has been in

Tuscany since at least the fourteenth century. These pigs have black hair and a distinctive pink band around the shoulders that extends to the front legs. One such pig appears in the famous painting *Allegoria del Buon Governo* (Allegory of Good Government) by Ambrogio Lorenzetti in Siena's town hall.

In the 1950s, when pigs with rapid growth rates were preferred over this one with its slow growth rate, the Cinta Senese was forgotten. By the 1990s, it was almost extinct, but ten years later, dedicated groups of Tuscan breeders created a consortium to promote the delicacies of the products from this special breed. The Siena Breeders Association and others have since put out great effort to revive the Cinta Senese, which is now off the endangered species list. Today, plenty of Cinta Senese products with the label Suino Cinto Toscano DOP can be found in the shops of Tuscany's provinces of Siena, Grosseto, and Florence.

My favorite product from this heirloom pig is prosciutto di Cinta Senese, and my favorite place to buy it is Maccelleria Falorni. This ancient butcher shop has been in the charming village of Greve in Chianti since 1729. Their products are small-scale and exclusive, made according to time-honored Tuscan traditions— the real deal. The eighth generation brothers who currently run it have an estate nearby where the Cinta Senese pigs roam freely, foraging on acorns. The resulting prosciutto reflects the strong flavor of juniper and has a feral saltiness that is exactly what I want in a prosciutto.

I watch the pigs taking pleasure in the mud, and then I follow a trail into the woods. On the other side of the woods looms a steep hill leading to Monteriggioni. Surrounded by intact walls with fourteen towers at regular intervals, this hill town is an impressive sight. It has stood guard on its isolated mound since the 1220s when the walls were built by the people of Siena as a defense against their enemy, Florence, and to protect the Via Francigena.

The climb to the town causes me to sweat even without my pack. When I get to the top, I drop to a bench in the piazza. Slowly eating the grapes and cherries I've brought, I watch German and American tourists crisscrossing the piazza, small children in tow.

The route after Monteriggioni leads along a dirt track through oak woods where the sound of cicadas beats through the trees.

I focus on how marvelous it is to have a body that can walk—and to walk through Tuscany, no less. My thoughts turn to Lorenzo de' Medici's poems and how they showed his love of the Tuscan countryside. I imagine him riding a chestnut horse, a Benozzo Gozzoli horse with a thick neck and a green and bronze breast plate. He's riding on an afternoon in woods like these, with calfskin boots and a wool cape lifting from his shoulders in rhythm with the horse's gallop, humming one of his carnival songs.

Spurred by an eagerness to arrive in Siena before getting too hungry, I'm able to make short work of the woods without a pack on. Outside Porta Camollia, I buy yellow and orange peppers, garlic, and cherry tomatoes. Back at Adam's, I turn them into a quick pasta sauce, delighted to cook again.

When Adam gets home from work, we have a glass of wine before he goes to his tango lesson. I cannot accept his invitation to go. The route tomorrow is a long one.

"What do you think," Adam asks me, "about those who would say a pilgrimage is an escape and not going to fix anything?"

"Good question. Is it supposed to fix everything? It's too much to ask for this one thing to fix everything. I think it just gives the pilgrim a chance to listen."

"To listen to God or to your inner voice?"

"Both. Are they maybe the same thing?"

"Dunno."

I swirl my wine. "Someone said, 'on the journey to progress we lost our soul.' You know, slowing down to this pilgrimage pace, walking daily, wondering daily about where to get food and where I'll sleep, and visiting churches and shrines, it puts me at a preindustrial pace, and that allows me to connect to soul, and to listen more."

"So the combination of self-reflection and solitude is powerful."

"Yeah. Not easy, but powerful. I trust the power of it. I trust that something begins to percolate. It's like a window gets opened that wasn't open before."

"Why has pilgrimage become popular? Because going on some kind of retreat isn't a thing in our culture?"

"Very likely," I reply.

"People want to get off the bus."

"Get off the bus and start walking!" I laugh.

"Yes, so that once in a while, you arrive somewhere with reverence instead of in a rush!" Adam says, joining my smile.

"Perfect!"

"I'm going to tango," Adam says, getting up.

"Have fun. I'll be going to bed early."

I remain with my wine, reflecting on how pleasant it was to hang out with a friend in Siena after many solitary days. Fun times with girlfriends in Italy flit through my head. Robyn had come through Florence with some friends of hers when I was living in Florence with Darrell. With her, I had a respite from the culture of deprivation. She, I, and her three friends hit up the sleek cocktail bars on the Lungarno, sipping mojitos next to the green river and laughing in the bronzed happy hour light. But one night we got serious. We were seated around the table in our apartment—me, Darrell, our expat friend Lorna, and Robyn.

Robyn turned to Darrell and asked if he'd learned Italian.

"Not really," he replied.

"But you're leaning," I said encouragingly.

"But why should he learn it? You dragged him here," Lorna stated.

I was startled. Why did she say it this way? Darrell had chosen to go to Florence, saying that the only way he'd get enough "kick under his butt" to finally start his own business would be to get out of his comfort zone.

I looked at him expectantly. Surely, he would set Lorna straight. He said nothing.

Later, as I walked Robyn back to her hotel, I said, "I don't get why Darrell wouldn't have corrected Lorna. This is the lack of teaming that keeps coming up. I want us to be a team, but it seems like we come across as adversaries. What am I doing wrong?"

"You know," Robyn said carefully, "I think he's getting something out of playing the hapless victim."

"What?" I pondered the words, puzzled. "You mean . . . on purpose?"

"Yes."

"Oh, I don't think so. I mean no therapist has ever suggested this."

"Well, some therapists aren't very good."

"I tried three."

"Well, maybe they never saw him in action like I just did. Look at Lorna's perception. Poor Darrell. He was dragged to Italy by Medusa. Why does she say it that way? Because Darrell's been presenting it that way."

"I don't know, Robyn. I just have to figure out how to team better."

Robyn stopped in the middle of the Borgo degli Albizzi. "Chandi! You're never going to get the teaming you want if he's playing the hapless victim."

Seeing confusion on my face, she gave me a hug. "Just think about it."

It was high season, and I was frantically busy with weddings. I didn't think about it until the end of the summer when Darrell and I moved home and an incident slapped away my bafflement.

Back in the cohousing community, we went to a meal in the common house. As I was helping to set tables with two community members, Vicki and Ursula, Vicki said gushingly, "Darrell is so good-looking since he got back from Italy!" She said it in front of me, but not *to* me. She nudged Ursula. "Isn't he?"

"Totally!" Ursula replied with a laugh. "He's really gotten good-looking!"

Was a reply from me expected? Ursula, like Vicki, seemed to throw her comment my way without specifically engaging me.

"Was it the wine or the gelato?" Vicki asked Darrell as he walked up to us. "You know, that made you get so good-looking over there?" The way she turned her face up and flashed him a smile reminded me of the popular chicks in high school.

I still didn't know if I was supposed to be included in this. The back of my neck felt flushed as I sat down at the table.

"Why did you guys move back?" Ursula asked, looking at Darrell and then at me.

I paused, waiting for Darrell to step in. He said nothing.

"Some things were a struggle," I said hesitantly. "We couldn't get residency. . . " I looked again at Darrell for acknowledgment. He didn't look at me, and I stumbled on. "With me being the only one who could deal in the language, you know, like arguing with Telecom Italia . . ." I forced a laugh.

Darrell remained silent. After the meal, Darrell walked to the deck with a few of the guys, and I began to stack plates.

Ursula turned to me. "Sounds like you weren't very supportive of Darrell in Italy."

"Yeah, you're such a bitch toward him!" Vicki interjected.

The floor seemed to drop from under me. I feared I'd break the plate I was holding. People didn't talk that way in our cohousing community. We did our best to use "right speech." Vicki, as a leader of "nonviolent communication workshops" claimed to use right speech more than anyone. In an instant, I understood what Robyn was saying, and I understood that I had to give up, that a dynamic of me as Medusa and him as hapless victim would always be presented.

A week later, Darrell informed me that Vicki was going to be his Buddhist therapist.

But she's a fellow community member and she's been friends with both of us. Isn't that a conflict of interest?

I didn't bother voicing my question. I'd given up.

I still wasn't familiar with the term passive-aggressive. None of my friends, therapists, or family members had ever used the term. Prior to Darrell, I'd never been with a man who was passive-aggressive. As odd as it might sound, I'd never encountered the behavior or the concept—thus, I had no tools for recognizing it.

The relationship was a tightly pulled knot that couldn't be undone. It wasn't just his passive-aggressive behavior or the culture of deprivation. There was all that rescuing I'd been so eager to do. And on top of it, I had drawn to me a man with weakened masculine energy because I had carried too much masculine energy myself. But I came to resent saving the day time and again, and resentment turned to sharpness. It was the sharpness that Vicki blithely defined with her one-word vulgarism.

Now, as I hold a wine glass in Adam's sink, I see the complexity of the marriage like a knot that grew as large as the Giant Ball of Twine in Cawker City, Kansas. Every year, every month, every week, and every day we were together, a layer of his behaviors and of mine were pulled and fastened around each other in tight knots. And we kept doing it, year after year, fastening knots around each other that bound us to unhappiness.

I turn from the sink, drying my hands, and I lift my head as a confluence of church bells intones on the air, moving me to the window. Each bell tower is passing a message to the next. The sound moves in tributaries along Siena's narrow streets, a cymbal for each beating heart of each person in each street, calling us, *Venite! Venite!*

I know what I must do. I slip on my Keens, put the apartment keys in my pocket, and enter the tributary of bells. There's a tiny church just a jot down the street. It must have been the first church the pilgrims saw after entering the Porta Camollia. I press on the door that is surprisingly smooth. It opens, and I step in. There's just one aisle with about six pews on each side.

Tenebrous twilight, thick like earth, squeezes through the thin windows. I take in the exposed trussed roof and plain apse as I slip into a pew. The pew's wood is dark and smells of musty books, like the very old spine-crumbling ones in my grandma's house.

The world is still except for the bells. My heart and soul empty and offer themselves to the sound. The bells of Italy are the closest sound we are able to make that might replicate the sound of God.

Sensing movement behind me, I turn to see an elderly woman approach the font of water. Others follow, Old World style with gray hair pulled tightly back, shapeless dark clothing, and slipper-like shoes. There's a priest now, behind the altar. Candles flicker, and the women and the priest begin to sing.

I close my eyes and see the yellow saint again, but this time, the saint is a woman. I think she's Saint Catherine of Siena. In my vision, I'm on my knees in her cell, my forehead pressed to the cold brick floor near her bare feet. Her hands hover above my head, pulling the anguish from my body, absolving me.

I lift my face and open my hands. "I forgive each one," I tell her. I don't have to name them, she knows and she nods.

I raise my palms higher.

"Each one, and myself."

"It is done."

I open my eyes. The singing has stopped. The church is swathed in soft darkness. I follow the maternal forms in black to the door, my body so light I don't feel my feet for the first time in weeks.

The lightness of absolution.

THIRTY-SIX

Arriving

While we are eating breakfast, Adam jumps up. "You need a seashell!"

I follow him out the kitchen door to a patch of green next to a brick wall with ivy along the top. On a table scattered with terra-cotta pots, Adam sorts through a pile of seashells.

"Christians in the Middle Ages on the pilgrimage to Santiago de Compostela wore the symbol of the scallop shell on their cloak or their hat," he explains. "Here's one with a hole in it." He holds up a flat, white shell. "What day of the pilgrimage is this for you?" he asks as he ties the shell to my pack with a ribbon.

"Oh, I don't know." I run through my stops with him, counting on my fingers. "It's day twenty. Halfway." Then I'm crestfallen. There aren't twenty more days left to Rome. I know there aren't without looking at my printouts. "You know what, Adam, I'm going to arrive in Rome sooner than forty days. It's because I skipped all that stuff between Aulla and Lucca. Darn. I wanted it to be forty days."

"It'll work out," he says simply.

"Yeah, you're right."

I let it go as I make my way south through the city toward the Porta Romana. It's already 8:00 a.m., a late start.

Adam's apartment, being next to the Porta Camollia, allows me to pass through the entire length of the city on the road that was paved on top of the exact path the pilgrims of the Middle Ages had taken. Nearing the center of town, I realize that the shell on my pack matches the scallop shell shape of Siena's *campo*.

As I head to the Porta Romana, I have a sensation that Siena has held me in the cocoon of her circling streets and her sturdy walls, and that entering Siena as a pilgrim is like coming home to someone who lifts my tired cloak, soothes my aches, and invites me into her embrace. I wonder if the pilgrims long before me felt the same.

Walking through the Porta Romana, I feel eased into the birth-light of morning. I think of the inscription on the Porta Camollia—*Siena opens her heart to you*—and I know that the butterfly wings of Siena's heart open in recognition of the pilgrim, whenever she returns.

The route begins on a quiet country road lined with abundant gardens and views over the gently rolling hills. The morning air is extra warm, and I swing my poles, turning over the gems of my time in Siena. I realize with surprise that I never went into Siena's cathedral. With a laugh, I tell myself that I am a very bad pilgrim.

And then I think of another church, the protestant one in Florence. Father Casparian, who I worked with on weddings, had kept an open invitation for me to attend a service. "We've got a community here you can plug into," he'd said. But Darrell and I never went until the week before we moved home.

I now remember something I'd forgotten about that happened during that service. There was a baptism after the sermon. Darrell and I both watched Father Casparian with intent, drawn in by the light of his smile as he lifted the child toward the heavens, by the richness of his voice, by the meaning he infused with every gesture.

He has such passion for what he does, I thought. And then I turned to see tears streaming down Darrell's face. My heart went buttery, and I knew instinctively why Darrell was hurting. He'd not found that kind of passion. He'd looked, he'd tried, and it had eluded him.

As I walk past a field of wheat, I understand one of the key reasons I stayed in the marriage as long as I did. I'd bound myself, even bound pieces of my identity, to helping Darrell find that passion.

I stop walking. My legs tremble, and I want to drop to my knees and give thanks. My greatest fear had been that I'd torture myself with my obsessing about my bad choices and my bad marriage memories. I feared that I'd be defined by these things, that I wouldn't slay my demons. And lord, how I'd wrestled with those demons. But in that act of forgiveness in the church, when I supplicated before a vision of Saint Catherine, the demons had perished. Their bones had turned to dust, and the dust had been vaporized.

And now, with the memory of Darrell's tears, I'm left with the underbelly of his sadness. The orange glow is no longer a small lantern in the distance. Right now, it's a garland of marigolds draped on my shoulders.

As the quiet road leads on to the busy Cassia, I brace myself. Originally a Roman road, the Via Cassia went north from Rome through Tuscany, joining the Via Aurelia near Liguria. The modern road is referred to as *the Cassia*. I'm on a tight curve, and a huge truck roars toward me. There's no room to squeeze myself off the white line, and the truck seems to lean, as if it might topple on me while barreling around the curve. After straining up a steep hill on the road's edge, the route turns off the Cassia, thank God, onto a dirt track.

It's already hotter than any other day I've walked, and I stop in the shade to check Alberto's kilometer indications. I've gone seven kilometers—only 4.3 miles—yet I'm limping on both feet.

The directions say to cross the courtyard of a farm house and take a cart track to the right. Wolfish barking resounds as I scuttle across the courtyard. I come to a pasture where horses and foals graze. I pause to look at them, but flies soon swarm around my legs and start biting. Flies are circling the horses, too, in great black droves.

Down a gully and up, I arrive in a place of plowed wheat fields. The stubby stalks are bleached almost white by a vehement sun. I pull my hat down further, but its brim isn't wide enough to shield me from the sun's ferocity. My back feels slimy wet against the pad of my backpack. The trail I'm following angles to the right and dwindles downward into another field. A small yellow pilgrim sign indicates a left turn.

I stop and pull out the damp-with-sweat directions. Yes, it says to go right. Pushing the papers back into my pocket, I frown as I suck deeply on the hydration tube that hangs over my shoulder. Do I follow what the directions say or follow the pilgrim sign?

A coin toss is as good as logic. I choose the pilgrim sign.

The heat batters me like cake made ready for the oven and the rocks press sharply at the soles of my shoes. *Why did I choose these trail runners instead of day hikers with thicker soles?*

The trail merges into more bleached fields where stubs of wheat scratch my ankles. The pilgrim signs have disappeared. My teeth clench at the pain in my feet.

What's happening? An inner voice startles me. *You're lost right after understanding that you've snuffed out your demons?*

My fingers grip the poles more tightly and a determination sets in. *I must not fail.*

Tripping over my feet, I stumble across the field, my eyes cast down, away from the fierce light.

Getting lost is a final confrontation with my shadow side. The thought comes as I pause by a dusty stone. On it is a faintly painted yellow pilgrim. My heart lifts.

A farmhouse comes into view, suggesting a greener, shadier route to come. When I reach the farm, the pilgrim signs disappear, and so does the trail. I shift my weight from one foot to the other, trying to relieve their ache and wondering which way to turn.

The sound of a motor causes me to look toward a field where a man on a tractor waves me over. As I walk closer, he calls out, *"Devi tornare indietro!"* (You have to go back.)

I call to him, *"Ma, quanto indietro?"* (But, how far back?)

"The signs are incorrect! Go back!" I hear his shouts in Italian as he plunges the tractor into chunks of earth and rumbles away.

I return slowly on the dusty tracks to the brittle fields. Finding a handkerchief-sized patch of shade, I take off my pack and sit on it. My head drops toward my feet. Silence reigns, as if in the piercing heat, even the crickets and birds have been struck mute.

I make the only decision I can make: heave the pack on and begin retracing my steps. Sweat threatens to drip into my eyes, and I stop to squint at furrows in the field—mini trails made by mice. Then on a hill above me, I see a tractor track and aim myself toward it.

After about twenty minutes of walking, the track leads me to a farmhouse, which appears deserted except for the jarring howl of caged dogs. I round the red-brick house.

"Ow Eee!" I leap sideways as a snake rustles in the dry leaves next to my feet.

I flail a trekking pole weakly at the snake and pull the handkerchief from my pocket to wipe sweat from eyes so I can see better. Was it a viper? It's now under the leaves.

I turn and hurry to the driveway of the house. It leads to a road that looks like the Cassia. Sure enough, it is the Cassia. Walking on it briefly, I come to a bus stop. Now that I've so clearly lost the route, I'll have to take a bus. The stop has no bench and no shade, but it does have a time schedule. There's a bus to Buonconvento in half an hour.

On the bus, blissfully off my feet, I again hear the man's words, *you have to go back.* And my call, *but how far back?* The man's words now seem like a commandment that relates to the demons I've wrestled with. I have had to go back—go back in my mind through the traumas of the illness and through the painful marriage memories. And I've asked, how far back? How far back through the shadow side must I go?

I have gone further back, beyond the marriage, to teen years and childhood and further still, to my ancestors who have shown me that they can be next to me if I turn to them.

When I arrive in Buonconvento, I call the priest whose number is listed in my accommodations booklet, and he tells me how to find the *parrocchia* (parish). His voice is cheery as he shows me to a room that has a handful of cots and an attached bathroom. I tell him about getting lost and how I'd taken the bus after losing the route.

He assures me that I did the right thing.

In the shower, tighter than a British phone booth, the sweat and grime slip down my body as I close my eyes and remember another time I'd gotten lost while traveling. Besides Istanbul and Thessaloniki when I was nineteen, there was Nepal when I was twenty-five.

This memory is like another guardian angel tapping me on the heart, saying, *reveal this to yourself again, how you loved the world.*

I'd never thought of it this way, but I suddenly do. Loving the world in those moments, like I did when I was lost in Nepal, is different from loving a person. Loving a person is great; it can easily be the best thing in life. But it is reliant on that other person. Loving the world . . . I remember how powerful that was. My glow. No wonder I was heartbroken when I could no longer find it or feel it.

Ted and I entered the Kingdom of Nepal after traveling for five months in India. I had gone to Nepal on my own four years earlier when I was twenty-one. On that trip, I'd chosen to not trek the Annapurna circuit since it was so populated. I'd found a less frequented one and had loved the authentic experience of staying in people's homes—not the crowded *teahouses* where Coca-Cola was offered to trekkers.

Could I find another one like that? Asking around, we learned about a route to the Annapurna II base camp that was not well known by trekkers. Indeed, we saw few Westerners during the four days we walked to the famous mountain's base.

We hiked next to silver rivers and green rice paddies by day, and by evening we were warmly welcomed into Nepali homes with giggling children. There we slept on hard earth floors next to family members.

On our fifth morning, we woke to a brilliantly clear day in which Annapurna II stunned us with her white flanks reaching unimaginably high in a cerulean sky.

Unfortunately, the giardia that had afflicted me during the past five months in India had gotten the best of me during the night. Ted was eager to get to the mountain base, but I felt too weak.

We decided I would descend the mountain slowly while Ted would do his usual high-speed hiking to the base of Annapurna II. We were told that the first village at the bottom of the mountain was called Kavri. We planned to meet there by late afternoon.

My slow descent traversed a wide stone path with grassy terraces overlooking expanses of mountains and valleys. The sound of water came from an unseen river somewhere far below. It was all green, and blue, and white, and wrapped in a ribbon of peace.

When I reached the valley floor, I asked a Nepali man the direction to Kavri. I was waved on.

After walking almost two hours in the valley, I began to worry. My destination seemed ever farther away. I kept looking back for Ted. What if he'd had an accident? I knew the weather could change quickly in the Himalayas, and I also knew I should get to a village for the night, even if it wasn't Kavri.

The amoebas were still having a party in my intestines, and I felt weaker as the afternoon wore on. I'd not eaten anything except a few nuts and dried apricots throughout the day. At a fork in the trail, I asked a woman washing clothes in the river the way to Kavri. She pointed at the trail that went steeply up, leaving the valley. This dismayed me. I'd been sure Kavri was located in the valley.

With hesitation, I began to climb, still holding out hope of reaching Kavri. Black clouds rolled down over the mountains and now, in addition to my stomach pains, I had blisters on my feet. I knew I'd have to stop in the next village for the night.

I entered a small settlement of yak-dung homes on the side of a windy cliff just as raindrops began to fall. The first dwelling I saw had three walls with one open side that looked over the narrow trail next to the sheer cliff edge. I shook off my pack, ducked my head to enter, and pulled my pack in behind me out of the rain.

Suddenly, I was utterly happy, surrounded by welcoming villagers. Was half the village in this hut? They crowded close, young and old, looking at me. I moved right in and sat down on the dirt floor, joining their afternoon tea party. I loved them immediately—their peaceful eyes, their fluttering brown hands, the way they squatted on their haunches to make *chai*, the way they accepted me.

In this little dwelling so dramatically close to the cliff edge, the storm was right there in our faces, reminding us of powerful things beyond our small lives. I was from the other side of the world, but that evening, I was one of them. We all needed shelter from the storm, something to put in our bellies, and a place to rest our heads.

By evening, the villagers retreated. I was left with a mother, father, and their daughter, who had two tightly braided pigtails with a red ribbon woven into them. She was barefoot and, like everyone else, wore only a thin shawl against the cold wind. I sat next to her on the floor, eating the *dahl-bhaat* (rice and lentils) I was offered.

Then a friend of the father showed up. The men sat on their haunches playing cards and smoking. The young girl curled up on a mat still wearing her clothes—braids and ribbons still in her hair. I got out my sleeping bag and lay down next to her. The men's voices were loud and coarse, and the girl began to sing quietly. I was awed by her sweet, clear voice and by the long shadows from her eyelashes that the candlelight sent across her high brown cheeks.

I might have been lost in the little dwelling on the cliff edge, with Shiva the Destroyer raging through the night sky, but magic surrounded me as I fell asleep next to that beautiful child.

In the morning, I understood that with those villagers in their humble dwelling against the storm, I'd found both the power and the insignificance of our lives.

I'd found the best of the world in that hut.

At almost 2:30 in the afternoon, I dread the possibility that the restaurants might not be open. Stepping out of the shower, I dress quickly, rush to the street, and come upon Trattoria Da Mario.

The kitchen is indeed closed, the proprietor says.

"I'm so sorry for arriving so late. I'm a pilgrim. Is there any food that might not necessitate cooking?"

The kind proprietor calls out to the kitchen, turns to me with a gracious smile, and shows me to a table. I adore him immediately.

He comments on the heat. "It's thirty-five degrees centigrade! *Insopportabile!*"

Yes, insufferable. I feel a rash around my ankles where my socks end. But it's so cool in his restaurant, and he brings me white wine saying, *"Ci vuole."*

It's needed.

Along with salad comes slices of tender turkey—that wonderful way the Tuscans roll turkey breast with pancetta and herbs and then roast it. The proprietor sets the plate in front of me as if he knows I needed protein.

It's the best happy trattoria yet. And not only that. With the Nepal memory fresh in my mind, I realize that here I am, eighteen years later, having been lost again as a woman alone, and I don't mind it one bit. I sense a connection to the glow I had in Nepal, to the trust in the universe that curled contently in my heart back then. And I'm reminded that if I open my heart with trust, the kindness of strangers will always be there.

I can almost reach out and touch it, the new shore.

Ad rīpa. To the shore.

THIRTY-SEVEN

Wander and Wonder

Buonconvento's name derives from the Latin *bonus conventus* (fortunate community). The town used to be surrounded by defensive walls, with the old Roman Via Cassia running between the only two openings, Porta Senese on the northern side facing Siena and Porta Romana on the southern side facing Rome.

At the post office, I send a few things to Rome. Reducing the weight of my pack is going to help my feet. It's another scorcher of a day, and I can't imagine needing my raincoat again. I feel ruthless about saving my feet, so I add it to the shipment.

On my way to the bus stop, I pass by where the Porta Romana once was and read a plaque that says *Qui sorgeva la medievale Porta Romana distrutta dalle truppe Tedesche nel Giugno 1944.* (Here stood the medieval Porta Romana, destroyed by German troops in June of 1944.) Anger rises. The Germans were retreating and destroyed it out of spite. What good did it do them to destroy this porta that framed the way out of Buonconvento on the Via Francigena? It didn't help their war effort at all.

How dare you disregard Italy's heritage! I want to howl at the troops.

Alberto's directions go straight south from Buonconvento to San Quirico, a town of medieval origin, encircled by fortified walls. But there's a diversion to Montalcino, just west of San Quirico, and to the Abbey of Sant'Antimo, a few kilometers below Montalcino.

I can't resist this detour. I haven't been to Montalcino or the Abbey of Sant'Antimo in ten years, and I yearn to see them again. There may be a trail between Buonconvento and Montalcino, but Alberto doesn't cover it and the priest doesn't know, so I take a bus.

I'm now in the famous Val d'Orcia region, a UNESCO World Heritage Site, which extends south of Siena to Monte Amiata, the extinct volcano at the southern end of Tuscany. I wish I could lean out the bus window. No, I wish I was in a topless Fiat. The lines of pointed cypress are almost black against the undulations of grey clay hills. Stone farmhouses curl like cats in the sun.

Why is it so idyllic? It's the merging of the grain, vines, olives, and hay, it's the total absence of fences, it's the way it looks like a Renaissance painting. Indeed, the artists of the Sienese School during the fifteenth century depicted this very land in the backgrounds of their paintings. This landscape is a rich throaty tenor. I can almost hear Andrea Bocelli's voice singing "*Canto della Terra.*"

The bus deposits me at the top of Montalcino. Buses and cars aren't allowed to enter the center of town. A plaque for tourists lists contact information for B&Bs and hotels. I select one to call. A friendly woman answers and offers me a pilgrim rate of €35 a night. To get there, she gives me directions that take me through the town and down steep steps to a road hugging the hillside.

Nada, a slender woman about my age with brown hair in a loose bun, shows me to a room that I immediately love. There are white lace curtains, a terra-cotta floor, and a large bed with crisp white sheets. The spacious bathroom has three luxurious-looking towels. I lean out of the window, which is cut into the thick walls, and see the town curving along the hill to my right, while straight in front, I view gardens that sport palm trees and olive trees. In the distance looms the dusky purple volcanic bulk of Monte Amiata.

Conveniently, there's a clothesline outside the window. I promptly wash all my dirty clothes and hang them to dry. Then I eagerly head to the town center and settle into a bar with a panino and a glass of Rosso di Montalcino.

Brunello has the big reputation here in Montalcino, but Rosso di Montalcino has its merits. Called Brunello's "little brother," it's smoother and not as tannic and complex. Rosso di Montalcino is made from the grapes of younger vines and aged less, perhaps making it nicer than Brunello to drink in warm weather. And it's another scorcher today. From the castle at the top that's been turned into an *enoteca* to the central piazza surrounded by wine shops proclaiming that they ship, the whole little stone town is an endorsement of Brunello and Rosso di Montalcino.

As I eat my panino I scan the *La Nazione* newspaper. In it, an article on stalking catches my attention. Stalking, the author explains, is an English word meaning *perseguitare* (pursue, victimize, haunt). "Even though it's a new word," the author says, "the crime has been around forever." The article states that thanks to the efforts of a woman named Mara Carfagna, stalking has become punishable in Italy by imprisonment.

In the US, the word was coined in 1989 in the aftermath of the murder of an actress by an obsessed fan. When stalking was made a misdemeanor in California, it was too late for me. And that law did little for victims. Finally, by 1994, California's stalking law was amended to protect the victim. This meant that by 1994 (at least in California), a person guilty of stalking faced up to a year in jail if the infraction was filed as a misdemeanor. If it was filed as a felony, the sentence could be up to five years in prison.

All of this was too late for me to have Mutton Head strung up by his balls as my Italian boyfriend had said. Nico was from Naples and I met him soon after I arrived in London when I was twenty-one. I'd gone to London seeking work and a way to prolong my stay in Europe after my semester program in Florence. When I told Nico that Mutton Head's father was my parents' stockbroker—as in, all their investments were done through him—Nico had immediately said, "But they stopped using him, right?"

"Oh, no. That would have been causing a fuss."

"*Dio Buono!* What's wrong with you Puritans?" he'd exclaimed. He'd gone on to say that if one of his sisters had been wronged by his parents' stockbroker's son, or by the son of their fishmonger, or anyone else, they would have pulled their business out from under the guy immediately. "And we would have strung the son up by his balls," Nico had said with a mix of ferocity and matter-of-factness.

Maybe Nico was on to something. Maybe the puritanical culture didn't fit me. My gut said an immediate *yes* to his description of a family not giving a flying hoot about making a fuss in order to stick up for their women.

After lunch, I browse one of the modern wine shops where big busty Brunellos line up to be tasted. This is major league wine tasting. I ogle the bottles of Vin Santos from the Avignonesi winery, a top maker of this typical Tuscan dessert wine. At a cost of more than €100 ($128) a bottle, I refrain from buying one. Drinking Avignonesi Vin Santo will have to wait.

Back at the B&B, I prop up my feet, write in my journal, and fall asleep. The dragon roar of pain in my feet wakes me. Despite a long nap, there's a palpable exhaustion in my body, but I'm hungry.

Putting on my dusty shoes, I ease myself to standing, and climb the steep steps to the center of town. The restaurants look sleek, and I have no idea if there's a cheap one. I choose an enoteca that appears simple.

I order only a soup. It's not enough. I want five bowls of it.

The waiter chats with me. "I hope to own a wine bar."

"A wine bar in a Tuscan town sounds fantastic."

"I work hard, but I'm not stressed. That's what's important—to be at peace. People think too much and create chaos when they don't need to."

"I could be guilty of thinking too much!" I offer.

"Why are you doing the pilgrimage?" he asks, pulling up a stool as if he's got all the time in the world.

I give him an overview, and he looks at me quizzically. "You still have pain in your body, don't you?"

How can he tell? I nod. "I've got this thing with my feet, it's quite painful."

"That's like self-flagellation," he says.

"Huh?"

"Look, I know how long the recovery is from acute peritonitis. I'll wager you're not fully recovered from that, and now you're walking all day with plantar fasciitis? You may as well be in one of those Mexican Catholic Easter processions where they whip themselves bloody as they walk through the streets dragging a cross!"

"Oh, goodness!" I laugh.

"There. Now you look less exhausted!" he says with a smile. "Would you like a Vin Santo?"

After having a Vin Santo with the waiter, I ignore my feet and take a little walk. I enter a silent park illuminated by bright patches of moonlight and come to a bench where the hill drops dramatically away. The valley below is dotted with silver lakes and storybook farms on round hills. A lovely breeze arises—soft and moist, not like the dry, harsh Colorado wind.

I sit on the bench, noting the weariness in my body and recalling when I'd voiced to Gregg that I felt exhausted and how he'd said, "It takes a lot of energy not to be you."

It seems long ago now. Yes, my body is plumb worn out, but there's a new stirring now in my soul. I take the iPod out that a friend lent me. The only thing loaded on it is Caroline Myss's *Sacred Contracts* book. Her words are, "How should I fulfill my life? This question won't usually have an answer, because it isn't supposed to. This question is supposed to lead you to wander and wonder."[viii]

I'm certainly wandering and wondering, and since Siena, I have not obsessed.

"Thank you," I whisper into the shadows.

216 | CHANDI WYANT

THIRTY-EIGHT

The Most Beautiful Abbey

The skies are cloudy and rain threatens, but I'm determined to do a day-trip walk to the Abbey of Sant'Antimo, which I had dubbed in my mind the most beautiful abbey in Italy after my one and only visit to it ten years ago.

Nada explains the route to me. I will go a few kilometers on the *provinciale* road and then make a turn onto a dirt track. Then I will walk a few hours through the woods to the abbey. She insists on lending me an umbrella. I'm unsure how to carry it along with my trekking poles, but once I have begun my trek, I'm glad to have it because it rains most of the time I'm on the provinciale.

The trail leading off the road is indicated by the typical red and white signs of CAI, *Club Alpino Italiano*. As I start on the dirt track, the rain lets up. Gradually, the trail descends over hills full of purple thistle and yellow broom where sandy-colored sheep and white goats graze. Then it leads into the woods. These are goddess woods, I decide, because the energy is so good.

I arrive at an agriturismo, Villa Tolli. Its stone houses have brown shutters and red flowers in window boxes. Nearby is a sweet chapel. I neither see nor hear any inhabitants. It's a bit like coming upon Snow White's house after wandering through a forest.

Under a large oak tree, I spot a flat, square stone where I sit to eat my lunch of focaccia, pecorino, and a juicy nectarine. A contentment comes over me. I'm so unencumbered, beholden to no one, and free to peregrinate through the countryside.

After Villa Tolli, the path leads through the woods for a few hours and then out of the woods and onto the crest of a hill. I look down to a green and yellow vale where the travertine abbey beckons in the honeyed light. Again I'm reminded of a fairytale.

On a hill beyond it is the village of Castelnuovo dell'Abate. The small windows of the homes look like children's eyes, peeking out from behind trees. Beyond that, another line of hills is knitted with varying shades of green. Far in the distance is a much higher range, blue and flat, like a paper cutout.

When I reach the end of the path, I walk next to a bright wheat field and gradually slow my pace as I approach. "Sant'Antimo," I say under my breath. All is harmony here. A green slope with a scattering of ancient olive trees extends from the back of the abbey. Beyond that, rows of vines and olive trees are layered in precise lines. Two rows of vines, followed by a row of olive trees, and again, two rows of vines, one row of olive trees—repeating along the slope of a hill in a charming contrast of spring green and moss green.

An ancient olive tree traces the abbey's façade—delicate silver branches on warm travertine. Next to the bell tower, a single cypress with an immense trunk reaches toward the bells. Fantasy animals are sculpted into the exterior stone, and the entrance is crowned with bas-reliefs of curving feminine shapes. Legend says the abbey was founded by Charlemagne in 781 as he made a pilgrimage to Rome. This legend hasn't been confirmed, but it *is* known that the abbey was founded in the era of Charlemagne.

Shafts of sun come through the narrow windows of the ambulatory like warm fingers touching the cool interior. A timber roof covers the nave and columns supporting it feature sculpted decorations. The bases of the columns, carved in alabaster, glow when the shafts of light settle on them.

The monks at this abbey are known for Gregorian chanting. Travelers aim to be here when it happens. I have no idea what time it is or when it happens, but serendipity is mine today. Soon after I settle into a pew, the white-robed monks file silently into place and begin their chants in Latin.

> *Oro supplex et acclinis,* (Low I kneel with heart's submission,)
> *Cor contritum quasi cinis,* (See, like ashes, my contrition,)
> *Gere curam mei finis.* (Help me in my last condition.)

I have an urge to lie down on the abbey floor and feel the song of the monks swing back and forth, over me, like a thurible of incense.

What a blessing to walk to this abbey through the goddess woods and arrive where the monks' voices turn into stars in the sky.

When their singing ends, I find a monk to stamp my pilgrim passport. My finger traces over the stamp. I have walked to this most beautiful abbey in Italy.

Back outside, with the lines of olives and vines, the shining wheat, the buttery stone, I cannot say if it is more lovely inside the abbey or outside. In this moment, I'm sure that the land around Sant'Antimo is the most pleasing in all of Tuscany.

It's like Byron's lines:

There is a pleasure in the pathless woods,
There is a rapture on the lonely shore . . .[ix]

I lean in to a cypress tree, feeling its strength under my palm. Will I make it to Rome? *Don't be attached to the outcome*, I tell myself.

Trust. Build a tower of your trust so high that you can paint the mountains and valleys of your pilgrimage on the sky.

THIRTY-NINE

Saint Quiricus of Abundance

When I give Nada €70 for the two nights, she gives me back €20 saying, "For your pilgrimage."

Feeling teary, I give her a hug even though she's expecting the more common kissing on the cheeks.

It's raining hard—almost a deluge—and Nada's husband, Sergio, insists on driving me to San Quirico. "You cannot walk in this rain!"

"Thanks. So nice of you," I say. "I believe a pilgrim should try to walk, even if the weather is bad, but I sent my rain jacket to Rome."

What an idiot I was to get rid of my jacket! I accept Nada's gift of the umbrella she'd lent me the day before.

Sergio exclaims, *"Senza giacca? Fa male il fegato!"* (Without a jacket? Bad for the liver!)

I laugh, remembering the Florentines crying out, *"Fa male il fegato,"* in the winter if anyone opened a window on a bus, and in summer, if the air conditioning was on in a building.

Sergio drops me in San Quirico near the parrocchia. A Philippine nun shows me to a dorm-style room with bunk beds and indicates the small kitchen where I can cook lunch. "Two male pilgrims called and will be joining you here tonight," she tells me.

At first, I feel apprehensive about two male strangers in the room with me. I want to be back in my sweet room at Nada's in Montalcino.

Although the rain stops, my two long-sleeved layers don't protect me against the cold as I walk down the main street to find provisions for lunch. Browsing through a shop full of pecorino cheese wheels and other delectable products of the region, I decide I'll make a simple *aglio e olio* (garlic and olive oil pasta). Behind the glass counter, I see *pomodori secchi* (sun-dried tomatoes) in oil.

Those would be good in the pasta, and I can use the oil.

I explain to the shop owner that I'm a pilgrim and have kitchen use at the parrocchia but no olive oil.

"Of course you shouldn't buy it. A bottle is too heavy to carry," she immediately replies.

"Might you add a bit of extra oil to the *pomodori secchi*?" I ask.

"Of course!" She weighs them before adding the oil. "It wouldn't be right to charge you for the extra oil," she says.

When I ask for parmigiano, she asks if I want it grated.

"Good idea. There might not be a grater in the kitchen."

"Walking alone must be lonely," she says, wrapping the grated parmigiano in wax paper.

"It can be," I reply.

"But perhaps sometimes it's better than dealing with someone else."

"Yes, that's how it is."

A woman who'd been in the shop a few minutes earlier reenters and hands me a tiny glass bottle of olive oil. "I heard you say you don't have olive oil," she says, taking me by surprise.

"Grazie infinite!" I exclaim. "It looks like great quality."

"Yes, it's good for *condire*." (Dressing.)

I thank her again as I hand the shop owner €3.00. She tries to give me back fifty centesimi, but I tell her to keep it. "This is why I always come back to Italy. You are all so kind!"

She replies, "That's what is important in this world. It's the least we can do."

The experience in the shop makes me think of Florence and how I loved food shopping in the Mercato Sant'Ambrogio, just around the corner from where I lived. One of my favorite vendors in that *mercato* was Giuseppe from Sicily who, depending on the season, sold blood red oranges, lemons, strawberries, fava beans, and cherry tomatoes.

He delighted in handing me slices of lemon with a sprinkle of salt on them, urging, *"Prova! Assaggia!"* (Try it! Taste it!)

I always did, with a laugh, and lingered to chat with him.

Then there was Urbano's stall. Along with selling prosciutto and eggs, Urbano doled out appreciation. I remember when I first stopped there, he looked me up and down and said, "You're very feminine. A woman should be feminine, and you have a lot of it."

Urbano always got me grinning as much as Giuseppe did. To top off my rounds, I would stop at the forno on the corner, outside the market, a few yards from my door, where Paola greeted me with *"Cara!"* and put warm just-out-of-the-oven *coccoli* (dough fritters made from flour, olive oil, and salt) into a bag for me. Before I reached my door, I would consume them, melting in mouthfuls of happiness.

Back at the parrocchia, I encounter the Philippine nun and the two pilgrims, Gianni and Enrico, who are both from the north of Italy.

They shake my hand and ask, "Where did you start from? And when?"

I learn that they each started at the San Bernardino Pass about a week before I started in Fidenza and that they began walking together in Aulla.

They depart to get food, and I make my aglio e olio, noting again that cooking pasta makes me particularly happy.

For the equivalent of only four dollars, I had bought a half bottle of wine—a Sangiovese-Merlot blend, 2007, from the Banfi Estate. The largest estate in the Montalcino zone, Banfi is known for its medieval castle and luxury hotel as well as its excellent wine. Opened in 2007, the hotel has its own enoteca, a balsamic cellar, and a swimming pool overlooking the gorgeous countryside. It also has a museum with ancient Roman glassware and Etruscan pottery that had been unearthed beneath the castle itself, as well as a complete fossilized skeleton of a five-million-year-old whale discovered in one of the vineyards. I haven't stayed there, but I'd like to.

The simple bunk bed room at the parrocchia is a far cry from Castello Banfi's lodgings, but I'm happy to sit at the minuscule table in the little galley kitchen, consuming my half bottle of wine and my spaghetti. Maybe someday I'll be able to stay at Castello Banfi.

Enrico and Gianni return as I'm finishing my lunch. Gianni immediately says, "I smell aglio e olio!" The shorter of the two, he has a stocky build, a bald head, a thick neck, and copper-brown skin. Enrico is tall with a muscular body, huge hands, and a mild manner. He's less talkative than Gianni. He tells me he's fifty-six, but he doesn't look over fifty and neither does Gianni, who is sixty. They cram in with me at the table, and we begin to chatter in Italian.

Gianni tells me he'd walked the Camino to Santiago in 2006—a year that 96,000 other pilgrims did that walk too.

"Ninety-six thousand!" I exclaim. I run through how many I've encountered. There was the Swiss guy, the ponytailed guy on the bike, the Belgian couple, and the Dutch couple in the restaurant in San Gim. "I've only run into six pilgrims before you two."

"Oh, this is a totally different thing," Gianni responds. "The Camino has thousands on it every day. You can't get lost because there are so many people. If you wander off the route, there's always someone to wave you back on it. The Via Francigena is harder not only because you can get lost, but the terrain itself is harder."

"And you may be alone for days," adds Enrico.

"I'm glad I'm doing the Via Francigena before it becomes popular and crowded," I reply.

Enrico says, "I'm not sure any of us are experiencing an authentic pilgrimage. We all have many more comforts than people in the Middle Ages did, but I think the Via Francigena is as real a pilgrimage as you can get in the modern world."

"And why are you doing it?" I ask him.

"I live in a small town, and it's limiting," Enrico explains as he tips back the plastic chair to stretch his long body. "People around me are caught up in the fear-based culture. They're afraid of what's out there. The media contributes to this." He pauses to see if I can follow his words in Italian.

"I know what you mean. I often feel that the culture in my country is fear-based."

Enrico nods and continues. "Good people don't make the news, but the world is full of good people. This fact gets confirmed for me when I take a pilgrimage."

Gianni leans in. "My motivation is my profound love for my country and for the wonderful people that inhabit it." As he gestures with his hands, I notice a gold wedding band on his ring finger. "And by walking, I'm discovering things and meeting people in ways I never would traveling by other modes of transport."

We sit at the tiny table talking for two hours—the longest discourse I've had in Italian on the trip thus far. Talking with Gianni and Enrico reminds me of my early solo travels through Europe two decades ago and the encounters with other travelers in youth hostels.

How quickly they became my friends for a night or a few days.

Back then, on the budget backpacking circuit, I had often enjoyed spontaneous bonding, roaming through a new city with young people from different countries and singing and guitar playing far into the night. In contrast, during the pilgrimage, I'm almost always alone. After all the silence, I am, this afternoon, a real *chiacchierona* (a big talker).

Starting in the tenth century, San Quirico became an important commercial center due to its position on the Via Francigena. It doesn't take long for me to circle the town, admiring the well-preserved walls that enclose it and the fourteen towers. I pause at tower number thirteen, realizing it's a residence. Stone steps lead up to a door, and a tiled roof and little chimney cover the top of the tower, which had probably been shortened from its original height. I see a sign saying it's a vacation rental. How charming to stay in a medieval tower in this friendly little town.

Saint Quiricus, the town's namesake, was a three-year-old child when his mother, Juliette, was arrested while fleeing the persecutions of Diocletian. The Roman magistrate threw her boy down some stairs, killing him, which Juliette had to watch. She was then tortured and beheaded. So the story goes. Now Saint Quiricus is prayed to for the health of children.

That evening, walking with Gianni and Enrico down the main street to a trattoria, I notice that my words in Italian are flowing ever more effortlessly now that I've been in Italy a month. It's happened before, at about thirty days into an Italian sojourn, this cadence and flow that comes upon my speech, as if I've joined a pod of dolphins.

I tell the guys about sending my rain jacket to Rome and how I need a third arm to carry the umbrella while using my trekking poles. I say how foolish I was for sending my jacket to Rome.

"Yeah, that was foolish," Gianni agrees.

At the end of the meal, Gianni says, "Walk with us tomorrow, Chandi. The route is through Bagno Vignoni and on to Radicofani for the night. The day after, we'll enter Lazio."

"Oh, I don't want to leave Tuscany!" I say with a laugh. "If we're about to leave Tuscany, I'd better drink a Vin Santo!"

"Good idea," Gianni replies and orders one for each of us. When it comes time to pay, Gianni says, *"Ti offro la cena."* (I'm covering your dinner.)

Back at the parrocchia, I don't have to share the room with Enrico and Gianni after all. They graciously take another room up some stairs, without me saying anything.

Trust that the universe has gifts for you, I tell myself. I had passed the afternoon in pleasant conversation with them, enjoyed dining with them, and even had my meal paid for. In fact, every experience in this town had been full of generosity. I'm ashamed that I'd felt apprehension earlier.

I fall asleep thinking about the baby saint and how the town has been a place of abundance. Saint Quiricus might usually be prayed to for the health of children, but for me, he's a saint of abundance.

FORTY

If I Have Washed Your Feet

The next morning, I depart at seven with my new companions. The air is cool and clear—no rain. Our destination, Radicofani, is thirty-three kilometers away, more than twenty miles, and Alberto's directions for this section use the word impegnativa.

My companions are much stronger than me, and thirty-three kilometers is daunting. I fret at the thought that I might not keep up with them. I don't want them to have to make concessions for me. I want to be as strong as they are, to match their pace as if it's a breeze. But what I want and reality are two different things.

Don't argue with reality, I tell myself. I have to accept my physical condition. I walk behind them repeating in my head, *accept it, accept it, accept it.*

Gianni leads, consulting his GPS, and I'm able to enjoy the countryside rather than concentrate on which way to go. In only three and a half kilometers, we reach what Alberto calls *la prima perla della giornata* (the first pearl of the day), a tiny medieval hamlet called Vignoni Alto.

Almost hidden on the green hill, the stone buildings huddle around a severed tower, which had originally been built to watch over the Via Francigena. At the end of the silent hamlet are thick intact walls and, one by one, we step through an arched opening.

There, the glory of the Val d'Orcia spreads below us.

A dirt and gravel road leads us down the two kilometers to Bagno Vignoni, Alberto's second pearl of the day. The only sounds we hear in the peaceful morning air are birds twittering and our shoes on the gravel. We pass tall cypress trees that press themselves against small stone buildings and push their emerald spires into the sky.

While the Etruscans might have known of the thermal waters

at Bagno Vignoni, it was the Romans—great connoisseurs of hot springs—who developed this as a spa town. They consecrated it to the Nymphs, with an inscription in Greek:

> Oh, Nymphs living in these vapors, liberating the eternal fire among the waves, restoring life to those who suffer, I salute you and gift you with copious waters. Spring forth and bring health to the infirm, and to the healthy, a sweet bath. For both, we will be grateful.

When the Western Roman Empire fell apart, Bagno Vignoni fell with it, but the town perked up again when pilgrims began to come through on the Via Francigena, stopping to rest in the hot, healing water. The pilgrims included emperors, cardinals, and Saint Catherine of Siena. By the Renaissance, the Medici had constructed a large pool at the center of the town where the thermal waters bubbled up. Lorenzo de' Medici visited Bagno Vignoni frequently, attempting to cure his gout.

Bagno Vignoni is the only place in Italy where the main piazza is a pool of steamy water, which makes for an evocative sight. Having the place to ourselves, Gianni, Enrico, and I spend time next to the pool taking photographs and absorbing the quiet scene. In the early morning light, the sandy-hued stones of the handsome square buildings are perfectly reflected in the pool's still water.

The guys plan to push on to Radicofani, but I tell them I want to linger in Bagno Vignoni and "take the waters" as Lorenzo had done. Being there makes me think of his poetry, and of his struggles with gout and untimely death.

Hoping healing waters will give me a boost, I check in at the pool at the back of the Hotel Posta Marcucci, where I'm given a pilgrim discount.

The pool is rectangular and manmade, with steam rising from chalky blue water. Two other bathers hang on the side in a corner. I float on my back, arms and legs spread like a snow angel, my eyes on the gray clouds that are layered like the Italian dessert, *millefoglie*.

After soaking in the pool for almost an hour, I sit in a lounge chair and eat an apple and a piece of cheese from my pack as the lukewarm sun comes in and out between the clouds.

As I leave Bagno Vignoni my destination looms far in the distance. Radicofani is a striking castle on a basaltic mountain. I've been there before, but in a rented van full of friends when I'd not been looking at the mountain from the perspective of a pilgrim. It looks much farther than a day's walk, rising incongruously a few thousand feet up from the rolling pastures, almost at the far end of my vision. On the top of the mountain I can make out a Legoland grey crenelated tower.

I can't imagine walking all that way and climbing that crazy mountain at the day's end. I tell myself not to focus on how daunting it is and instead decide that I'll be provided for.

I'm starving. The apple and piece of cheese have done nothing, but my spirits remain strong, even though the millefoglie clouds begin to release rain above me. Along the road's edge, I walk, holding my umbrella in one hand and both trekking poles in the other. Luckily, the rain stops after twenty minutes, and the emerging sun unveils a stunning landscape.

Enraptured by the artistry of cypress-lined drives curving up little knolls, I stop constantly to take photos. The land displays a myriad of colors. On my left, a bright green pasture is full of white flowers, while on my right, a field is patterned from the cutting of the hay, and round hay bales glint gold when the sun emerges.

Beyond the hay bale field and up on a ridge, I can see the village of Castiglione d'Orcia with its turret and crumbled castle. Then I pass fields the color of chocolate. Beyond those are clay hills that look almost violet, and the low sky over them is all chalky and periwinkle-colored where it is still raining.

Next to me, a strip of wheat catches the sun's rays making a waving line of bright ochre. It creates a spectacular contrast with the rich dark earth just beyond it.

My eyes, heart, and soul embrace the landscape with rapture. The thought comes that I am nearer now to happiness.

I think of Freya Stark. In her book about her travels on the Aegean coast of Turkey in 1952, she wrote, "To catch even the echo of a thousand times weakened and repeated of the authentic voice of happiness, is worth a journey." [x]

After two hours of walking, I come to Gallina, with its few homes and a restaurant lining the road, and slow my pace. My feet have had enough of the asphalt. I decide to hitchhike. After five minutes, I'm picked up by a young guy who is an off duty *carabiniere*—a member of the national military police of Italy, which police both military and civilian populations. He tells me he works in Montalcino but lives in Viterbo.

His way of talking is strikingly different from how Tuscans speak. I'm awed that his speech is so different when Viterbo is only about thirty minutes south of the Tuscan border.

As we near the towering basalt mountain on which Radicofani stands, my driver comes to a stop. "I was going to stay straight on the Cassia, down to Viterbo. Are you going to walk up *that*?" He points to the road winding upward. I lean forward to get a look at it out his window. "Holy Cow!"

Then, in Italian, I exclaim, *"Caspita!"* turning to him with wide eyes.

"It's very steep, and there's ten kilometers of it," states the young man.

"And a pilgrim is supposed to climb that at the end of the day after already walking thirty kilometers?" I marvel.

"Look, why don't I just drive you up there. It's really not that far out of my way."

I don't even attempt to protest.

He stops at the entrance to the grey stone town, and as I exit the car, pelts of rain are released from the sky like hoplite arrows. I rush down the narrow cobbled street wincing and haphazardly scanning the houses for the Casa d'Accoglienza, a free place for pilgrims run by volunteers of the Confraternità di San Jacopo. Through the arrows of rain and obscured light, I find the door and ring the bell.

A middle-aged man sticks his head out from a window above. *"Vieni! vieni!"* he calls out in a cheery voice.

Up the narrow stairway I trot with a last burst of energy. I'm greeted by Gianni, Enrico, and two volunteers, Romano and Pierluigi, who are probably in their sixties.

My pack is wet and I don't know where to put it. The galley-like room contains a few kitchen appliances along one wall, and a small table is tucked at the end, by the window. Romano offers me tea, and after I wrap up in a wool blanket and drink two cups, I finally feel warm.

The contents inside my pack are wet, but not from the rain. I'd had a rain cover over my pack. The cap on my water bladder has come open. My only change of clothes is wet, so I'm not going to shower, but that's okay. The access to the shower is through a door in the kitchen that opens to a bathroom in a closet. I don't really want to shower and step out right where the four men sit.

Pierluigi invites us to mass. Gianni and Enrico immediately decline, which does not surprise me because they had shared with me their views that religions are hypocritical and nonsensical, but I don't feel polite declining. Plus, I don't have anything else to do. Pierluigi holds out a warm-looking coat, which makes the excursion palatable.

The short mass has some nice singing, and Pierluigi introduces me to the priest, who is jolly and talkative. Both he and Pierluigi exclaim how *brava* (fantastic) I am to come to mass, not being Catholic. The priest chats with me about the concerts featuring special international choirs that are hosted in the church because of its great acoustics.

Back at the apartment, Pierluigi puts on a brown cape with pilgrim shells on the shoulders and tells us to take off our shoes. Romano fills a pitcher at the sink.

I whisper to Gianni, "I have no dry socks!" I don't relish the idea of cool water being poured over my already cold feet.

Gianni, familiar with the ceremony, replies, "You have to go with it!"

"Is it a thing in the Bible? Foot washing?" I whisper to him. He jabs his elbow in my side as Romano approaches us with the pitcher.

I take off my shoes and socks, looking at Gianni for clues. But Romano comes to me first. He holds my feet in turn, while Pierluigi pours water over them. Romano dries them and Pierluigi kisses them. They do likewise for my utterly nonreligious companions and say a prayer about our feet taking us to Rome.

Then it's dinnertime. My hunger is galloping in my stomach. I watch as my hosts open a can of tomato sauce and pour it on the cooked spaghetti, throw some butter lettuce leaves into a plastic bowl, and set a few boxes of wine on the table. Before we consume the food, Pierluigi reads from a script about God blessing our pilgrimage.

The food doesn't satisfy my hunger. They don't know how big an eater I am, I think to myself as I drink too much wine to supplement the food.

As the only foreigner and the only female with four older Italian men, I wonder if I'm managing to blend in. Pierluigi recounts a tale of his walk from Rome to Jerusalem, and Gianni shares anecdotes from his time on the Camino. Romano tells us he volunteers on the Via Francigena because he deeply cares about it remaining a spiritual endeavor and doesn't want it to become a business like the Camino has.

That night, I share a small room with Gianni and Enrico. They both snore, and the rain, like a rousing rugby song, doesn't stop all night. Is there a saint of sleep? If so, he gives me no blessings this night.

FORTY-ONE

The Freaky Hostel

We walk for three hours to Ponte a Rigo, mostly in silent comradeship, passing tranquil countryside, stopping at times to look back at the wonderful views of Radicofani's castle on its mountaintop—something an illustrator would draw for a Hans Christian Andersen fairytale. In Ponte a Rigo, our route again joins us with the statale. Gianni and Enrico make a beeline for a truck stop bar, and I follow.

Over coffee, Gianni says, "The rest of the way to Aquapendente will be on the statale. It will be hard on your feet. I'll ask about a bus."

The woman running the bar tells us there's a bus to Aquapendente in an hour.

"Good," I say. "I'll take it."

We consult our accommodation lists and Gianni calls the Hotel Ripa. "A bed with real sheets is what I want," he says.

"Yes, please. I'll have a room," I say.

"I don't care about such luxuries," Enrico says, but he reluctantly lets Gianni book a third room for him.

My companions leave me outside at the gas station where the bus is supposed to come. The arrival time of the supposed bus comes and goes, and I realize I'll have to hitchhike. It isn't appealing loitering at a truck stop. I watch drivers park and walk into the bar. They're all men. Shifting on my aching feet, I push my toes into the dust, wondering if women ever drive on this road.

I try to intuit which driver might be safe to approach, but no one seems right until a camper pulls up. The man who steps out strikes me as Dutch or German—that's who tends to drive campers around Italy. When he returns to his camper from the bar, I ask if he's headed to Aquapendente. Yes. He says his wife is bicycling in the region and he's the designated driver. He's Dutch, and I am sure he's safe.

In Aquapendente, I find my way to the Hotel Ripa, a basic but decent place offering a discount to pilgrims. After checking in, I'm thrilled to sit down in the hotel dining room and eat French fries, grilled eggplant, and salad. But the town itself seems *tutto grigio*. The stone streets, the stone buildings, the sky—all gray. And the main piazza is a car park, rendering it unattractive.

I dine with my companions that night, and we plan to meet at 6:30 in the morning to tackle the long route to Bolsena. My alarm goes off and I thrust myself out of grogginess. I don't want to be late. I fill my water bladder and pack my backpack just so, putting a new battery in my camera, keeping out my bag of protein powder to add to hot milk for breakfast, and putting tissues and sunblock where I can reach them.

We walk until ten in the morning, when we arrive in San Lorenzo Nuovo, a town with a lovely view of Lake Bolsena.

"It's so big, the lake," I say to Enrico.

"The largest volcanic lake in Europe. You've never been?"

"No, I had no idea," I reply, trotting to keep up with him as he follows Gianni through a busy market. We come upon a bar with outdoor tables where we each eat a slice of pizza and Enrico drinks a beer. When he offers me one, I laugh and reply, "If I have a beer at this hour, I'll be done walking for the day!"

We pull out our phones and our lists of places to stay. Gianni calls one convent in Bolsena while I call the other. To our dismay, both are full. Gianni then calls a youth hostel. "We can stay there," he says, clicking off his phone. "It's a few kilometers before Bolsena, but we have to call the guy when we arrive. He has to come with a key."

"Okay," I reply reluctantly. The nun I had spoken to sounded so sweet. I want to stay at her convent. She told me there'd be room the following night, and I resolve to stay there if I need a day of rest in Bolsena. From San Lorenzo Nuovo, it's about twenty-four kilometers to Bolsena, which is twice as far as what I'm comfortable with—pathetic as that makes me feel.

After San Lorenzo Nuovo, the dirt track cuts through fields above the large lake that stretches out to our right. The golden wheat fields are strewn with vermilion poppies and slope down to a line of pines so dark they're almost black. Behind them, the lake is a saturated cerulean. As I walk behind Gianni and Enrico, I'm overcome by an urge to lie down in a field and ask the angel Gabriel to deliver me—where or to whom, I don't know. I only know that whenever I think I can't take another step, the meadows of poppies next to the trail lure me like a drug. Almost deliriously, I steer toward them, and Enrico gently steers me back to the trail.

What I've learned about Catholic angels and saints comes from Renaissance art, and all I know of Gabriel, besides the story of the Annunciation, is that he's the angel of consolation and mercy. Oh, mercy me. I want to lie down in a meadow and never get up. Instead of doing that, I focus on Gabriel, of Fra Angelico's image of him in the convent of San Marco in Florence. To distract myself from the dragon roar of the fastidio and the aches all over my body, I try to recall the details of that fresco: the classic Renaissance setting in which the angel appears to Mary under Brunelleschian arches; blond Mary, tall on her wooden bench and looking decidedly Scandinavian; Gabriel, his long golden curls and a pink dress, sporting outrageous psychedelic wings.

In spite of my exhaustion, I giggle. He reminds me of someone in Haight-Ashbury in 1967. Enrico's startled stare seems to suggest that I really am delirious as I stumble, barely holding myself up with my poles.

Then, as if he's picked up on my thoughts, Enrico begins talking about angels, telling me that Gianni is his angelo custode. He tells me that he pushes himself too much, while Gianni walks at a nice, steady pace and helps him to moderate.

"For example," Enrico says, as he slows to walk next to me, "the day I left Passo della Cisa, I kept going when I reached Pontremoli, and I walked all the way to Aulla."

"Enrico! That must be over fifty kilometers!" I exclaim, coming to a stop on the dirt track. I recall how I had walked only half of the route from Passo della Cisa to Pontremoli and arrived at Adriana's B&B absolutely exhausted. To then continue from Pontremoli to Aulla is astronomical.

"It *was* a bit insane. See, I don't know how to moderate. That's why Gianni is my angelo custode!"

After Enrico's words about angels, we fall to silence and I lag behind. The track goes on for miles, sometimes turning into a trail that winds through orchards of olive trees, then back to a track in wheat fields. Below us, I see the road that heads to Bolsena. *I'm going to have to go down there and get a ride! I'm going to have to . . .* But because I'm with Enrico and Gianni, I hang on. *Just one more kilometer.*

There's a gremlin in my shoes stabbing at my heels with a knife. I try to use my mind. I tell myself I don't feel it. And then comes the hunger, squeezing my stomach and snuffing out the air in it. My insides are concave, flaccid. But I continue, mile after mile.

Finally, we come to a large Madonna shrine at an intersection of two small roads. It's not a little shrine up in the wall. Rather, it's at road level and big enough to sit in, which I promptly do.

"Non posso muovermi," (I can't move) I say flatly to my companions.

Gianni consults his GPS. "The hostel is up there," he says, indicating a narrow potholed road that leads steeply upward.

"Nevertheless, I can't move." My voice is faint, my head between my knees.

"I'll go check it out!" says Enrico, who I'm sure could walk from this Madonna shrine to Moscow without stopping. I vaguely turn to see him trotting like a Clydesdale up the hill. Gianni sits next to me and phones the caretaker of the hostel.

"He's coming." Gianni sets his phone down, pulls out a handkerchief, and mops his head.

We sit in companionable silence on the smooth stone with the Madonna behind us. I doubt Gianni would say the Madonna is comforting, but for me she is. I think about ice, food, and a bed. Dear God, how heavenly it would be to have my feet in a bucket of ice and eat a bowl of *ribollita* soup. Then a small car the size of a sewing machine slows to a stop at the corner. Cheery voices call through the open windows, *"Pellegrini?"* (Pilgrims?)

Gianni nudges me. "Get a ride with them, Chandi!"

I manage to put my aching feet under me and stand. "Are you going up?" I indicate the steep road to the hostel.

"Sì! Anche tu?" they call to Gianni.

"No. I walk. Always," he replies as I climb into the backseat.

The driver bangs the little sewing machine of a car into potholes, and I note a sign for an agriturismo. After more potholes we come to the hostel. It's in a clearing backed by woods.

I climb a few stairs to a deck where Enrico is kicked back in a chair. *"Manca una birra!"* (I'm lacking beer!) he says.

I collapse in a chair next to him. "God help us if there's no food here. I can't possibly walk anywhere to get any!"

"Food and beer need to greet a pilgrim at the end of every day, don't you think?" Enrico replies.

Gianni trudges in on foot just as the caretaker's car pulls up. The caretaker whizzes about like a fly, quickly unlocking a part of the hostel that contains a few rooms: bunk beds, a bathroom, a sitting area with one couch, and a TV. He asks for €20 each and tells us to lock up when we leave.

"Um, is there possibly any food here?" I ask when he's done with his instructions.

He shrugs and says he'll unlock the kitchen and have a look. "That's all," he says, handing me a bottle of juice and relocking the kitchen.

"Take it, Chandi," Enrico insists. The caretaker buzzes away, and the three of us drop to the couch.

"Twenty euro! It's too much!" Gianni exclaims. "There's no food here, and Bolsena is five kilometers away!"

"No beer," Enrico says.

"No ice," I say, pulling a chair in front of the couch so I can elevate my feet.

"Twenty is too much. They can't charge that for a bed with no services," Gianni says.

"You guys wanna split this juice three ways?" I ask.

"No, you have it," they both answer.

"I believe I have a panino in my pack," Gianni says, his eyes lighting up. He digs around and pulls it out.

"How *old* is that?" Enrico asks.

"Um . . ." Gianni pauses. "Three days."

He takes out a knife and cuts the panino into three pieces. It consists of a crusty roll of white bread and slices of pecorino and salami. "You know," he says as he hands us our portions, "this place is like that horror movie, *The Hostel*."

"Oh, I can't stand horror movies," I say, alarmed.

"Yes, there's one where backpackers go to this hostel—"

"Basta!" (Enough!) I put my hands over my ears.

Enrico turns on the TV. Scenes of the movie *Elektra* come into focus. I sit with my feet up and my stinky clothes on, slowly eating my little portion of the three-day-old panino and watching Jennifer Garner speak Italian.

Shouldn't I be writing in my diary and contemplating spiritual aspects of the day? But no. I'm aware only of hunger, pain, and the odd way the Italian language comes out of Jennifer's lovely lips.

Gianni had seen the same agriturismo sign, and when *Elektra* ends and I come out of my stupor, I learn that Gianni has booked us dinner there.

As desperate as I am for food, I'm not sure I can walk.

"Maybe we can find a wheelbarrow to put me in, and Enrico, the Clydesdale, can push me," I joke.

Instead, I shower, get my poles, and walk between the two men.

What a lovely agriturismo, with a big white house, a green lawn, and a view of the lake. We are the only diners. A large carafe of red wine is on the table, and each of us promptly receives a plate of cheese, green olives, and prosciutto.

Perfect! I can eat cheese, olives, and prosciutto for hours!

Then comes a generous plate of pesto pasta. Oh, the taste of basil and olive oil sliding over pasta! Bless these people and all their ancestors!

After the pasta, we are each given a whole fish from the lake and a green salad.

"We should have stayed here!" Gianni exclaims.

"They might even have had a beer for us when we arrived!" Enrico chimes in.

"Or a cup of tea!" I say.

"And," Gianni leans forward as if to share something special, "breakfast is included. Plus, it doesn't cost that much more than the hostel."

"The freaky abandoned hostel," I add.

The meal costs €20—more than I've paid for any meal yet on the pilgrimage. But I'd also never had three courses, and it feels like the best €20 I've ever spent. In fact it feels like Christmas. What's more, when the proprietor learns of my foot condition, he insists on driving us to the hostel. Not even Gianni protests.

"We've got thirty kilometers to do tomorrow," Gianni says as we prepare for bed. "Enrico and I plan to leave at five thirty. Do you want us to wake you?"

"Oh, yes," I reply quickly. "I'm leaving with you two no matter how darn early it is." I'm too freaked out about the hostel to stay there alone. "Only as far as Bolsena though. I'm going to stay with nuns there."

FORTY-TWO

Ave Maria

To walk for an hour and arrive at my destination before 7:00 a.m.—as a non-morning person, this feels utterly strange. Without the benefit of tea or coffee to rouse us, we emerge drowsily from the hostel in the dusky dawn and walk for fifty minutes to Bolsena.

Entering medieval cobbled streets that are hugged closely by square stone houses with terra-cotta roofs, we follow our noses through the silent town and make our way to the main piazza. Just before it, we stop at a small bar for coffee. The cappuccino tastes so good, I order a second one for the equivalent of only ninety cents each. I make an *offerta* of buying coffee and pastries for my companions, and then it's time to say good-bye.

"I want to advise you about the last part of the route," Gianni says to me as we leave the bar. "When you get close to La Storta, the roads become dangerous for pedestrians. And after La Storta, the last twenty-five kilometers to Rome, you really should take the train. The route goes through a dangerous and ugly periphery of the city." He uses the words *pericolosissimo e bruttissimo*, giving emphasis to the words dangerous and ugly.

We wish one another *buon cammino*, and then they're off. The sound of their large boots on the cobblestones of the otherwise empty street echoes back to me as I stand alone. A sharp slant of morning sun hits the stone facades on one side of the via, while the other side remains in dark shadow. I'm sad to see them go, but I move toward the sunny side of the street, gathering inner strength and preparing myself to be alone again.

Walking down the street, I count off the remaining days of my pilgrimage. If I take the train for the last two parts—from

Campagnano to La Storta and from La Storta to Rome—I'll have five days of walking left. Five days sounds immense, especially if they are as exhausting as my walk from Aquapendente to the freaky hostel.

I remember hiking in the Apennines with a Florentine friend who said, when we scrambled up a mountainside, *"Non ce la fo."* (I'm not gonna make it.)

Non ce la fo my mind now tells me. God help me. I'm not gonna make it.

The convent of Santa Cristina faces the piazza from behind a large gate. I desperately want to curl up in a bed, but would it be impolite to ring the bell this early? It's only 7:00 a.m.

I ring, and a tiny nun wearing a gray habit, her head barely reaching my chest, greets me warmly with a cheery voice and smiling eyes. *Thumbelina* I pronounce her in my head. "The room won't be ready for a few hours, but you can put your pack here," she says, leading me to a sitting room off a wide hall. "And you can come to mass with us if you'd like. Here's some coffee." She points to a large vending machine. Since I can't curl up in a bed, I follow her and two other nuns across the piazza to the Church of Santa Cristina.

Cristina, the church's namesake, lived in the third century AD. Her pagan father was a wealthy Roman magistrate. When Cristina was approximately twelve years old, she converted to Christianity. She destroyed her father's golden idols of pagan gods and gave the gold pieces to the poor. In response, her father imprisoned her and ordered her to worship the pagan gods. Instead, she remained steadfast in her commitment to the new religion.

As the story goes, Cristina was then tied to an iron wheel with a fire beneath it. While the wheel turned, her body burned. But that night, an angel appeared and healed her wounds. Seeing her unharmed, her father gave orders to have her drowned in Lake Bolsena with a stone around her neck. Rescued by an angel, Cristina came out of the water and reappeared before her father, who said he would execute her in the morning. However, he died suddenly that night. His successor arrived and resumed Cristina's torture, ordering that she be locked in a red-hot furnace. After five days, the furnace was opened and she was found alive and unharmed. Seeing this miracle, many in the town came to believe in Christ.

How did her name come to be Cristina, I wonder? If her father was pagan, she couldn't have been named Cristina at birth. She must have changed it at her conversion.

I immediately like the feeling inside the church. A rustic looking trussed roof reminds me of the barns of my childhood. The nuns move through a marble portal on the right side of the church to the New Chapel of the Miracle, built in 1693 to preserve the relics of the Eucharistic Miracle of 1263. This story tells of a medieval priest who walked the Via Francigena and struggled with his faith. He stopped in Bolsena to pray at Saint Cristina's tomb. As he prayed, blood flowed from the host—the bread and wine of Eucharist that Catholics take in communion—staining the surrounding stones. This miracle caused Bolsena to become an important place of pilgrimage in its own right.

There are six other worshippers in the chapel, and I slide in and focus my breath, finding peace in the rhythmic sound of the nuns reciting the *"Ave Maria" lode.* I've heard it only once before, when I stayed in a nunnery eleven months ago, after the three weeks in the hospital. But then, I was too ill to consciously absorb the words. Now the words drop like Newtonian apples, my mind recognizing each one of them.

I pray at the end of the service that I'll manage to walk for five more days.

Then I explore the church and enter the grotto where Saint Cristina's tomb—a simple fourth-century coffin—was found during excavations in 1880. Hollowed into the rock, the grotto is clearly the oldest part of the cathedral complex. In the dim light, I move toward the altar, where the Eucharistic miracle took place. Under a stone balustrade with four beautiful Corinthian marble columns, the altar displays the stone that was hung around Cristina's neck when she was thrown into the lake.

I'm unsure how to get to the catacombs under the church. But knowing they're there, learning the story of Saint Cristina, and wandering in the cold grotto evokes the period of Late Antiquity. This tumultuous time, when Christianity was supplanting paganism in the Roman world, was a new topic for me in grad school.

Fighting an overwhelming desire to sleep, I wait for my room at the convent. About nine-thirty, Thumbelina leads me upstairs to a clean, undecorated room with its own bathroom and a view of the convent garden.

How delightful to lie on this narrow bed with crisp white sheets. I barely wake up in time to get to a trattoria for lunch. Following Thumbelina's suggestion, I go to a simple place that offers a fixed price of fifteen euro, but for pilgrims it's fourteen. At a little plastic table next to the cobbled street, my fourteen euros gets me a lasagna, a pork steak, a salad, and a fourth liter of wine. I consume it quickly. The young waiter smiles at my clean plate and returns with a Limoncello.

"Un'offerta," he says. "Because you're a pilgrim."

Now I have cause to linger. The quiet cobbled street and mellow atmosphere of Bolsena please me.

At the nunnery, I wash my clothes and Thumbelina shows me to a clothesline on an upper deck. "What's it like being a nun? Is it peaceful?" I ask her.

"It's peaceful, but it can be busy because we pray so often," she replies, handing me clothespins.

Busy because we pray so often? What an unusual kind of busyness that must be.

Thumbelina adds, "Do *you* feel peaceful?"

I pause, wondering how to answer. "With you in the church this morning, I felt peaceful. But life in general, where I come from . . . well, I guess most people wouldn't describe it as peaceful," I finally reply while hanging my well-worn socks on the line.

The nun leans her tiny frame against the wall of the deck and a breeze lifts her pale gray veil. "Do you feel you're on the right path?" she asks.

"I'm still trying to figure that out," I reply, smiling at her. "How did you know that being a nun was the right path for you?"

"Oh!" She clasps her hands to her heart and raises her eyes to the sky. "If you're called to do it, it's the most beautiful thing!"

Another nun appears on the deck and asks if the pilgrimage is challenging. I tell her about my feet. "Then you must take the bus to Montefiascone tomorrow," she says. *"È tutto in salita!"* (It's all uphill.)

"I don't want to take buses too often," I say hesitatingly. "My friends donated money so I could make this pilgrimage on foot."

Thumbelina chimes in. "Your friends donated because they want you to be healthy and happy, not because you *must* walk to Rome. What you *must* do is take the bus to Montefiascone tomorrow. If you ruin your feet, how will you visit the basilicas of Rome?"

"*Si, cara,*" the other nun interjects. "Visiting the basilicas in Rome is important!"

"Okay, I'll look into a bus," I reassure them.

Back in my room, I telephone the nunnery in Montefiascone to ask about a bed for the following night. Hearing my accent, the nun asks if I am German.

"No. *Americana.*"

"*Ah! Va bene!*"

Why did her voice perk up? It couldn't be due to residual feelings left over from the war, could it?

That evening, I walk to the lake down a straight avenue lined with magnificent plane trees—big grey and white trunks slanting toward the sky like the Leaning Tower of Pisa. I arrive in front of a restaurant on stilts. It's located over the water like something in the South Pacific. Next to it is a small strip of dark sand where two people in folding chairs sit, each holding a beer. Their faces turn toward the sunset.

I think of the nuns and how their life had looked momentarily appealing to me. But no, becoming a nun wouldn't suit me. My thoughts turn to the beaches I love in Mexico—Playa del Carmen and Tulum—and how good I feel with my bare feet in sand and those moist warm breezes on my skin. But if I move somewhere like that, I would miss Brunelleschi's dome, and Raphael's *Madonna della Seggiola* with the Arabian scarf framing her girlish face, and that blond doe-eyed Madonna of Lippi's in the Church of Santo Spirito.

The sun sets beyond the crater-made lake and Venus comes out in an indigo sky. Thumbelina's words play over in my mind: *If you're called to do it, it's the most beautiful thing!* It's a good life for her, here with the lake, and Venus, and Saint Cristina.

That night, in the narrow convent bed, I whisper the "*Ave Maria*" *lode* in Italian.

Whispering it in the language I love is the most soothing experience since that evening on Manarola's wall after the swim in the sea.

"*Ave, o Maria, piena di grazia . . .*"

FORTY-THREE

Vinum Est Bonum

I stretch in the bed and the cry of pain in my feet is the first feeling of the day. Ignore it, I tell myself stubbornly.

Dozing under the eiderdown, I think of the way these nuns open their hearts. They remind me of the Italian word *genuinità*. Genuineness. It comes from them in abundance like that stained glass of Saint Zita with her flowers in Lucca.

My legs swing over the side of the bed and my feet gingerly press to the terra-cotta floor, preparing to bear my weight. Downstairs, as I examine the vending machine, in walk three young guys with packs and hiking boots. They greet me in Italian and show me how to procure an espresso from the machine.

"We're from Rome," the one with dark curling hair and thick eyebrows says to me. "This is my bachelor party. We're going to walk from here to Rome."

"Veramente?" None of them look a day over twenty-five. They could be out partying up a storm for a pre-wedding send-off. Instead, they're walking for five days. What lovely young men.

"Are you walking to Montefiascone today?" he asks.

"Actually, I'm taking the bus. I've got this *piccolo* fastidio in my feet," I say, trying to make light of it.

I check out in the afternoon, and when I say good-bye to the nuns, I cry. They tell me not to pay for the night or the extra time in the room, and they give me a folio of prayers and call me *cara*.

I shoulder my pack and smile through my tears. They encourage me with calls of *"Forza! Coraggio!"* and I wonder how to gather all their faith and tranquility and take it with me.

As the bus climbs the hills to Montefiascone, I realize that when I feel sad or afraid, my heart closes. But all I have to do is open my heart like the nuns do and the joyful things in life enter.

The streets of Montefiascone leading toward the nunnery are almost vertical, like the steepest streets of San Francisco, but much more narrow. I feel like a squirrel heading up the trunk of a redwood tree as I scramble up them.

The nuns are *chiusura* (secluded—not leaving the convent). A small grate in the door is slid open after I ring the bell, and a pair of eyes peers out.

"*Sono la pellegrina!*" (I'm the pilgrim.)

"*Entra,*" says a disembodied voice as the thick door creaks open.

I step into a dark hall in a building that must have been built in the Middle Ages. In front of me is a black-skinned nun who asks me in Italian if I'm the one who phoned. She points to a narrow bench along the wall and asks me to sit while she gets her superior.

She has an accent, and I figure she comes from Africa. It's rare now for Italian girls to join the vocation. Most new candidates come from Africa and Asia. She returns with a wisp of an elderly woman dressed entirely in black who walks with her head pushed forward from her rounded shoulders.

"*Ma sei così giovane?*" (But you're so young?)

"*Insomma!*" (Not really!) I reply with a laugh.

I follow the elderly nun upstairs while the African nun settles back into a chair by the door. The dormitory room is lined with narrow cots that have thin, sagging mattresses. The bathroom is down the hall.

I spread my sleeping bag on one of the cots and head out to find food. An impossibly steep street leads me to a tiny piazza where I'm drawn to a wine bar. It is after lunch and before dinner. At that hour, a wine bar will likely have at least a plate of cold cuts. A pleasant man behind the bar named Angelo greets me happily and tells me to sit wherever I want.

I order a plate of *formaggio* and prosciutto. He suggests I try the white wine called Est! Est!! Est!!! that has made this town famous.

The story goes that in the Middle Ages, a German bishop who was very fond of wine set out on a pilgrimage to Rome. He sent his runner ahead of him to mark the inns serving the best wines with "*Est!*" on their doors in chalk. (*Est* being short for *vinum est bonum,* the wine is good.) In Montefiascone, the wine was so good that the runner wrote *"Est! Est!! Est!!!"*

It's said that when the bishop arrived in Montefiascone, he forgot about his pilgrimage and stayed there until his death, indulging in the local wine. Apparently, he was buried in a church in Montefiascone with a tombstone that states, "He died from drinking too much *Est*."

Angelo presents me with an abundant plate of *capocollo*, *bruschetta* with olives, and exquisite green tomato *marmelata* in addition to the formaggio and prosciutto. Then he brings over a bottle of the infamous white wine and sits down at my table. There are no other patrons, and we talk for the next hour.

"My wife and I moved here from Rome because it's more peaceful," Angelo explains. "But there are drawbacks to small town living. Within a few weeks here, people knew everything about us. In a small town, people love to gossip, especially about newcomers."

"Yes, it's like that in small towns."

"You see, I'm Roman, so I have an open mind, but the mentality in villages is so provincial. Teenagers get their licenses at age eighteen, but do you know that most of them here haven't even been to Aquapendente?"

"People are afraid of the unknown."

"Exactly. And the corporations that control everything want people to be afraid and only educated enough to operate a machine—not think critically. The uber-rich and the big corporations, they allow this thin sense of democracy, but this extreme inequality corrodes democracy."

"Yeah," I agree. "There's a huge concentration of wealth at the top in my country. I think it's something like twenty individuals at the top own more than half of the population of the country. And they get involved politically only to push for their self-interests."

"The top small percent has so much of the wealth and so much control over the media and politics, how does the bottom ninety percent even begin to get some power? They have us by the balls," Angelo says, giving the "I've had it" gesture, which symbolizes imminent explosion of testicles.

He fills my wine glass a second time and begins speaking so fast that I struggle to follow his Italian. Wishing I could speak about the topic more easily in Italian, I count my blessings. Here I am in another town, alone, and I've walked into this bar where the owner has given me a bounteous plate of food with a pilgrim's discount and chatted with me for an hour.

At the convent, I ask the African nun if there's a grocery store nearby. I need to get provisions for the next day's walk.

"At the bottom of the hill," she says.

I know if I go in search of it, I'll have to clamber like a squirrel back up the crazy steep streets, and my feet aren't up for it.

As if reading my mind she says, "I've got some Philadelphia and crackers you can take for tomorrow."

"Oh, thank you!" I'm touched and carry the plastic container of cream cheese reverently to the dorm room.

There are no other guests in the convent. Just me, the stranger from seven thousand miles away, here behind these thick walls with the closed-in nuns and their silent reverence. Just us and the inward-looking stones that have been here for seven hundred years, absorbing prayers.

FORTY-FOUR

Locked Up

It's a cloudy morning when I leave the silent convent in Montefiascone and head to the top of town, as my instructions indicate. The street is so steep, the hill so narrow and pointed, and the presence of buildings on it so improbable, that I feel I'm in a Dr. Seuss book.

I stop in a bar and add the last of my protein powder to hot milk. Continuing to the tippy-top of the narrow street with my stomach protesting that it wants oatmeal, I arrive at a park, a view of Lago di Bolsena, and a crumbled tower. Alberto calls it a pilgrim's tower, and his directions instruct me to take a stairway from the tower to a parking lot. From there, I find a small street heading downward.

I walk to an arch—one of the charming barrel vaults seen often in Italian hill towns, that appear to hold back the walls on either side. This particular vault has, in the middle of it, a rectangular window with brown shutters and white curtains. Red geraniums burst out of a window box. Passing under the vault, I stop near two pine trees at the edge of an escarpment. Through the pine branches, the bright blue of Lake Bolsena twinkles far below.

My route drops me to a flat plain, one that stretches from the bottom of Montefiascone's steep sides to the city of Viterbo, tucked at the base of the Cimini Mountains. I'm pleased to walk on dirt tracks, with an occasional gravel road, and not on asphalt. When the sun comes out at about 9:30, I stop at the side of the road to retrieve my hat from my backpack, and a man in a truck slows to a stop.

He leans out the window and says, "Are you crazy to walk to Rome?"

I'm not sure how to reply. "It's a pilgrimage," I say and concentrate on pulling out my hat. I feel relief when he drives off.

Famished, I sit down and eat all of the cream cheese and crackers, and then for more than an hour, I follow the yellow pilgrim signs along the tracks between fields of wheat, corn, and olive trees until I arrive at the hot springs mentioned by Alberto. The land is flat with little vegetation, and I see no place to change into my bathing suit. Being Saturday, the visitors—including lots of women and children—are plentiful. I remind myself that Italians often change very casually on beaches. It won't be a big deal to duck behind a clump of pampas grass to put on my swimsuit.

After relaxing in the hot pools, I'm getting back into my clothes behind the pampas grass when I hear thunder barking across the plain. I put the cover over my pack and, as I begin walking down the gravel road, the rain starts. I awkwardly hold my umbrella in one hand and my poles in the other. When the rain pelts me at an angle, I tip the umbrella toward the deluge and manage to stay dry, except for my feet. Hunger gnaws at my stomach and I sense my blood sugar dropping. The cream cheese seems to have done nothing.

Nearing a cemetery after walking a few miles, I can tell I'm reaching the outskirts of Viterbo. I turn onto a large paved road and speeding cars spew waves of water at me. My hunger drains my energy, and as an even more forceful downpour descends, my spirits begin to feel as drenched as my feet.

I take refuge at a bus stop. After about ten minutes, a local city bus approaches. I stand up and wave. The driver stops and opens the door, and I call out, *"Centro Viterbo?"* For some reason, the driver laughs at me, as I stand in the pelting rain, before he waves me onto the bus.

The bus circles Viterbo's walls interminably. How many times can it go through a large porta into the historic center, then out into the modern areas, then circle the walls again and enter through yet another porta?

I check with the driver again. Has he understood I'm going to the *Instituto Adoratici Sangue di Cristo*? He speaks in a dialect, and I can hardly understand him.

Finally, outside the walls and up a hill, he stops. "It's that way," he says, pointing across the boulevard to a series of streets leading up a hill.

Crossing the boulevard, I look for street signs but can't find any.

I stop in a beauty salon to ask for Viale 4 Novembre, but neither of the girls know where it is. Then, when I finally find the right street, I can't find the convent. After walking the length of the road and standing at the top of it, the same bus lumbers up from a road to my right and stops. The driver leans his head out of the small window and laughs at me for a second time.

"You've passed it! It's there—in that street!"

Too weary to find it funny, I take a breath and reply, "I didn't see it."

He tells me to go back and look carefully on the left for a small sign in a wall.

Indeed, imbedded in a wall is a wallet-sized sign that reads *Instituto Adoratici Sangue di Cristo*. Filled with relief, I ring the bell.

The nun's greeting is nothing like Thumbelina's in Bolsena. This nun, tall and angular, has a pale face and a sour expression. She leads me to a room with a bathroom attached. I fervently hope she will offer me tea. I mention I'm famished and dehydrated, and that I've been caught in the rain. But no offer of tea comes.

"Might there be a place open nearby to eat?" I ask. "I may have missed the lunch hour."

"There's a bar down the street," she says with a shrug.

"Shall I ring the bell to get back in?" I ask her, concerned about interrupting the nuns' prayers. I use the verb *entrare*, to enter, and she thinks I've said *cucinare*, to cook.

"*Cucinare?*" She sounds alarmed.

"*No. Entrare,*" I say.

"Yes, just ring. We're not a hotel!"

I bite my tongue.

As soon as the nun leaves my room, I hastily strip off my wet clothes and take a hot shower. My body is slightly revived from the shower, but now I have a shoe problem. My shoes are soaked. I'll have to put on my keens instead, although they're not good for the plantar fasciitis because I can't put my inserts in them. My feet will quickly get wet and cold in either pair.

Oh, I'm dying for tea and food. My blood sugar has dropped to my knees—worse than any other time thus far on the pilgrimage. I find a bar at the bottom of the road outside the city walls. But there's no food. I tell the proprietor I've walked from Montefiascone and have missed the lunch hour. I ask if anything in the center might be open, and he assures me I'll find something there. Although I'm limping like the sad dogs I've seen on the streets of New Delhi, I will walk farther to find good food.

Through the big porta and down a cobbled street, I see a little trattoria. Closed. Farther along, I come upon an enoteca with a grotto-like interior. It's empty except for a guy clearing tables. I greet him and explain why I'm walking in so late. No acknowledgment shows in his face. He wipes the top of a glass case where I see delectable-looking cheeses. I tell him I'm starving and just need a bit of food—anything.

"We're closed," he says dispassionately.

I resist a desire to leap over the counter and tackle him for a wheel of cheese. Instead, I turn to stumble outside. My head is light, as if unattached to my body, while my feet are heavy as lead. I manage to steer myself down another street, where I see a bar. It's not the homey trattoria with hot soup I'd envisioned, but it will have to do.

Selecting a premade tomato and mozzarella panino and a *limonata*, I settle into a plastic chair at a tiny plastic table. On TV, two short thick-bodied men in tight spandex leotards are wrestling.

The panino doesn't make a dent in my hunger, so I go to the counter for another. This time with tuna. Maybe the tuna will give me energy. Seeing beer behind the glass door of the fridge, I think of my housemate who I'd squeezed into my tiny house this year to help pay the bills. She loves Boulder's homegrown breweries. "Beer fixes everything," she's fond of saying.

Maybe a beer is what I need.

But after the beer and the second panino, I don't feel an ounce better. I want to pass out. But where? Can I manage the walk up to the convent?

On TV, the wrestlers continue their ritual of slamming each other to the ground and locking their bodies together as if death itself can't part them.

I am still waiting for the food and drink to revive me. Maybe I need coffee?

"Un caffè per favore," I say, giving the bar guy a wan smile. I've never before tried so many drinks to revive myself.

I will the coffee to give me sustenance to hobble up the hill to the convent. Although exhausted, I don't want to go to bed at 4:30 in the afternoon and risk not sleeping during the night, so I wander into the convent's lounge and leaf through a magazine. A pale-faced Italian, somewhere between a boy and a man, enters and sits near me.

"Where are you from?" he asks. He then quickly explains he's with a seminary, training to be a priest. "Do Americans have the same mentality as Italians?"

"Uh . . . I'm not sure I can speak for all Americans," I reply.

"But *I* can speak about the mentality of all *Italians!*" he exclaims, looking perplexed.

"Well, in my country, we come from many different backgrounds." I wonder if I should explain the melting pot, but I lack the energy.

"In Italy, we are all one thing!"

"The US is very diverse, you see, while Italy has experienced immigration only recently."

"I don't know what you mean by diversity, but I know everyone is rich in America. Like on the TV shows," he says, his pale face serious.

"Well, not everyone is rich. Some people are homeless."

"What do you mean homeless? I didn't see that on TV!"

I realize I'm too wiped out to manage the conversation. "I'm sorry, you'll have to excuse me," I say, fleeing the lounge on my tortured feet.

From the window of my room I watch the rain heave itself onto the plane trees, and I remember that here in Viterbo, the concept of a papal conclave was born. Back in the thirteenth century, when Viterbo was home to the papal court, an interminable papal election occurred, lasting almost three years. After two years of squabbles, the cardinals still hadn't elected a new pope. The frustrated city officials locked the cardinals in a meeting hall and reduced their diet to bread and water. When their bickering and intransigence continued, the city officials took the roof off the hall so the cardinals would suffer from the cold as well as from hunger. Finally, the cardinals made a decision—or so the legend goes.

The cardinals finally elected Pope Gregory, who decreed that future papal electors would remain strictly locked up until they named a new pope. Their meals would be reduced to one a day if their deliberations took more than three days. *Conclave* comes from the words *con chiave*, with key.

I feel a bit like those thirteenth century cardinals—cold, and hungry, and locked up, not by a conclave, but by a body that's in pain again. No amount of work with my mind will make it go away. My body waves at me like a white flag of surrender.

I'd slipped into surrender so smoothly in the hospital when they'd wheeled me into the operating room, when I'd felt only trust, gratitude, and surrender.

The branches of the plane trees yield gracefully to the rain, fluidly without resistance, dropping and rising. My forehead rests on the cold glass of the window. I close my eyes and whisper, "Trust, gratitude, surrender."

FORTY-FIVE

Ancestors

A cough begins in the night that keeps me awake. In the morning, my usual hobble to the bathroom ends with me slumped on the toilet with stomach pains and diarrhea.

Yikes. How does a pilgrim walk with diarrhea?

At breakfast, when the young priest-in-training sits down at the table across from me, I tell him I'm ill. I fear I'm not up for more discussions about whether everyone is rich in America.

I wonder about staying another day, but I don't feel particularly comfortable at the convent. What about my thoughts of surrender? Can I walk another day? A stubbornness comes over me, and I decide to try walking one more day.

Alberto calls the route to Vetralla impegnativa because there are no towns along the way for water or food. Plus, it's twenty kilometers, over twelve miles.

Exiting out a porta in Viterbo's wonderfully preserved medieval walls, I stop to read the directions. *Prima della recinzione del marmista giriamo a destra.* Before something of something, turn right.

What is *recinzione* and what is *marmista*? My brain is foggy. I tell myself to break down the first word. Surely the verb *recintare* means to enclose? And *marmista* must relate to the word *marmo* (marble).

Marmista would be someone who works with marble, and *recinzione* must be a fence. Oddly, I've never run in to either word before. After passing along the edge of a two-lane road, I see a right turn and, indeed, there's a fence, although I can't tell if anything to do with marble is happening behind it. There's my friend, the yellow pilgrim on the fence, and I begin to walk more confidently as I turn onto a narrow one-lane road with high green banks.

Spontaneously, a message comes to me: *Drop along the trail the weights of the past in order to receive the gifts of today.* It becomes a mantra that stays with me as I continue on the leafy lane.

I start to name the weights and metaphorically drop them as I walk. My list, said aloud and witnessed by the oak trees, goes like this: "My divorce. Okay, but what about my divorce? The idea that I'm flawed because I got a divorce. *Do I have that idea?* Okay, drop it on the trail anyway. The idea that it's stuck in my body. *Yes, that's a good one.* Drop it on the trail!"

I start to swing my trekking poles and point them at the weights I drop, which I picture as plate-sized dung heaps.

"Umm . . . what about . . . how I choose the wrong guys? Let's drop that too, and Mutton Head. Good riddance!" I stride on, down the car-less lane. "I'm dropping the idea that I shouldn't be in my power."

"I'm dropping the fear of speaking my truth." *Why do we do that? Play small?* "Drop it on the trail!"

In my mind's eye, I see the dung heaps behind me while the gyrations in my stomach warn me that I need a bathroom. The only option is to scramble up the roadside bank and find a spot in the corner of the field. Oh, this diarrhea isn't convenient!

I relieve myself, slide back down to the road, and stand with my pack resting on the ivy-covered bank. My heels feel like shards of glass are pressing into them.

Non ce la fo. I'm not gonna make it.

The sound of a scooter makes me turn. It's a woman in a powder blue dress showing a stretch of bare legs above black boots. She slows the scooter to a stop. Her skin is the color of whipped honey.

"You're a pilgrim?" she asks with curiosity.

"Yes."

"What town are you walking to?"

"Well, I was hoping to walk to Vetralla, but I don't think I can make it."

"It must be hard. And you're alone?"

"Yes."

"Coraggiosa!"

I laugh. "Do you know if there's a bus?"

"To Vetralla? Not from this road. Do you have a GPS?"

"No. No GPS, no compass, no maps, no iphone."

She raises a delicate eyebrow that I can just see under her helmet.

"By choice," I add, not wanting to appear as ill-prepared mentally as I am physically.

"To take a bus, you should backtrack toward Viterbo and head south. On the SS2 there will be a bus to Vetralla."

"Um, okay." I hesitate. Backtracking is not appealing.

"If you keep going this way, you'll get further from a bus route," she says, seeing my hesitation.

"*Senti.*" (Listen.) She pats the scooter seat behind her. "Get on the back and I'll take you toward the SS2. It's not out of my way."

"Really?" Now I'm raising an eyebrow. There's room for me *and my pack?*

"*Certo!*" she says with a laugh. "It will be my good deed for the day! *Forza!*"

"At least I walked *some* of the route," I say.

As we take off, in an instant, I'm light—as light as the air in my face and the sun dancing in and out of the leaves above. The shards of glass are momentarily gone from my heels.

She's an angel in a blue dress.

Drop your weights along the trail and receive today's gift! Indeed.

The bus comes without much of a wait and deposits me near a gravel road leading to the nunnery in a quiet countryside area just outside the town of Vetralla. An African nun answers my ring at the gate of *Monastero Regina Pacis.*

I follow her black robes down the corridor.

"I'm sad about Michael Jackson's death," she says over her shoulder.

Could a nun really be a fan of his music?

"I don't know if he'll make it into heaven. He may not have had a chance to ask God for forgiveness."

"Ah, yes," I say.

She opens the door to a small spartan room with no bathroom attached. "I'm praying for him," she says as I set down my pack.

"That's good." I try not to show my weariness.

"You are tired," she says.

"I have stomach problems. Diarrhea. And a cough."

"Come," she says, and she takes me to a central *sala.*

She leaves and returns with a stooped, ancient Italian nun who holds out a glass jar of homemade syrup.

"I made it from the nuts of the tree outside," she says.

She pours a spoonful, her hands thin and worn like scratched eggshells. *"Ti fa bene!"*

"Mille grazie." I drink from the spoon. "Which tree?"

Holding my elbow, she steers me to a doorway. "That one."

"Alloro?" (Laurel?) I squint at the tree.

"Take it with you." She presses the jar into my hand.

That evening, I eat by myself in the sala. The nunnery is silent. I'm served plain spaghetti, nothing on it except olive oil and a dash of parmigiano.

Maybe they want it to be as plain as their lifestyle.

After the pasta, a young nun brings me a plate with a small piece of meat and some stewed cabbage.

"How does it work, being closed in, when you need things from town?" I ask her.

"The *fruttivendolo* and the *fornaio* come here." (The greengrocer and the baker come here.)

"Fruttivendolo!" I say, laughing. "That's my favorite Italian word!"

The nun looks at me politely, but I imagine she thinks I'm not the brightest nut on the laurel tree.

The problem with the English words—*greengrocer* or *fruit and vegetable seller*—is that they end in consonants, which describe an occupation in a flat way. Whereas, the word *fruttivendolo* becomes a festival of people in Carmen Miranda hats, grinding organs and juggling oranges.

Finishing my modest meal, I think about the life of the closed-in nuns, and my thoughts turn to my female ancestors who have been showing up prominently on my journey. It occurs to me that my inner journey seems more salient now than my outer one.

I have the last letter Gerald Heard sent to Aunt Margaret. Dated December 29, 1963, it's five typewritten, single-spaced pages, mostly about death and how to let go when the time comes. When I reread it before I left on the pilgrimage, I noticed his words about pain: "All pain is our unfinished evolution demanding that we develop further."

Wasn't that the very reason for my pilgrimage? My pain demanding that I develop further?

"We are always in touch even dimly now. In prayer there is no absence," he wrote at the end of the letter. I love those words, *always in touch even dimly now*. It's like that for me with my grandmother.

As I lie down on the narrow bed with threadbare sheets, I decide I need to stay with the nuns the next day more than I need to walk. In the morning, I go with them—all African except the ancient Italian one—to the small church next to the convent for their lode, which lasts about thirty minutes.

Then a priest arrives to give mass. His sermon is about faith. Bald except for a few long hairs swept over his head, he wears a red cloak with a white dove on it. "Faith is believing in what's invisible, not only believing in what can be seen and what can be verified," he says.

I think of the Muslim family I'd stayed with in Kashmir on my first travels around India. The father had said to me, "We don't worship idols or cows like the Hindus because we have faith in something that's invisible."

The priest goes on to talk about the pope. He calls the pope a martyr and a saint because of the criticism he has received from TV and newspaper reporters. "You have to be very strong to withstand that criticism," he says.

I'd hoped to find a sense of prayer for myself during the service, but there's too much getting up and down when I want to just sit, breathe, and find my center.

At breakfast, I notice the convent's bread is moldy, so I eat a few biscuits with my tea. Not very satisfying. My stomach is still off and the cough kept me awake again. The potion from the nun is all I have, so I take it and head to the garden to see if I can find the peace that had eluded me in the church.

Like the building and meals, the convent garden is simple. It consists of a few gravel paths, some rose bushes in pots, a wrought iron table with chairs near a wall where a jasmine vine suns itself, and an adjacent grove of cedar trees. In this setting, I turn on my iPod to listen to Caroline Myss. What she says is eerily appropriate: What's the significance of forty days? It's the incubation period through which the spirit manages to become stronger than the physical world. [xi]

A small grey dove flies in front of me as I walk toward the cedar grove as Caroline continues.

Write a prayer and put it away for forty days. Ask for a revelation. Ask for guidance for how to move forward with your spiritual life. Put it away for incubation. Await the answer in forty days. [xii]

I pause the iPod and think of the requests I'd written in the Church of Santa Maria in Trastevere before embarking on the pilgrimage. I had put the requests away, planning to take them out again at the same church after forty days. I think about the answers incubating and I remember when my grandmother said, "Now I'll have insight instead of outsight!" when her eyesight began to fail.

Had I ever been that positive?

I feel an existential panic as I wander under the cedars. I'm privileged; I'm able to take the time to do a pilgrimage. How many of the world's women are dealing with civil unrest, violence, scarcity? Fifty percent of them?

My divorce wasn't such a big deal.

The grey dove scratching at the ground lifts itself into the blue light. I feel a release, as if a wind has blown through me, sweeping up debris inside me and scattering it to the sky.

My divorce doesn't matter. My connection to my ancestors does.

So many letters came in when my grandmother passed away. I didn't know how all those people, some in other countries, had heard of her passing. Many letters resembled this one:

I have spent some time today thinking about Ena—what a mighty spirit in that tiny body, a fierce warrior fighting for what she believed in. I have such lovely memories of tea in her little hobbit house, of our long talks on life, of death, of love, of children and their education, of injustice and justice. She was totally alive to life, an indomitable spirit, a wonderful and giving friend, an educator, a wise woman, and a true world citizen as she wished to be.

My grandmother started her process of passing to another realm at my parents' house during Christmas of 1992. She was bedridden but wanted to see the daffodils, which were blooming in January, thanks to the mild California climate. But my mother and I knew we couldn't lift her to take her outside to see the daffodils. Then my boyfriend, Ted, arrived. He picked her up—though her tiny frame had become heavy—and carried her outside. Impressed by Ted's strength, we followed, none of us thinking to bring a chair. Ted bent a knee to the ground and managed to hold my grandmother on his thigh while she absorbed the host of golden daffodils in front of us.

At the garden table where I'd left my notebook and pen, I write this passage:

I have reclaimed my story, and perhaps the stories of the Isherwood women. I have stronger roots now, my feet are firmly planted now, as I look to the future with my female ancestors at my back.
"We have been here all along. You only have to turn to us."

I think of my grandmother standing tall after a painful divorce, holding her children's hands on the dock in Genoa as they got the last boat out of Europe to the United States. How brave to leave her children with a family in Philadelphia when she went to New York for a job. She had lost her marriage, she had lost her beloved community at Dartington, she had gone to another country, and then she had left her children with someone else in order to get a job. Somehow, she still had the energy to create and run a camp in Maine for British refugee children. This is resilience. Through reflecting on hers, I find my own.

Leaving my journal and pen on the table, I go back to the cedar grove. The trees have dark shadows on one side and bright light on the other, like a Caravaggio painting. I sit at the base of one. Sunlight touches the swirls of a cedar cone on the ground. My grandmother used to take me into the redwoods, pointing out the circles of light on the forest floor, and telling me it was where fairies danced. I tip my head to the Caravaggio highlights above me, and I tell myself, *we are always in touch even dimly now. In prayer, there is no absence.*

FORTY-SIX

Surrender

After resting half the day at Regina Pacis, I take a bus to Sutri, the next stop on the route, which Alberto's directions say is 22.5 kilometers away. Fourteen miles is definitely more than I can walk. With my stomach problems and a cough that won't quit on top of plantar fasciitis, my body is giving up.

The stooped nun who gave me laurel berry medicine asks for €37 to cover the night and two meals. As I walk slowly away from the nunnery toward the main road, I wonder if I'll have enough to cover the rest of the trip. Given my finances, Sutri probably *has* to be the last stop.

My poles click on the black road and sunlight flickers through a canopy of leafy green as I walk toward the bus stop. Feeling nostalgic, I realize I'd dreamed of Florence in the night.

In all my time abroad, when contemplating "home"—whether it was Santa Cruz, California, or Boulder, Colorado,—the thought never made me teary. Oh, I love the way those towns uphold a healthy lifestyle, I love the intellectual buzz of their universities, and I love their organic food stores and progressive politics, but Florence is the only place that makes me teary from missing it. Just a month ago, while working at the computer, I glanced at Facebook and saw a friend's photo of a street in Florence. My heart had such a pang in it and I felt so utterly displaced that tears stung my eyes.

The bus comes on schedule, and I settle into a seat with my pack next to me. Lulled by the soothing green countryside and the bus's motion, I think about what Florence has given me: a place where my soul sings. Maybe some people get that in a good marriage—in a really strong partnership—in knowing that someone is there for them no matter what. For me, it hadn't happened that way. But I have Florence. The knowledge fills me with gratitude, and I feel a sense of abundance like never before. I can't find any of the grief.

The bus drops me at the Sutri amphitheater. Legend says that Saturn founded Sutri—*Sutrinas* to the Etruscans and *Sutrium* to the Romans. The town is built on a tufaceous cliff and was one of the last strongholds of the Etruscans—a pre-Roman civilization from which the Romans derived some of their cultural and artistic traditions.

Immediately taken with the ancient atmosphere, I wander around the amphitheater before calling the convent. When I had phoned the Oasi di Pace earlier in the day, I was told to call back when I arrived in Sutri, and a nun would come down the hill to fetch me by car.

The amphitheater could be a Roman creation but it may be Etruscan—perhaps the inspiration for the coliseums the Romans later built. Instead of constructed with stones, it was carved from the tufa rock cliffs. The rock—at times red and at other times gray—is dappled with green moss. The floor is grassy green. Mediterranean pines and oak trees grow along its curving top. It's unlike any I've seen.

The amphitheater is nearly devoid of visitors, and I'm reminded of the ruins I'd stumbled on in Greece. In the 1980s, I'd spent three months there, mostly off the beaten path. When I came upon ruins in a spring meadow with not a tourist in sight, the ancient pulse was palpable. For hours, I walked dreamily around the great columns whitened by the sun, most of them resting on their sides. I bent to wipe the dust off a fragment of a mosaic that lay on the chalky ground. Only the poppies and I were young, and I felt like a Hellenic maiden heading to the Eleusinian mysteries. The connection I felt was deeply feminine, as if I could sense the energy from thousands of years ago when ceremonies were held to the goddesses Demeter and Persephone. This amphitheater of Sutri holds a similar resonance.

A Filipino nun pulls into the parking lot. She appears about my age and immediately says to me in Italian, "But I thought there were two of you!"

"No, just me," I reply, realizing that even though I'd said *"io"* and not *"noi"* when I spoke to her, she had assumed I was traveling with others.

"Coraggiosa!" she exclaims, her face burnished the color of an incense cedar cone in the late afternoon light.

We drive through a residential area at the edge of town and arrive at a modern-looking nunnery. Immediately, she offers juice or tea.

All the nuns I see at the Oasi di Pace are Filipina, and the energy is cheery and light. Once again, I'm the only guest.

After leaving my pack in my room, I take my journal to their attractive garden where I find a chair beneath a shade structure. Low, white flowering plants line the garden paths and red and pink roses fill the beds next to the stone walls. A large area edged by a curving orange-tiled bench is full of tall purple iris and hydrangea bushes with bright green leaves and plump white flowers. I stop writing to observe the nuns setting up chairs in a semicircle facing the open door to the chapel.

"We're having mass outside," one of them says. They wave gaily and settle into their chairs.

The now familiar "Ave Maria" lode floats on a light wind. Their headdresses ruffle like prayer flags and their sweet voices reach me in the blooming garden.

There is sustenance that culminates in a deep peace, a surrendering peace. I feel myself opening to their way, to a way that's foreign to me, setting aside all I know. There is only trust and faith now, golden, like the mosaic in Santa Maria in Trastevere.

This is more important than walking into Rome. I only have to wander until I'm still.

And I am still in this moment with the nuns. I recognize what they've created: a peacefulness that so many of us want. They have it because they've surrendered. While we all want that peace, we don't want to surrender, or we don't know how.

I feel a merging with the nuns, as if my spirit has entered their circle, as if their spirits and mine rise and circle each other like Botticelli's graces.

Tears of gratitude slip slowly over my cheeks: gratitude for the Italian doctors; gratitude for the steady strength of those who helped to keep me alive; gratitude for the nuns and their prayers; gratitude for my pilgrimage and my health.

FORTY-SEVEN

Testimonium

At dinnertime, a young nun with a delightfully bright smile tells me she joined the nunnery at the age of twenty-two. "You've been away so long? What about your family?" she asks.

"I have parents in California." I pause for a moment and then add, "I'm divorced, and I don't have children."

"No children?" The nun gasps.

"I have a cat!" I add quickly.

"Un gatto?" Her eyebrows lift with alarm.

"Sì! Un gatto!"

This time, I don't mind saying *sono divorziata*. A month ago, this same conversation would have made me sad. But today, these things have no charge.

That night the fastidio will not let me sleep, and in the morning, I can't walk at all. I take an ibuprofen and massage and stretch the fascia until, finally, I can stand and hoist my pack on my back. As I walk gingerly out of the room, this thought comes: *Your body is done, but your mind has just begun.*

The golden-faced nun takes me to the train station in the neighboring town of Capranica. On the way, I ask her why so few Italian girls choose to become nuns.

"Young Italians have many comforts," she answers. "They're indulged by their parents, so why would they give up a comfortable lifestyle?" She shifts gears and heads up a narrow country road. "Young Italians like discos and fast food. But you cannot hear God when your life is loud and fast. Africans and Filipinos want to come to Italy as nuns, they have trouble getting permits to reside in Italy."

"What do you think will happen? It's such a significant part of Italian history."

"We pray for a solution," she replies.

As I climb out of the car, she leans toward me, and with a smile in her eyes says, "Remember, in order to hear God, you need to be still."

With its frequent stops, the regional train to Rome from Capranica takes an hour and a half—a distance that would have taken only forty-five minutes by car. The first few stops are ten minutes apart, but in the last hour, the train stops every three minutes at small, graffiti-covered stations. In the shadows of these stations are skinny men, immigrants from North Africa carrying large blue plastic bags over their shoulders.

Do these bags contain their worldly belongings?

Near the tracks, teenage boys throw glass bottles. I remember Gianni's words, *Pericolosissimo e bruttissimo.*

I'm told that for those who walk, after the nasty part, there's a lovely view of Rome from Monte Mario that gives pilgrims a sense of the grandeur of Rome in a special way that only walking to Rome can give. But still, for me it was the right choice not to walk. It doesn't feel anticlimactic because I had those moments of deep peace and surrender with the nuns in Sutri. And I still have some moments to anticipate: going to Saint Peter's to get my *testimonium* and going back to the Church of Santa Maria in Trastevere.

I exit at the small Trastevere station and walk up the hill to Abigail's apartment. Abigail is a friend of a friend who has lived in Rome for more than twenty years, and she offered to put me up after the pilgrimage.

The crowds press close around me, and my back sweats under my pack. I pass a small alimentari and note that I feel dehydrated, but the idea of moving through the narrow store aisles with my pack on seems too much. Even though I have walked about 425 kilometers (264 miles) in the past month, I find it hard to walk the four blocks up the hill. My body is flat-out exhausted.

Abigail, a busy musician, is out most of the time teaching music or playing in concerts. I see little of her during my few days in Rome. After a day of rest—during which the most I could do was hobble out for pizza—I walk up the river to Saint Peter's. It is only day thirty-two of my pilgrimage, not day forty. But I know what I'll do about it. I'll go to my uncle's house, my British uncle who lives near Urbino, and then return to Rome and go back in to the Church of Santa Maria in Trastevere on day forty. To do this on day forty feels supremely important to me.

Pilgrims arriving in Rome can take their pilgrim passport with all its stamps to an office, the Opera Romana Pellegrinaggi, on the edge of Saint Peter's square, to receive a certificate. Surprisingly, despite my foot problems, I outwalk the hordes of tourists in the Via della Conciliazione. Entering Saint Peter's piazza I find the Opera Romana Pellegrinaggi. Who should be walking out but Gianni!

"Ciao!" he calls, quickly coming forward to kiss me on each cheek.

"Non ci credo!" (I can't believe it!), I say, happy to see him. "I thought you'd be long gone from Rome!"

"No, I'm waiting for my wife to join me here. She arrives tomorrow."

Gianni follows me into the office, and we recount snippets of our last days on the route.

"Do you think it's okay if I ask for the testimonium?" I ask him as I pull out my pilgrim passport. "I didn't walk all the way."

"Of course it's okay! The requirement is only that pilgrims have covered one hundred kilometers."

"I've walked more than four hundred," I say with a smile.

As the clerk prepares my testimonium, I again contemplate my guardian angels. Almost always alone, I'd walked more than 250 miles, relying on my wits and the kindness of strangers. And I had been safe.

The testimonium has the official Saint Peter's seal. The date is in Roman numerals and my name is written in Latin. We step outside into the grandeur of the piazza, and I wave my testimonium.

"You did it!" Gianni says.

"High five!"

"Now, do you want to eat?"

"Definitely! A happy trattoria!"

"Huh?" He looks at me oddly and I laugh.

We walk down the river to Trastevere and choose one of the many restaurants with a fixed-price lunch menu.

"How odd to be able to choose from so many *trattorie* for lunch!"

"Feels luxurious," Gianni agrees, smiling. *"Voi un po' di vino?"* (Want a bit of wine?)

How I love those words! There is nothing else in the world I want more than to be having pasta and *un po' di vino* at a little outdoor table in Trastevere.

"You made it, Chandi!" Gianni raises his glass. "How are your feet?"

"My feet? They're destroyed."

After lunch, we meander down one of the neighborhood's narrow streets, and Gianni startles me by asking, *"Faresti l'amore?"* (Would you make love?)

"You mean hypothetically?" I manage to respond, tripping over my words. His use of the conditional tense of the verb confuses me. "What do you mean by *would I?* In general? With anyone?"

"No, con me, adesso," he says firmly. (With me, now.)

"What, here in the street?" I squeak, glancing at the alley to my right, laundry hanging across it. Does he want to take me down the *vicolo* and press me against a wall in the middle of the day? "You have a wife."

Gianni proceeds to go into such a convoluted explanation of why it's okay to proposition me—in spite of being married—that I can't follow his Italian. At the end of it, I respond in the same conditional tense he'd used—the answer would be no.

"American women don't let go so much," Gianni says.

"It just seems very out of place with my pilgrimage," I reply.

"Peccato" (Pity), he replies simply.

With nothing more said about it, we go back to talking about pilgrimages until we reach the tram and say good-bye.

On the tram, I reflect on the fact that I am not bothered by a man's direct and upfront proposal when he asks in a straightforward way and when he simply says, "Pity" when I decline.

I think what many of us in Anglo-Saxon cultures don't understand is the element in Latino cultures that views pleasure as something healthy to have. They are unapologetic in their enjoyment of pleasure—whereas puritanical cultures are almost antipleasure. When a man is direct, like Gianni was, it defuses any potential for weird underhanded ways that might feel threatening.

The sentiment that American women could loosen up is one

I've heard more than once when I'm in Latino cultures. I guess that's why Anglo-Saxon women flock to countries such as Italy, claiming they feel more alive in them. Within these cultures, one feels more permission to indulge in pleasure.

Pleasure. As I step off the tram, I think again of the lines of Byron that had come to me at Sant'Antimo. *"There is a pleasure in the pathless woods, / There is a rapture on the lonely shore."*[xiii] I'm smiling as I let the crowd move me from the tram to the sidewalk.

"Bel sorriso" (Pretty smile), a man says to me.

FORTY-EIGHT

Glow

B ack in Rome on day forty, after visiting my uncle, I sense the Church of Santa Maria in Trastevere waiting.

I enter it near sunset, through the olive green door. The earthy scent of incense shifts my senses from outer world to inner world. Everything is tinged with gold: the colors of the priest's robes, the gold-plated thurible that he swings as he comes down the long aisle, the mosaic of the open-armed Jesus. A service seems to be beginning. How serendipitous.

I slide into a pew as worshippers continue to enter until the pews are full. Some even stand at the back. At the altar, the priest sings psalms while a group of men in robes below him respond antiphonally.

Is this what's called divine liturgy? This praiseful singing lifts me—lifts all of us—and places us at the core of western spirituality. Communal blessedness envelops us, and I feel it spinning gold through our hearts. I know no one here, and I love them all.

An epistle is chanted, and then prayers recited. People bow their heads and I do the same, and then I bring out the small notebook in which I'd written my intentions forty days ago. Silently, I read them and then close my eyes, going through each in my mind.

- I will know how to trust my heart and trust the universe.
- I will regain strength in my body and empowerment of my spirit.
- I will experience surrender.

Yes, yes, yes.

I feel my heart absorbing the prayers and the gilded light of the church. Then my mind wanders and I tell myself, *just be here now, and open your heart.*

Then I'm *there*. With the ancient hymns, with the reverence, and with the heavens opening. In my mind's eye, I see a shower of gold light wash over me and then pour *into* me. I *become* the gold light, my body weightless, my heart shimmering.

To arrive with reverence. This is what it's like to arrive with reverence to the new shore.

I enter the piazza and feel I'm floating for two blocks before I have a sense of coming back to earth. Back to the cobbled streets on a lively summer evening. Back with the Italians in tailored shirts sipping Campari at outdoor tables. Back with the tourists walking in their practical sneakers holding cones of gelato. Back with the artisans displaying their jewelry and paintings. Back with the wonderful sound of Italian voices and and the wisteria running along the apricot-colored walls shouting, "Look at me!"

The moon slips into place over the rosy rooftops, and smiles down on the Trastevere scene. I say aloud, "I have my glow back."

It is not only the red balloon of my heart pulling me eagerly toward explorations. It stretches like long morning light across the length of my life. It stretches back to my ancestors who have been restored inside me to an honored place. They are tall and bright now like kukui trees giving me the air I breathe and lighting a lantern in my soul.

The pilgrimage has reminded me where my spirit really resides.

Like the lines of the Mary Oliver poem when she suggests that no matter how lonely you are, you can heed the message of the world that calls like wild geese.

It had not been domestication where I had thrived. It had been the call of exploration like wild geese, the call of the world with its history, its stories, its secrets. In this world, I'm continually curious and growing.

It's where I learn to read timeless stories of the land and of the people.

It's where I come to know the stories of my own soul.

It is where I learn trust, gratitude, and surrender.

It's where I return to glow.

Acknowledgments and the Raising of this Book

A very heartfelt *grazie infinite* to those who contributed to my pilgrimage (in the order the donations were received): Kimberly Beck, Katherine Fibiger, Lisa Hall, Juliette Levy, Stefania Maci, Larry Burgess, Sheryl Reiss, Rob Myers, Suzette Simonich, Joe Rahill, Margaret Leon, Eric Kloor, Rivvy Neshama, Linda Pierce, Deborah Knox, Phil and Lydia Ferrante-Roseberry, Connie Chow, Gopal Gopalakrishnan, Laurel Kallenbach, Pat Califana, Alice Park, Daniela Bigatti, Lee Burton, Camilla Raeburn, Sandy Martin, Susan Taylor, Candace Johnson, Dario Castagno, Kate Rider, William Craig, Geoff Laughton, Marina Bianchi, Frances Cottingham-Kelly, David Walthall, John Henderson, Lynne Barnett, Jeni Moretti, Cassandra Kimble, Judy Witts Francini, Rosa Magruder, Rebecca Shelp, Randall Nishiyama, Jim Ashley, Dawn Johnson, Lin and Anne Wyant, Ben Wyant, Devi Kumari, Christina Summers, Wendy Wyant, Annetta Ove McCarty.

Special recognition to Dawn Johnson for taking care of my cat in my 40-day absence. Your contribution was crucial and there was no better person to be with my baby.

I am indebted and deeply grateful to Suzanne Da Silva, Andrea Sacchettini, and Teresa Centoducati who gave enormously and selflessly during my illness in Florence.

Accolades to the medical system in Italy for the generous care I received. I am forever grateful.

A special acknowledgment goes to my mother. For vinegar in the searing streets, for *Rebecca* on the cigarette terrace, for extraordinary stamina.

My heart is full of blessings and thanks for the nuns, monks, priests, and B&B owners who I stayed with on the pilgrimage, and for the guardian angels who gave rides and sustenance along the way. You are remembered with joy.

I'm immensely grateful to my beta readers who volunteered their time and who gave such honest and essential feedback, and to all the friends, too numerous to mention, who willingly responded to my requests for feedback on the subtitle, the cover design, and the back cover description.

I also bow in appreciation to the editors I hired, and editor friends, who helped me learn to craft memoir. Thank you to Barbara Kyle for nudging me along the hero's journey. Thank you to Lindsey Alexander for pushing me to be more vulnerable. Thank you to Melanie Mulhall for going the extra mile and for the approach of, "where life is concerned, we're all in this together." Thank you to Candace Johnson for being *sempre* available with answers and encouragement. Thank you to Peggy Sands for stunning generosity and for turning the tedium of interior book formatting into a fun activity.

I wrote this book in many places. I first began it in Boulder and I was immediately stumped. There was the rudimentary A to B walk of the pilgrimage, which I saw as a skeleton, and around that skeleton was a mélange of emotions that somehow had to be crafted—the emotional experiences that caused me to take the pilgrimage, along with my emotional experiences while on the route. Little did I know when I began my first draft that it would take me years to learn to craft those emotions.

In Boulder while part of a three-person critique group I wrote the first draft. The camaraderie and support that I received from our threesome in those beginning stages hold a special fondness for me. Thank you, Lori Stott and Andi Stanton for wading through the mess with me. Most of all, thank you for the laughter.

Reluctantly I left that group eight months later, when I moved to Santa Fe. I ignored the manuscript for my first year in Santa Fe, but during my last six months there, when I rented a tiny studio out in El Dorado, I plugged away at it again. Without a critique group, I tried my best to breathe life into the chapters, still having no idea how to craft memoir.

Then I got a job in Qatar. During the first nine months there, I spent many weekends inside, hiding from the heat, and hashing through the manuscript again, determined to continue learning how to improve it. I found a few beta readers and was able to afford to hire an editor for additional feedback, which served to show me how much I still didn't know. With a desire to give my all to my students, and with doubts that the manuscript would ever come together, I set it aside for the next two years in Qatar.

Upon returning to my hometown of Santa Cruz, five years after writing my first draft, I decided to give the manuscript one more try. I renewed my effort to learn the craft, found a few more beta readers, and another editor, and it finally felt like things were falling into place—the skeleton had more flesh, maybe even a heart—and perhaps could stand on its own.

Brené Brown said, "The original definition of the word courage was to tell the story of who you are with your whole heart."

I heeded the call of the pilgrimage, and then the call of writing my story. The courage required for the pilgrimage was small in comparison to the courage required of me to now send my story into the world.

I imagine what it's like to be a parent, sending a grown child into the world. Does the parent struggle to be brave as she wonders what her child will encounter—how much negativity and indifference, and how much love and acceptance? It's with a mix of fear and hope I imagine, that the parent gives the goodbye hug, as her child leaves for college, or for a first trip abroad.

This book is not of much consequence compared to having a child, but it is what I have. The process of birthing it, and raising it to be something decent, demanded far more of me than I ever imagined it would.

I've gathered my courage and I stand with my book at the threshold, as if with a daughter who is leaving home.

Coraggio! Have fun out there.

Notes

i Freya Stark, *Baghdad Sketches: Journeys Through Iraq* (Tauris Parke Paperbacks, 2011).

ii Dylan Thomas, *The Collected Poems of Dylan Thomas* (New Directions, 2010).

iii Walter De La Mare, *The Listeners and Other Poems* (Kessinger Publishing, 2004).

iv Gertrude Bell, *A Woman in Arabia: The Writings of the Queen of the Desert* (Penguin Books, 2015).

v Hilaire Belloc, *A Path to Rome* (University of California Libraries, 1916).

vi Both plaques were taken down by the new mayor in April of 2015 and put in the town's Museo della Memoria.

vii William Burnlee Curry, *Education for Sanity* (W. Heinemann, 1947).

viii Caroline Myss, *Sacred Contracts: Awakening Your Divine Potential* Audio (Sounds True Incorporated, 2001).

ix George Gordon Byron, "Childe Harold's Pilgrimage" (George Routledge, 1892).

x Freya Stark, *Ionia: A Quest* (Tauris Parke Paperbacks, 2010).

xi Caroline Myss, *Sacred Contracts: Awakening Your Divine Potential* Audio (Sounds True Incorporated, 2001).

xii Ibid.

xiii George Gordon Byron, "Childe Harold's Pilgrimage" (George Routledge, 1892).

Page 76: Permission kindly granted by Kraft Heinz for use of the Oscar Mayer Weiner song.

Made in the USA
Lexington, KY
04 May 2019